BANGKOK TO BC

BANGKOK TO BC

Chasing Sunsets

Wolf E Boy

Book Guild Publishing
Sussex, England

First published in Great Britain in 2007 by
The Book Guild Ltd
Pavilion View
19 New Road
Brighton, BN1 1UF

Typesetting in Times by
Acorn Bookwork Ltd, Salisbury, Wiltshire

Printed in Great Britain by
CPI Bath

A catalogue record for this hook is available from
The British Library.

ISBN 978 1 84624 063 8

Contents

Getting the Ticket

I'd only really gone into Brighton to buy a book, taking the train from Shoreham, armed with camera, rucksack, writing material and a Robert Capa biography, *Blood and Champagne*, for the quiet moments. Brighton's always a good place to bring your camera, from its wonderful Victorian railway station, down to the sea front and the two polar piers, West Pier battered into submission, the cynically renamed Brighton Pier (formerly Palace Pier), and a fair amount in between.

After a lazy, enjoyable jaunt around the town, and an unsuccessful attempt at book buying, I stopped off at one of the ever-increasing number of coffee shops springing up all around Brighton, in Cranbourne Street, just off Churchill Square. There I was, minding my own, when Chris and Gav wander past the shop front and we spot each other. They were on their way to STA Travel in North Street, to pay for their trip to India which would be a couple of months further on. I tagged along with the intention of getting a beer in after they'd concluded their business. Well, their business took quite some time, and while waiting patiently out of the way, I watched as all the other potential travellers came and went, and the staff keep telling me it's my turn. 'No, it's alright, I'm just waiting for these two', pointing at Chris and Gav. Anyway, after about the fourth time of asking, and no real sign of Chris and Gav getting anywhere, I decided just to see what's on offer. No harm, I thought. The upshot of the situation was that I ended up walking out of there having shelled out for a ten-stop, one-year, round-the-world travel ticket.

I'd sold my house a few months earlier, and was contemplating a trip somewhere; I'd been thinking of buying a van

1

and travelling around Europe. But all of a sudden there I was, after a chance meeting with a couple of mates, a convincing travel salesperson, and most importantly, a great-looking trip for only just over £1,000, which included a solid travel insurance for the year. Probably the first time in my life when I'd been in the situation to afford, both in time and finances, to do such a thing on a whim.

I don't really think it sunk in properly until the actual day of departure. I still hadn't bought myself a proper rucksack until the day before, preparation not being my forte.

Thailand, Laos and Cambodia Journals, 29th Sept 2002 to 20th Dec 2002

Depart Heathrow 29th Sept 2002, Bangkok bound

Booga said to me at the airport, 'You look like someone going to the gallows', I felt like it, but didn't want to speak about it and give my fear away – or rather, confirm their suspicions. This was meant to be the trip of a lifetime. They were all jealous as, but I was in a state of bewilderment wondering what the fuck I was chucking myself into. I mean, South East Asia, on my own, why?! Impulse? Bloody-minded stupidity? Bit of both, probably; I couldn't say.

After a flight to Singapore, stuck between a Paddy and a woman that needed two seats and had a wind problem, I was grateful for the airport massage service there. The nerves had somewhat decreased by now, although that was quite likely down to the endless selection of movies at my disposal on the seats – whatever next!

Fairly uneventful really all the way to Bangkok. Even there it was a doddle, hordes of Thais after your business for taxis even before you're out of the airport. I paid at a desk, got given a ticket for a cabbie and off we went. 'Expressway, please,' I said, while pointing skyward to the huge concrete motorway sailing over the top of the city. 'You want go quick cost 70 baht for toll.' Looking at the ever-increasing wedge of mayhem traffic developing in front of us, this was no contest, Booga's first little gem of advice put to good use on arrival: 'Get the expressway unless you fancy moving hideously slowly through dogshit traffic.' He'd explained it well.

After just a day in Bangkok your eyes are opened to the virtually no-holds-barred traffic system which keeps buzzing 24/7. Traffic lights seem to be just a guide rather than a law, with swarms of mopeds, tuk-tuks, and motorbikes always at the front at red, revving up ready for the off, which itself is an experience as they all simultaneously thrash the living daylights out of their machines, leaving plumes of smoke clouding the rest of the traffic. I noticed many of them had masks over their nose and mouth – no crash helmets, mind you – and it occurred to me how pointless it would be to quit smoking since I arrived, walking around this place must qualify as the equivalent of chain-smoking Marlboro full-strengths; you can actually taste the shyte. I quickly noticed and took up the habit of holding a hanky to my mouth and nose for a few 'fresh' breaths, with earlier mopped brow sweat adding to the filter. Many things Bangkok may be, but good for your health ain't one of them.

Unpacking my kit in the sparse but respectable Royal Hotel room, I was happy but surprised at the ease with which it'd all gone. I'd been texting Mon in Oz throughout the journey to let him know the Wolf was on his way and he was giving me a few tips on what to eat, where to go, and every text ended 'WEAR A RUBBER' in capitals. Sad that I'm held in such low regard by my compadres.

Next step, navigate the area, and the first visible problem is how to cross a road where there's at least one part always in perpetual motion. Having seen a couple of locals take on this seemingly suicidal mission with ease, I gave it a stab myself and dodged around about eight lanes to get across to some squalid-looking market behind Khao San road. Welcome to Banglampu district. What can I say about the Khao San road? On a par with their traffic at the very least, almost every Thai you come across is trying to sell you a service or a product, and the smell of veggie Pad Thai being cooked up in the street permeates the air even above the tuk-tuk exhaust fumes, 15 baht with egg and I lived on it for a week and nothing else. The entire road is a seething mass of street vendors, backpackers, tuk-tuks, taxis, and little room left after. It was easy to see why everyone told me three days in Bangkok would be more than enough, Xanadu it aint! More like a giant khazi that regularly flushes out on to the streets.

First night there, and some London scumbag had me phone away while I was playing pool. He'd been at a distance earholing as I was having a laugh with a couple of Dublin lads, 'Awright, geezers,' he said in an excessively chummy fuckin' manner while shuffling his chair closer to our table. 'We should all go down to Phat Pong for the sex shows.' Like he was our best buddy already. I'd been texting Mon so wasn't paying too much attention, and left my mobile on the table as I played my shot. Me and the Paddys weren't tanked but we'd had a few so I thought nothing of the loudmouth London twat being gone until this old guy comes up and asks me if I still have my phone. Looking around and checking me pockets firms up my worst fears: mugged off on me first bleedin' night. 'He looked like a snide straight off,' says the old guy, another Londoner. Part of me suspected every single human being in eyeshot at first, like I was the victim of some mass conspiracy against me. I belted out the place and wildly looked into the sea of madness that is Khao San road, knowing I had no chance of achieving anything. I went back in and the old guy comes up to me, 'Sorry, son, but I didn't see it, I can only tell you I've seen his sort before, wouldn't 've noticed but for the fact I was about to come over and ask to borrow your phone to make a call, when I saw him and your phone not there.' 'Bollocks' was all I said. I'd been careless and paid for it. The scumbag even had the front to come back in later, 'you seen my phone around' I asked pointlessly. 'Na, mate, you wanna watch these Thais, they'll nick anything.' I just wanted to belt him, but what could I prove? You can sell

5

anything on the Khao San road with no questions asked. He
wouldn't have waltzed back in still with it, and the Thais are
more than capable of stopping a fight and dishing out their
own retribution. Lesson number one, day number one.

<u>Dog'gone</u>
('dog and bone' = phone)

Banglampu and the Khao San road
Where my phone got nicked by a cockney toad
I was playing pool when he starts his patter
Left my phone for a second,
didn't think it'd matter.

He'd gotten all chummy, said
Let's do Phat Pong,
Though he couldn't pay his bill
I never thought 'what's wrong?'

Then this old guy says,
'ere son where's your blower?'
And me guts twist up as I'm feeling lower.
I'd been doing quite well,
And on top of my game,
Then I find to my cost, some
Scum's doing the same.

The cockney's disappeared
And the dog's gone too.
I try to look around,
but they're out of view
It's only day one
And I'm a mobile down –
My advice,
Keep your eyes peeled in this town.

Next day I decided to put it down to experience and 'fuck it', one less thing to worry about losing. Trouble was, it just made me ten times more paranoid and directly responsible for my next and wholly self-induced disaster. Having met up with some Yank traveller who was waiting for his mate to arrive, we ended up going on the piss and thought it'd be a crack to check out Phat Pong, but every taxi driver just took us to some backstreet sex show in dead-end city shitholes of which Bangkok is amply filled. After the third or fourth attempt, and even having to run away from the drivers as they demanded to know 'Why you no want boom-boom', we ditched the idea and got a state cab back to Khao San and went back to our digs. Come the morning and I'm thinking of booking a trip out to the islands, and when I check my wallet for credit cards, they're not there. Well, after the phone incident there's only one thought in my mind, I've been fuckin' done again, and every single person in Bangkok and surrounding districts is a candidate suspect. Sweating like a bastard and cursing my every fibre, I turned my room upside down to no avail and pondered why they'd have my credit cards away but leave all the cash. But fuck that, I had to get to the police station, report them stolen and get the cards stopped to limit the potential damage. I didn't need this shit on day fuckin' two! I cursed my teeth to my toenails all the way there, stopped the cards, made a report, and as I waited for the report to be processed, 'You go sit wait, this take 20 minutes', I got out my phrase book to ask for some water and, to my overwhelming embarrassment and hideous annoyance, the pages opened up freely to reveal the cards in the middle of the book. What a twat. I'd stashed them for safety sake before shooting off to Phat Pong, and totally forgotten.

KOH TAO (TURTLE ISLAND)

Written 13th Oct 2002

Well, there you have it, one part slack vigilance and one part super paranoia coupled with dogshit memory equals no phone, useless cards, and vastly reduced cash survival kit for South East Asia duration. Well it's not all bad, because, after a 14-hour coach trip down to **Chumpon**, and a few more hours on the boat across, I'm now writing this in Koh Tao (Turtle Island), two islands up from Koh Samui, and I've just finished a four-day scuba diving course with Buddha View dive resort, in some of the most amazing open waters and outstanding marine life, all for a 100 quid and room included, so my chill level is restored and hopefully I'll be a little more relaxed in my approach to travelling for the rest of the journey. We'll see!!

Koh Tao is a world away from Bangkok, even though they're still after your money, but here the Thais are far more chilled. Four-wheel drives everywhere, mopeds, off-road bikes, rough terrain roads with craters, cracks and dogs to contend with all over. The turtles have long since left this place that was named after them: coconut trees are the most evident and abundant sight here. It's grubby, but not too much. The main, or perhaps only, attraction of Koh Tao is its location amidst some of the most amazing corals, pinnacles and general marine life which the diving schools exploit to the full, and if you have the time then you can combine a holiday with diving lessons and leave the island as a qualified open water scuba diver for less than half the cost of the British PADI courses, and do it in an infinitely more pleasurable environment.

I had no intention, when I left home, of doing a dive course, but it turned out to be a great way to meet people in the first part of my travels, and also gives me something I can do in many of the places I have yet to travel to.

Well, the course has been cool, not too taxing, the company good and the instructors relaxed and approachable, but mainly, the diving has been awesome. The variety of species of marine life, the vivid and hugely varied colours, their ease of accessibility, with multitudes of traditionally built Thai boats leaving every day to take out the even more numerous multitudes of new divers to the many dive sites. Even snorkelling here is amazing with coral reefs and tropical marine life just 50 yards' swim from the golden sandy beaches. I've seen plenty of outstandingly beautiful creatures and marine plant life, but by far my favourite was the 5-foot giant green sea turtle we saw on a night dive. At a location called the Twins, just off **Koh Nang Yuan**, it was nestled under one of the Twin pinnacles with Remora sucker fish attached to it, and as we shone our torches on it for a proper inspection the turtle decided it wasn't having any of that, and matter-of-factly spun around, glided gracefully through us all, and made off with us in hot pursuit playing our torches after it. For a while it kept going ahead level, with its sucker fish trailing like tassels as they clung on for the ride, then it began to ascend with us still in tow. We had been at 20 metres or so down, and now looking up as this magnificent creature flew through the water like an angel rising to the stars, I could only watch in awe and thank my good fortune to have been lucky enough to have witnessed such an incredible sight first hand, something I shall always remember. A better reason to continue diving I can't imagine. That night I saw many other beautiful creatures, including an impressive blue spotted stingray, and the dive was more than a success, but that flying turtle would have made the whole trip worthwhile on its own, especially as it has been such a long time since they left their home after the human settlement, a bitter-sweet situation really.

And then came the shits! (Three days.) I'd been stead-fastly vegetarian during my time away so far, to cut down the chances of food poisoning. Then one night I fancy the look of a chicken meal on the menu, and bang, within a couple of hours at most I've got the raging squits and stomach cramps. Another lesson learnt.

KOH PHANGAN

(written) 15th Oct. 2002

Koh Phangan now. Met up with a Scottish lad, Niall, on the Fastcat boat from Koh Tao to **Thongsala**. We'd met up at the Buddha View dive resort a few days before. He's only 18 and travelling on his own, fair play to him, quite an intelligent bloke and not without humour, so an unexpected bonus to have someone to have a laugh with on the next stage of the journey. A sense of humour would be tested by the road from Thongsala down to **Haad Rin** on the south of the islands – positively suicidal roads and drivers. The Bali bombing was also all over the internet that morning. Niall gave me what details he knew on the boat across, things getting a little closer.

Koh Tao turned out to be good therapy and the diving course proved a fine way to meet new people, however temporary – something I shall have to get used to. Initially feeling a bit dumb on the course as I'd missed the intro, I eventually caught up and enjoyed it, having gained confidence. Peggy was my first friend made as we were paired up as dive buddies; a lively Dutch girl, instantly matey and amusingly bubbly. Also two Swedish lads, Danny and Magnus, became good friends to me during the seven days I spent there.

I barely drank during my time on the island, but on the

one night when most of us pushed the boat out, just having collectively passed our open water diving course, Danny was there to guide me back across the island and safely to my apartment. I'd accepted a challenge to down a bucket of Thai whiskey on my own and that, pretty much, proved to be the end of my night. There was a group of three girls on our course that were out on the celebration with their boyfriends. One of the boyfriends, a Scot called Alan, enjoyed his drink like myself, and after I'd held court with a piss-take of our instructors (drinking skills 1–5), he laid down the bucket challenge. I should know better, but hey, I'm a Ramii, and when it comes to drinking, we like to have fun, or *Sanuk* as they say out here.

It was a shame it had to wait until we finished the first course for us all to get together, because we had such a good time.

As usual after a big night out I couldn't remember half of it, so next day was 'Poirot' time once again, piecing together the clues to work out what had happened. I didn't have to travel too far for clue number one – two of the glass slats of my apartment window stove in (only costing me 300 baht). I obviously couldn't even find my keys in my own pockets and broke in, in my drunken impatience – the first indication that I may not want to find out any more. Unfortunately there are always witnesses, and even though Danny got me safely back, my noisy drunken display had caught the ears of some amused locals, laughing and pointing at me next day.

I'm writing at the mo from the sheltered cover of the Family House bungalow restaurant, with coconut tree palm leaves all around. Set on **Sunset Beach** at Haad Rin with the sea just 20 yards away, a pleasant sea breeze blowing in to cool the midday heat, Koh Samui taking up most of the horizon, and as always, traditional Thai-built fishing boats dotted all along the shore, gently bobbing around.

11

Last night (14th) I set off with Niall to check out the Haad Rin metropolis, a motley patchwork of dirt tracks with shops, bars and massage parlours stitched together randomly, and never too far from the call of 'You wan'?' followed by whichever service or product. You have to learn to accept ignoring people while keeping a smile on your face.

Sunrise Beach was beautiful, lush golden sand, and beach-front bars all the way along built in oriental style, each with a different variety of music either pounding or carousing the area directly in front of it. With its night-time lighting, it has the power to seduce all but the most ardent 'get away from it all' traveller. Just remember to avoid the 'happy mushroom' products on sale all over the place, unless you're into hallucinogens, of course.

16th Oct 2002

Up with the larks this morning, or more accurately the roosters. In Koh Tao it was a mixture of dogs, roosters, mopeds, pick-up trucks, and early morning dive oriented beings which acted as my alarm call. Here it's just the roosters, and I have to say it's quite a pleasant way to rise, no clocks required, but just the steady and reliable squawk of nature to let you know that breakfast has in all likelihood been laid. This morning I have more time to write as I've been informed by my hosts that our feathered friends have not yet performed, which brings a smile to our faces. With a view such as this and a gentle morning sea breeze, waiting is not a chore. The whole place is as it's named, a proper family-run concern, and having digested my mushroom omelette (normal!) with toast, as if to enquire whether the eggs were up to scratch, out comes the rooster and family, mother hens, chicks and all, pecking, clucking, grooming and strutting their way around the dining area. 'Yes, thank you, my little feathered friends, very nice indeed.'

Last night my Scottish fellow trainee traveller called around to see if I was up for food and a couple of beers over on Sunrise Beach, also giving me the low-down on his efforts out the night before. We'd both been warned in advance that Haad Rin was a bit of a nightmare owing to the rave scene, half- and full-moon parties, but I have to say I've found the place quite relaxing, although it helps to be staying on the other side of the small peninsula which separates the Set and Rise beaches. Niall, while being amusing company, always seems to sneak in a line about having a lack of confidence and insecurities regarding travelling on his own, and yet each time I see him he has a new friend won the previous night, using exactly this line of approach. I'd told him it was a winner on our way over on the Fastcat from Koh Tao, and it looks as if he's formed the same opinion. Confidence is one thing I'm sure he doesn't lack, from my observations of him in action. The girls love him, he gives them the routine, and that, coupled with his youthful good looks, ready wit, love of music (he bounces around to tunes while he's chatting), and no shortage of cheek, I'm pretty sure the boy will do well wherever he goes. Funny thing is, he wins over new mates in the same way: interaction is one of his fortes.

19th Oct 2002

With the full moon party only a couple of days away, I'm already thinking I've overstayed my time here. It's been good doing almost nothing, but I'd like a change of scenery, so after the party I'm off. Last night there was a downpour so torrential we couldn't see Koh Samui across the water, which is quite something as it gobbles up most of the horizon on a clear day. Niall was leaving the island so we had a meal and a couple of beers around the corner, having waded through the rivers flooding down the streets. He's heading south to Malaysia to cross the border and get another 30 days on his visa before heading up north to Chiang Mai, still a bit gutted about having to ditch his surfing plans in Indonesia. All the news bulletins and European embassies are now warning Westerners to avoid the place, or get out if there already. I've still got a couple of months before I have to make a decision, so I'll see how things go until then.

Took a boat trip the other day on one of their long-tail boats. A really sleek bit of kit they are, with big old engines sat atop the transom, with long poles leading to the prop which they use to steer as well as propel by levering in and out of the water, and push from side to side using the tiller, which is just another pole attached to the lump, and it all moves as one. They sound like a small aircraft taking off, and have plenty of kick in them. The trip itself wasn't amazing, just a couple of nice beaches and a ropey-looking waterfall which had a myriad of blue piping winding all the way up acting as the supply for the brown water to the resort below. Nonetheless it was a day out for only 300 baht with a meal thrown in for the evening, plus another chance to meet new people which was OK but a bit transient (I think).

Laying off the beer for a bit as it's eating into the budget, and that Chang gear is wasting me.

21st Oct 2002

Full moon party tonight. During the week Haad Rin has been swelling its tourist ranks by two or three times and latecomers are having trouble finding rooms. This place must be bedlam in high season. My laying off the drink didn't get off to a very good start, having finished my book (*Germinal*–Emile Zola) and having that deflated feeling I always experience at the finish of a good book, I took a wander down to **Sunrise Beach** at around midnight, the place was rockin' with the majority of the beach packed and good tunes belting out. So I bought a beer and sat down, as I thought, for just the one to soak up the atmos for a while.

Back home, going out for just the one is always fraught with obstacles as you never know who you're gonna bump into. Here I considered it quite safe. I know no one, or so I thought, so I sat contentedly watching it all going on for some time and feeling a little envious of these chiselled lads (mainly Israelis) homing in on all the European darlin's with apparent great success. Looking at my almost drained bottle I gave thought to the saddo walk back from a party just beginning, when Chiem, a Thai local, came over and beckoned me to the music bar which had attracted the biggest crowd. Nothing odd here, he's Yot's mate from the resort I'm staying at. Yot used to go out with a girl from my home town, Shoreham, and she'd put me onto his resort address to look up should I make it out this way. Anyway, I shouldn't have worried, I'd been here nearly a week, said 'Hello' and 'How ya doin'' whenever our paths crossed, and occasionally asked 'What's on where', just being sociable and enquiring without being overbearing or pushy. Last night they'd spotted me on my own and decided to take me under their proverbial wing. There you have it, or, there I'd had it, Thai bucket whiskey once again doing for me quite spectacularly. Yot found me staggering around the shanty shop village later, poured me across his moped and took me back to my bungalow, where he left me. The rest I've had to piece together from vague memories and witness accounts backed up by stifled, or not so stifled, giggles in my presence. After he left me I'd stripped naked on the porch and fallen akip in the hammock. Not so bad you might think, but these bungalows are about the size of a seaside beach hut, and not much further apart. Next to me is a group of Scandinavian girls, and their return obviously

15

woke me from my drunken slumber, so I stood up and staggered around starkers on my porch, still battered and having exhibited a rather pathetic display of human condition, retired back into my room. Their screeches were, I thought, just part of a curious dream until the evidence was pieced together next day, courtesy of Yot and family, coupled with the irritation caused by the million mozzie bites I received from the voracious little bastards feasting on my exposed flesh; my popularity with the insect world remains painfully undiminished.

Yesterday I laid off the alcohol and bought an Irvine Welsh book, *Ecstasy*, to keep me occupied, but tonight as I've said, is the big party, so watch this space, I guess. I hear the mosquito community has booked its tickets in advance, confident of a bumper crop of lily European flesh to bite into, bzzzzzzzzzzzz.

Still the 21st, midday-ish. Taking my camera for a walk to document what for me are the more interesting aspects of this little stretch of the island, such as the reptile element neatly ironed flat into the dusty roads, and their expansive recycling unit, otherwise known as the beach. Didn't see any 'crazy hairs' today, they're normally grey-haired hippy looking types resembling leather-skinned suntanned New Age travellers without the shithouse convoy of crapped-up vans, dogs, horses, screaming kids, tea leaves and attendant refuse heaps. There's always a gentle smattering of them about the place, but today they're lost among the 'backpackalanche' which is what moves me to scribble now. The past few days have been steady, but today it's like the D-day landings with boats coming from all directions laden with 'full-mooners'. And now I've got some irritating wannabe bongo drummer giving it the Les Dawson across the way. Everyone's gotta learn sometime: I just wish I didn't have to hear it on this bongo novice's first day. But then, joy! As I write he's packed up, bongo and all, to join

16

the rest of the trainee circus acts all over Sunrise Beach. At least you can turn away from the jugglers if you feel like it. Everything's pointing to an interesting night ahead.

Well, this is turning into a busy day, it's about 5 or 6-ish and the ferry pier is still busy, but now we appear to have been delivered a police force from somewhere, complete with a fleet of shiny gleaming new 4 x 4 meat wagons. I haven't seen a copper since Bangkok, not on Koh Tao or here, and now there's a small army of them watching all the decadent Western pill-popping, dope-smoking, beer-swilling, raveheads clambering off the ferries and on to a night of unrestrained oblivion under the studious eye of the full moon police, for that's the only time you'll see them. I've also noticed, during my afternoon stroll, an unmistakeable increase in the amount of British accents, from almost none at the beginning of the week, to maybe half the entire travelling contingent around here. It looks a bit like we have all the ingredients for a bumper payout for all concerned, be it bars for beer, dealers for gear, shops for wares, or boats for fares. Those dumb enough to get pulled by the full moon police may also find themselves in a Thai jail, a place I'm informed you don't wanna be, and with a nice fat fine to pay before release. I'm taking my camera out tonight.

23rd Oct 2002

It's 9.30 a.m. and ferries are filling up with the 'mooners' heading back to wherever they came from. Doubtless Haad Rin will resume its previous likeness to an Israeli settlement; the *Haad Rin Queen* (one of the ferries) has another busy day ahead. The party on the night wasn't what I'd call amazing, Brighton between the piers on New Year's Eve 2000, and Fat Boy's party on the beach 2002, they were amazing for sheer weight of numbers alone. The full moon party was however a great night (and the following day) for

17

all sorts of reasons, the fireworks, light displays, party animals, boats big and small, stretching along the Sunrise Bay, which had delivered many of the evening's guests and would escort them home afterwards. And the music had changed for the occasion. There had been just the one bar playing hard house and techno trance every night to virtually no audience, while all the others played from reggae, indie, ambient pan pipes, blues, or anything other than 'bang'. On this night the whole place was rockin' to the bangin' tunes of the rave generation and the crowd were lovin' it, with waves of smiling faces bangin' it out as 'ard as the music.

Yot and Chiem invited me over to meet some of their friends from Hat Yai (south) who were having a pre-party eat out with Thai whiskey and weed. I avoided the whiskey but decided that a bit of the weed could do no harm, and as I'd eaten already I could hardly just sit there twiddling me thumbs when the only words in Thai I know are, 'Thank you', 'Hello', 'I'm fine', and 'How much', somewhat strangling the conversational chances at birth. In fairness, as usual, I was once again put to shame by their grasp of a reasonable smattering of the Queen's stuff. Two of Yot's mates, Jum and Tu, made great efforts to keep me involved, and they were a couple of interesting characters to say the least. I reckon if there is such a thing as reincarnation then Jum was, or will be a cat, and if I get a photo of him you'll be half way to seeing why, with his wispy goatee and 'tache, sleek glasses, and rat-tail hair, he looked cool as a cat. Tu's personality leaps out at you quite literally, but not easy to define in words; let's just say not backward in coming forward.

Having got split up from Yot's crew in the mêlée snaking to the beach, I sat down with a beer and watched it all starting to kick off rave-style, and noticed that almost no Israelis, with their short lycra shorts, thongs (on the men!)

and puffed-out hairy chests, were around. We heard during the day that the heavy police presence was due to the perceived threat of terrorism after an attack on the US embassy in Malaysia, and not a counter to the pill-popping generation, which I have to say I rejoined for the night, more because I knew the alcohol would slay me while a decent 'beanie' would keep me up, happy and off the booze.

I had no idea that 'disco biscuits' were even available on the island, but having caught up with Yot and crew, I got talking to a couple of girls they'd been amusing, and after a brief convo about where from, what doing, where going, I discovered they're pillin'. 'Where'd you get them from?' I was curious. 'There's a little old Thai lady at The Frog a couple of streets along. Why, do you want one?' The thought hadn't occurred, but seemed like a bit of a life-saver for this particular occasion, long night and bangin' tunes coupled with my inability to survive for long at the hands of Thai booze. 'Would you show me where?' And that was it, once again a guest member of the 'beanie brigade'. I necked three 'smile smarties' during my involvement in the celebrations, and obviously the girls became lifelong buddies over the next few hours, 'love puppies' with saucer-size pupils floating in and out of the dance houses and talking the tits off each other in between spine tingling head massages, always a winner when you're off it. Kate and Charlotte were their names. Like so many others, they'd come from round the island for the night, and after chatting a while, it turns out we're on more or less the same route, so emails were swapped in case we should be in the same area on our travels and meet up again. I'm aware that this is becoming a bit like back home where you collect numbers that never get rung afterwards, but we'll see.

I was armed with my little Olympus for the beginning of the evening of the party, and the Maglite in case of any losses in the dark. Ironic that of the two things I lost that night ... you guessed it, the bleedin' Maglite. I was off to change cameras and score some more pills for the girls and myself, they gave me a 1,000 baht note and off I went, but when I got to my bungalow to get some money, I found I'd lost the girls' thousand, at the same time as I realised I'd lost the torch.

I began to wonder about the wisdom of taking out the big camera, a not inexpensive piece of kit, especially as it only had six shots left in the can, but the beanie was still in control and I confidently pressed on. Having made my way to The Frog, the comedy of the situation hit me. This little old, gentle-looking plump Thai lady was reclined on a mattress and smiling at me like I was a grandson come to visit. Obviously I hadn't 'accidentally' returned to the quietest part of town when everywhere else was throbbing to the 'bang'. Patting the space on the mattress/seat, 'You come sit here,' she said, while giving furtive glances up and down the dirt track passing as a road as she went off to a back room. When she returned, I decided I should see about reducing the price, having already mislaid the girls money, we'd paid, or rather the girls had paid, 700 baht earlier, I'd paid 660 for my first, so I pitched for 600 and she went straight for it. 'Bollocks,' I thought. 'Should've gone lower.' But never mind, next time maybe.

The next few hours are a bit of a blur, but somewhere along the line the girls left on one of the boats to wherever they came from, and I met back up with Yot and company who were off up into the jungle on the hill where the party was carrying on away from watchful eyes. By this time it was pure endurance, although I had just scored my third beanie so that'd keep me going for a while. They have a club tucked away in the forestation at the back of the resort looking out to the horizon where the sun sets. It's got two levels, downstairs for dancing, upstairs for chillin'. I progressed my batteredness downstairs, foolishly accepting the Thai buckets too often passed my way. At the second time of hurling I decided enough was enough. That was about eleven o'clock in the morning. There were some weird fuckin' dudes in that place, and not just the 'crazy hairs' because I've become accustomed to those, almost to the point of feeling let down if I don't see one. Two of these weirdos stuck out as if they had neon signs above them saying 'can you believe this?' One had hair desperately trying to escape from his head, and a strategically shaved stripey beard the like of which you never see, but amuse yourself by trying sometimes while in the confines of your own bathroom, but are never dumb enough to leave that way. The other one would give you nightmares; a skinny individual with semi-tight black cotton trousers pulled halfway up his belly, no top, his body contorted in to an 'S' shape, and his boat race, well, what can I say? Sharp chin out, forced grin that looked like he'd had the sides of his mouth stapled to his cheek bones, a very Roman, distorted eagle's nose, long narrowing forehead, and frizzy hair pulled back and tied in a bun at the top of his 'chest out, head back' cranium. As he ponced around with his head back, it was like he had an imaginary pair of glasses he was trying to look underneath. He should buy himself a cage, get in, and put a bowl outside – he'd make a fortune. I'm gutted I didn't have a camera then, but no one would believe it, they'd say I digitally manipulated it.

Finished reading Irvine Welsh's *Ecstasy* yesterday. Not bad but a bit of a rip-off, big words (large print) and loads of spaces, 276 pages which in normal print and no unnecessary spaces would probably be lucky to make a 100. I could easily compete with the second two stories, but he wrote *Trainspotting* which made me think I can't write at all, so who am I to say jack shit? I was gonna get *Acid House* by the same author, but gone already, so I picked up *High Fidelity* by Nick Hornby, 245 pages but small print and no unnecessary spaces. Page 59 and quite amusing so far.

TONSAI BEACH

24th Oct 2002

I'm now down near **Krabi** after another marathon ferry, coach and long-tail boat journey. Left Koh Phangan at 8.30 p.m. and arrived at **Railay Beach** about 4 p.m. the next day. We were packed in like sardines on the ferry from **Thongsala to Surathani,** so no sleep there and not over-comfortable, but whatever. Once on the long-tail boat the view was breathtaking, like mountainous pinnacles which have risen out of the water, half green with vegetation and half multicoloured rock, pretty awesome. But like every-where I've seen so far, it looks great from the sea, you land ashore and you're in the middle of a building site.

I've struck lucky this time though – all the places I'd tried wanted 500 baht a room, but I spotted a girl on a trek up an unreasonably steep path, seemingly into the back of beyond, ropes there already to assist, and a Thai lad to help with her rucksack. She tells me there's a quiet beach the other side and much cheaper. Unassisted I gulp and follow warily. Half-hour later we're on a much better, much quieter, and five times cheaper beach. The bungalows are a hike up into the jungle. On the way, we had to move out of the path of a 2 or 3 foot-long chunky-looking lizard being chased by a Thai girl using a palm leaf to steer it down the path towards us, which made me twitch a little. All in all it's so specta-cular here it's worth a try-out; without doubt the best-looking place I've stayed around. It's called **Tonsai Beach**; it's also full of nutters climbing up sheer rock faces. No thanks.

25th Oct 2002

Big old thunderstorm from early evening and through the night, cool as, kept the black spiky frogs 'gribbepping' all night too. I think I'll stay here a few days. The only downside, as everywhere, is the fuckin' insect world (flying variety). It's like some annoying git in the pub that irritates the skin off your back but can't take a hint and fuck off out of it, even after you've abused, then punched them, finally changing tables. The scientists should come up with an all-day spray which gives them a hideously slow, debilitating and painful death the moment they enter your 5-yard personal parameters, fuck 'em and make it hurt. Meanwhile my struggle continues and I maintain a firm grip on the wooden spoon, although in my moments of extreme malice one or two insects pay the price of my childhood apprenticeship in insect dissection and endurance (i.e, how long they'll last, and hope their mates are watching). More lizards spotted today but camera in bag (bugger). The plant life is pretty incredible too, like something out of Jurassic Park with leaves the size of table tops and ominous rustling beneath it almost continuously.

My bungalow here is much the same as the Family House bungalow in Koh Phangan, size of the bed plus walkway alongside, door in off the porch, and door out to shower/ toilet, difference being here there's no roof over the shower/ toilet so it's shower 'n' shit al fresco. Also this bungalow is on stilts owing to the steep gradient of the hill it's on.

4 p.m.-ish. Just as I'm snaking my way down through the jungle to buy some water and poem paper, feeling supremely bored with my own company, I hear the dense vegetation which skirts the route rustling, and stop in my tracks to pinpoint where the main sounds are coming from, thinking maybe a smallish lizard. But no, a decent-sized silvery grey monkey who stops shaking the bush for a mo, takes a brief

23

look at me and off he goes. Or should I say 'she,' as I have the same effect on the human variety. I had my camera but the beast was gone before I could get the lens up, no Freudian slip intended. The fur was quite fine-looking and splaying out from its face and body, making it look quite wide, but I'd say from the branch it was on it must have been quite light.

That's enough of the Attenborough stuff. Mid-downpour headed off for sleepy-head lotion (beer). This place is dormouse quiet, but strike up chat with barman Eag, or vice versa more like, pick up a few more Thai words, earwig a Brummie chatting up an Aussie bird with the killer 'my car back home' stuff, and it's working! Time to leave.

Backpackers Gold

Bamboo, mahogany, quality shacks
With al fresco shower and bogs
Ten minute yomps up through wilderness tracks
And lizards the size of small dogs.

The black spiky frogs are quite noisy at night
And doubly so when it rains,
Which affects all the power for fans and the lights –
They haven't a trip for the mains.

The jungle's a noisy collection of life,
And the view is a sight to behold,
And paths are lit up by the coconut lights,
To lead on the backpackers gold.

26th Oct 2002

Extreme sports rock climbers, you'd love this place. All day every day there's loonies scaling the rock by the restaurant where I'm staying; it doesn't just go up, it goes up and out.

To me it looks like madness, not fun, but obviously to some it's what gets you up in the mornings. The rock must be at least 200 feet high and with a ridiculous overhang at the top, although I've not seen anyone get all the way up yet; maybe not poss as it's quite some overhang.

27th Oct 2002

Sitting down for brekkie on my last morning at Tonsai Beach, and it takes an American on his own, diving straight in at the deep end with the locals, to make me realise I've still got far too much of back home in me. They invite him over and pat a seat next to them, get him to sit in tight, and can't be helpful enough to the guy. A bloke pats a seat and looks at me and my initial thought is to knock him out, thinking he must be of the opposite persuasion. They're so happy smiley (and after our money of course, I ain't totally blind) it disarms you, so alien to my home life experiences. Big trouble is, though, I feel like such a dummy not being able to communicate if they can't speak English, but that's crap really 'cos this Yank can't speak a single word of Thai and somehow or other there's a level of communication going on between them. Mind you I'm not sure if each party knows what the other's trying to get across. From what I can make out, I know he wants to go snorkelling but the crowd they've directed him towards are off on a boat to another rock-climbing destination. Nonetheless, the point is that I should be making more of an effort instead of sitting on my own all the time.

KRABI

27th Oct 2002, 11 p.m.

I can't believe the guide books talk about Krabi as some

nice little town; it's a fuckin' shit hole. The only good thing about it is its location as a gateway to the fantastic-looking islands around it. One day here will be more than enough. Having discovered that Trang, where I was going next, is even worse, I've changed my plans and am heading back to Bangkok for a couple of days before going up to Chiang Mai. Had another Thai massage this evening, number five since I've been out here. Have to be recommended and always over too soon; not bad value at 200 baht for an hour.

BACK TO BANGKOK

30th Oct 2002

Arrived back in Bangkok 6 a.m. yesterday and got lucky straight away. All the dumps were full and overcharging, but got in at the first time of asking at the D&D inn in the Khao San road, best one of the lot and same price as first time around, 450 baht. Bit pricey by the tightwad brigade's standards but worth it for the comforts, I say, and a rooftop swimming pool with city views, well.

Today I actually ventured out towards the river Mae Nam Chao Praya (Bangkok's main river) and got as far as the National Museum where a Thai information guide got chatting to me and gave me a list of things to see and marked them on my Lonely Planet guide book map, wrote the names in Thai script too for the tuk-tuk drivers' benefit, and even told me how much the tuk-tuks should charge and what to say if they tried it on. '30 baht, no more, *pang nai* mean too expensive.' He was so friendly and keen that I should see all the sights, pointing out all the free sights and telling me I should come back next day for the English-spoken free tour guide of the museum. So off I went, content to walk, but I'd only turned one corner when another Thai man sees me looking at this Thai college and just starts talking. 'Flee dance festival tonight, you come see', as he's pointing to the building we're walking past, then 'Where you come from?' 'Angkrit'. 'Oh! Angkrit, vely good football team, my team Chelsea.' They all love their *fitba* out here. But he asks me all the usual, 'been here long', 'what seen so far', 'where going', before, after my answers he launches into a similar spiel as the guy before did, telling me which tuk-tuks to get, 'Lite prate, no yerrow, cheaper' (white licence plates, no yellow), and 'You go Dherves Export show and buy loobies and saffries' (rubies and sapphires) – a chance, apparently, to buy gems at wholesale prices which happens for only one week each year, and is mainly for Thais to use as a chance to buy and sell abroad to pay for either their travels or student fees. I was starting to feel a rosy glow at all this friendliness being showered on me. He even flagged down a white plate (government) tuk-tuk and told him the price, 30 baht to take me to three sites and back to Khao San road.

I went and saw Wat Samphraya first, the temple of the Lucky Buddha, where yet another friendly Thai tells me the main temples are closed while the Buddhist monks take their exams, and how one particular monk instituted education into their Buddhist training. Then he showed me around the site and its smaller temple with a smaller (but not small) statue of Buddha with hands cupped holding a bowl into which you can chuck coins and buy some luck, I missed a couple but got one in eventually. Apparently he was using this half-hour, before he picked his wife up, for a little meditate, but he spent it instead telling me all about Buddha and asking me the same as the other two guys, and once again advising me all about the gemstone export company with their once a year opportunity (once every three years for tourists he said).

27

I had no money for gems, so no opportunity for me, and owing to a complete absence of knowledge (or interest really) regarding gems of any sort, not a particularly interesting visit. Then taken to see a big Buddha at the temple Wat In, snapped away for a while, and then left to find my tuk-tuk driver only to find he'd done a runner. Funny, that, but shouldn't it be the other way round? I mean, I hadn't even parted with any money. Maybe this was a repayment from the lucky Buddha. Or maybe (more likely) I'd just been through one of the well-publicised jewellery scams which operate all over Thailand, and the driver realised this particular westerner was a waste of his time. So there I was on the other side of Bangkok, not entirely au fait with the area, and a long walk back, which with more helpful Thai assistance along the way, I managed.

On my return I see that Khao San road is being set up for a big Halloween party run by MTV, and a vast influx of police and dogs is swarming over the area. I can only assume this has something to do with a terrorist threat.

4th Nov 2002

On the Halloween night I bumped into Dan, the Swede I'd met in Krabi. Said hello and got chatting again, then ended up going on the piss with him, or rather, met girls and he pulls a Claire Sweeney lookalike while I end up on the pool table. My territory, his territory.

Met up next day, his last of a year travelling. He's done some cool shit while away, sheep shearing in Oz, deckhand on a New Zealand to Fiji ferry (which he got to steer at night, how funny), and some nasty business in Indonesia from the religious nutters. He comes from quite a privileged background, private schools with princes there, nearly made it into pro ice hockey, but pretty down to earth and into the travelling, good company. He leaves after we've sunk a

28

couple and I carry on, play a bit of pool, and end up with the usual story. Day after that and it's the same old again, with a little difference, met up with some Brummie lads and headed off to Phat Pong to see the bars and shows. Upset a ladyboy by pointing it out to the lads, had to leave as a result while it all kicked off behind me with the ladyboy and one of the house girls tearing it up. I sat outside waiting until the lads came out and told me all about the drama I'd caused and missed. We headed back to the Khao San road for cheaper beer; Phat Pong = double-charge booze. Turned in at about seven in the morning. Gotta stop doing this shit.

KHAO SAN ROAD STUFF

Blind dudes with their Karaoke beat box amps and mics, pigeon-stepping through the street. Groups of Thais sat in circles at the side of the street on mats, with Thai buckets in the middle (street party). *Thunderbirds*-style security guards, with the hats and crisply sharp-pressed shirts. Everywhere, stalls selling Pad thai, rice, BBQ everything, pancakes, all so good, and cheap at 10–15 baht. Bars with winner-stays-on-pool, and only pay if you lose. The Thais that play, don't drink, and often change the rules on you, but hey, it's their place after all. And always a game of footy showing, from Europe normally, and English mostly. Any cheap, snide clothes you want too, everywhere.

THE NORTH: CHIANG MAI

Three days of trekking out of the way, a day's rest, and I'm still worn out. There were 14 of us in the group, Eirik, the Norwegian Viking, I had met as we waited for the coach from Bangkok to Chiang Mai, turned out to be quite a character. In the 13 hours I had to get to know him, I was glad of the fact he had a lot to say and pretty much most of it was of interest. He comes from a town near Bergen in Norway, and although quite young, he's had a fairly full life so far by the sound of it. He lived in Thailand with his parents from six to eight years old, and has a useful grasp of the Thai language, which I have tried my best to capitalise on during our time travelling together, asking him continually the meaning of his exchanges with the locals, mainly bartering – *pang nai* – too much, *lud noi* – give me discount, and *mai chop* – not interested, plus a few other things which I've tried my best to grasp. Doubtless I shall find out in the next few days how much has actually sunk in. Eirik has also done his national service back home so I knew once we had decided on trekking together that he'd be a useful travel companion, on what I had no idea I was letting myself in for. He'd already booked a trek to start on the day of our arrival, and I'd decided since talking to him (or rather, listening), that I'd go, but only after a day's rest. On our arrival he changed his arrangements, grateful for a day's rest after travelling through the night, and was booked on the same trek as me.

TREK DAY ONE

In the morning it's prep time and try to bring as little as poss. Well, what I wanted to bring wouldn't fit in my small rucksack so I took the 'Wolf pack', and it was full. That nearly proved to be the breaking of my spirit. Everybody laughed at the sight of it, at least double the size and weight of any of theirs.

I tried not to think too much about what was ahead, and was relieved to see that stage one of our trek was on an elephant, which turned out to be quite an enlightening experience (and a little sadness for the animals). The dexterity of these huge creatures along such absurdly narrow routes simply amazed me as they weaved through this unkempt jungle with grace and intelligence, each foot delicately finding the foot hole in front, left by so many other treks, never a tremble and steady as a rock no matter how steep or how narrow.

Having alighted from our majestic beasts at the end of their shift, we were fed, and then came our turn for the hard work. It was about here that my pity and respect for the elephants would magnify beyond question, and at the same time the realisation of how dumb I'd been to bring a full pack set in along with the cramps which were in the post.

The relief with which I greeted the tribal village at the end of our first day was only tempered by the knowledge that elephants had done half the work this day, but the following day was all on foot. That's not meant to detract from the unspoilt sights of nature along the way, just the muscles and bones of a middle-aged body giving the brain a little notice that it may not wish to endure such stresses for too much longer. Eirik, I have to say, was a first-rate hike mate, every inch the Viking spirit, and although I felt acutely knackered, we had at least led from the front almost continuously. The air at the village was so refreshingly clear that we all recovered fairly rapidly from our days toil, and soon were tucking in to our guide, Mr Whiskey's, freshly cooked soup and rice with fruit to follow.

The village overlooks distant misty mountains and valleys, and is a collection of chalet huts of bamboo, straw and logs, with fresh stream water redirected from the falls to supply the very rudimentary shower and toilet facilities. Very fresh indeed, and gratefully received too. They also have a shop – here we are in the middle of nowhere and we can actually buy booze, crisps and obviously, souvenirs.

They don't miss a trick, but who can blame them, certainly not I. Everybody stocked up with Sang Som (rum), the cheap Thai gut rot that blows your head off, and we set about the time-honoured tradition of getting pissed together in order to get to know each other. I failed.

All I can say is, that I drank lots, tried opium with the locals, spent half the night insisting it had no effect, and woke up none the wiser as to any of the names or stories of the people I was travelling with other than Eirik. He got wasted too and admitted the same to me in the morning before we set off again trekking. It amused us both at the time that everyone knew who we were, while we were clueless as to their identities. Something we'd try to remedy, maybe.

I was forgetting two things there. We were entertained with songs and dancing by the children of the village, although I'm sorry to say I wasn't in much of a condition to fully appreciate their efforts; one thing struck me, however – my ears were alerted to the familiar sounds of 'Frère Jacques', the French nursery rhyme, being recited much to our amusement. Also, I had a dubious and uncomfortable Thai massage from two of the village women, but they only wanted 100 baht so I'm not aggrieved.

TREK DAY 2

Up bright and early for egg, toast and fruit, pack up and push on. As usual me and Eirik darted to the front, refreshed after our rest, and soon we were back in the thick of the jungle, always staggered that no matter how high the climb, how narrow the path, or steep the drop, always before us were the telltale footprints of elephants. I looked down a couple of times and eventually thought better of it. If you fall down it's a long way, and if you make it back up it won't be in any hurry.

I don't know how long we trekked before reaching the waterfall, but we'd crossed a good deal of brooks and streams to get there and Mr Whiskey said there'd be plenty more to come. At arriving, though, all thoughts of what had been before just evaporated as we dived into the pool under the falls, one of the high points of the trek. We stayed there a good long while, relaxing, enjoying the giant jacuzzi and gathering back the strength for the next stage.

Eirik had explained, on the coach going up to Chiang Mai, his theory about travelling – that we were collecting together things to complain about, so that when we return home the story-telling would sound more impressive because of all the hardships suffered. A not unreasonable theory I supposed.

As we set off after the restful break at the waterfall, we were unwittingly about to be the cause of our own hardship out of pure bull-headed stubbornness. From the beginning of the trip, Mr Whiskey's assistant guide had been winding the group up continuously, sending us down one route then laughing as he walked off in a different direction. He had a childish laugh, and we came to the conclusion he probably wasn't playing with a full deck, most of his behaviour seemed to back this up. It was amusing at first, but after a while the novelty wore off, and I'm sorry to say he was starting to irritate me a little.

We'd been on the move up and down the mountain (mainly up), when we came to what seemed an unnecessary stop by the standard set so far. Mr Whiskey was, as usual, bringing up the rear with Teresa, one of the three Czech girls, who was always a while behind us, so me and Eirik looked at the only visible path ahead, which was up still further, asked our infantile guide if it was the way or not, and he just stood there doing his oft-played silent trick as he studied his machete from behind his lensless black plastic-rimmed sunglasses. Bored of waiting and wondering, Eirik and I said 'Fuck it' and made for the route ahead and up, while the rest of the group stayed rooted, unsure of what to do. We just thought that if the hill has to be climbed, then sooner rather than later. Then Mr Whiskey arrived from the rear and, after a brief consultation, was following us up the hill while the rest of the group followed the hyena who was laughing like a drain.

And with good reason did he laugh. We went up, and steeply; my pack was pushing me with its weight as I lent forward, falling up the mountain, hoping against hope that at least our extra exertion may have the benefit of short-ening the journey. This blissful oasis of thought was soon to be utterly dispelled on our arrival at the summit as Mr Whiskey informed us of our blunder in choosing this route – not just the gradient difficulty, but the extra distance adding half an hour to this stage.

It was at least all downhill from here, we thought. Well, yes, it was all downhill, bloody near vertical, dry, dusty and knee-breaking. I was on my arse twice, and nearly many times more before this supposed easy stage was over. Sure that my left knee was on the verge of crumbling to dust, I was learning, as usual, that downhill is not necessarily a good thing when trekking. Eirik was boundless as ever in his energy, yomping down the hill with increasing gusto in his black Bushman's hat, cheerfully singing, and occasion-ally calling back 'Come on old boy' in his part-Nordic, part-Yank, part mock posh English mixed-up accent.

When we eventually came across the village where we were to stop, at a mid-point in a valley, I could barely speak. The rest of the group had been there ten minutes already, so despite the pain we'd made good time, although I was in no state to care or recognise the depth of our achievement. I sat in a daze for a while in the shade until we had to leave, and here at least was some respite.

Our group had stirred a little interest within the village. Children, dogs and chickens seemed to be investigating the motley assortment of *falang* in their midst, and after a deal of sniffing, pointing and laughing, they'd become bored of us before we left. Passing the pig pen on our way, which the hyena had decided we should all closely inspect, the look I was giving him at that moment had its roots firmly back at the point where Eirik and myself took our 'alternative' route. It was of course an entirely wasted look, as is any kind of visual reproach with a Thai, and especially this gormless specimen staring back at me through his lensless sunnies.

We left the village and I could only wonder as to how far I would get before physically breaking down and embarrassing myself. Gamely I headed for the front with Eirik and we seemed to be back in the thick of the trek again, elephant footprints guiding the path, before we see the hyena, once again, laughing at us and heading off to a much easier-looking route. Fucker. We'd already shouted to him to ask if this was the route and he'd given us the silent treatment while sliding his machete blade down a piece of bamboo. Once we'd made some distance he began to laugh. We weren't getting fucked over twice by the little monkey, one look at each other and we were heading back to the easy option. First and only good move.

From there it was all flat. I refused to believe it would remain so easy until having reached the river, our destination for the day. After a few swims downriver with the current, the world seemed a much improved place to be.

That night the Canadians, Germans and Dutch entertained themselves with a card game I've not seen before (Kings), involving truth, dares and rules (odd), while the rest of us listened to Mr Whiskey strumming his guitar with Western tunes which he didn't know the words to. We got drunk and stoned, happy in the thoughts of no more trekking – let the boats do the work tomorrow.

TREK DAY 3

With other trekkers arriving to begin as we prepared to leave, there was a hive of activity with elephants loading up, boats being unloaded, and very little organisation apparent. We were herded into our inflatable with no instructions or crash helmets, and pushed out into the midstream to embark on our white water rafting experience. White water, big rocks, fast-running rapids, getting soaked, laughing, shouting, me and the Czech girls having a ball, splashing the other boats while close enough, then concentrating on navigating our way through the rocks and troughs of the bolting stream of H_2O surging along. Fluid anarchy, fantastic.

The river raft was cool, but not quite so for Eirik and his boat behind us. When we saw their oars coming down the river it was clear that all was not well. Mr Whiskey told me he thought as much without so much as a bat of the eyelids. 'Isn't that a bit on the dangerous side?' I asked him. 'Why?' he replied. So I asked him if perhaps being tipped out of the inflatable in rapids without crash helmets might prove somewhat hazardous. 'Why?' he repeated innocently. 'Oh, I don't know, just a wild idea that rocks might be tougher than skulls or other associated bony objects.' But no, still the same dumb questioning look returning at me, signifying what I took to be a total underestimation of the potential magnitude of the situation in hand. I prayed silently that the members of that inflatable may be blessed with a similar indifference to their plight. To my mind, this seemed a worthy situation for their famed, 'Oh my Buddha' exclamation.

As we soon found out, they'd been lucky and no one was badly hurt, but plenty of source material had been gleaned for the travellers' tales, of how Nate had looked like he was seeing death while under the inflatable after it had overturned, but hadn't lost his glasses, and Will just couldn't forget that look as he was opposite Nate at the time. Becky the Jonah added a cut to her shin to the many wounds she's been accumulating on her trip, as she was hurled through the rapids glancing off rocks as she went. Eirik the Viking swimming back in to the furious flow, from the safety of the riverbank, to help Kendra who wasn't having an easy time of it. 'Head up, legs forward', he shouted as he guided her to safety too. And for pure comic effect, there was Nate shouting ahead to Han, who'd been in the boat in front, to rescue the plastic drinking bottle that had their ganja in it. Without a second thought Han was in the river and swimming like a demon to retrieve the evening's gear. When next we all met up for the bamboo rafting stage there was an excited air as the individual experiences were being recounted for the first of many times to come, and not on that day only, I'm sure.

The bamboo rafting was a quiet relaxing wind-down to follow the white water excitement, but not without a little humour. The Thai steersman had, as with most of the guides, been into his high jinks, and after he'd turned three of our group into the river, his turn had to come. Knowing what a strong fucker he was, it was a case of just launching into him full tilt, so I was going in with him. In we went, and wet we got. Unfortunately he got his foot stuck between the bamboo poles as I bundled him off, and although unbroken, his leg had him wincing for the rest of the journey. So at least there was no more looking over our shoulders from then on.

That evening back at the Royal Guest House in Chiang Mai, the trekkers had arranged to go for a meal together, so for one last time we could swap bullshit about the endurance trial we'd survived. I talked football with Becky for most of it, and told her how Eirik and me had her and Kendra marked down as aerobics instructors, neglecting to mention a few additions we had made to our description. Email addresses were being moved around the table as Kendra could be heard proudly talking about her lovely embossed address book with elephants on the front, and how her 'special' travel buddies were all in it. Shortly afterwards she tore a piece of restaurant receipt paper from its pad, and slid it towards Eirik asking for his email. 'And yours, of course', she hastily added after catching my eye. 'So there you have it, mate', I told Eirik, 'Save a girl's life in the rapids and you don't even make it into the address book.' He'd already seen the humour of the moment. The German lads seemed keen to be friendly, as they had been throughout the trek, but for some reason we hadn't really clicked as a group and I'm pretty sure Eirik is the only one I'll keep in contact with. Next day the Canadian girls, Will and Eirik pushed off to Laos, they to see Laos, and Eirik to get his visa extended. Quiet day ahead.

Pai now, four hours' local bus ride north of Chiang Mai and I'm at the most chilled-out place I've seen so far. It's a central village-cum-town with lots of smaller villages surrounding it, and everything is ringed by mountains and a fast-flowing river running through it. So cheap here, so laid back, so friendly, so amazing to look at, and just so cool.

Eirik had come back from Laos with his visa extended and next thing he wanted to go see the long-neck Karen tribe and Buddha caves, so we booked up for the day trip. Once again it's easier for me to let someone else do the thinking. The Buddha caves were quite special, I thought; they go deep underground and have water-level markers to let you know how far the rainy season will raise the rivers inside, submerging many of the Buddha shrines carved out of the cave walls. Once again, many pictures taken as Eirik and I buzzed all about the place. Other than that it wasn't much of a trip really, all completely geared up like a shopping trip. Apparently the custom used to be that only

38

girls born on a certain day during the year had the right to wear the neck rings; now they all have them because it's good for tourism. I left my camera in my pocket as my heart wasn't in it, although there was one image I was tempted to frame – one of the little Karen girls wearing pink-rimmed plastic sunglasses. Then I see this Japanese guide herding this girl and two other long-necks in line for him to take a photo, yanking them by the arms, bloody rude I thought, then he barks at the little girl to take off her pink sunnies. Best reason for the picture was her glasses I reckoned, oh well.

Where they took us after that was a sad joke, the tribe of unwashed, living in filth, with occasional flash buildings and new cars in between sewage outlets and wildlife, and, as everywhere in Asia, Premiership football shirts worn aplenty.

At the end of the day we sat by the bar and began analysing the other travellers. We spotted a reasonable-looking tanned, mousy blonde, tall girl that seemed to glide through the place in her long draping black skirt, always on her own. Eirik had been teaching me a Norwegian comment, *skulle vor kukast*, which he informed me means 'she'd get it'. We were in agreement that this girl deserved the accolade. I was surprised to see her sat down with him later after I'd been to my room. I presumed he must be chatting to her out of intrigue as he was leaving the next day.

Well her name was Kitty, a Canadian that's travelled around Cambodia, Vietnam, Laos, just recently arrived in Thailand and heading next day for Pai. I'd already heard good things about the place, but meeting Kitty sealed the deal. She was travelling alone and happy for some company en route. After Eirik headed off to Bangkok, Kitty and I went out for some alcohol-fuelled retail therapy in the Chiang Mai night market where we got a hat each, she got

39

a ring, and I practiced my Thai bartering. I was probably a bit on the noisy side because the Thais I was bartering with kept gesturing with their hands to keep it down while Kitty was laughing, enjoying the entertainment. The night market has some great handmade stuff for sale, from clothes to sculptures and knick knacks, all at silly money, and plenty of it.

PAI

Arrived Pai 14th Nov 2002

Bright and early Kitty and I took a local bus up to Pai for 60 baht, a quaint old jalopy with electric fans strategically placed hanging from the roof to keep us cool, Thai music on the tape deck, and of course the 'bus nutter' sat in front of Kitty and myself. Some Dutch guy on a mission (apparently) to find an elusive 'no one's heard of it before' hideaway lodge, asking Kitty questions like she's some kind of tour guide before his attention was diverted by another woman, wearing futuristic-looking ear phones – he liked those.

When we got to Pai I was a bit surprised at the size of it. I'd expected a small village but it's more like a small town, and a rapidly expanding one at that. Kitty was off and running straight away, so I just kept in tow and she led us to a bamboo bridge over a fast-flowing river and we'd found our home for the next few days, 100 baht a night, with an unspoilt view of the surrounding landscape (rainforest-clad mountains), fresh baskets of juicy fat bananas, papayas, mangos and other fruits put out for us every other day. Bamboo-built shade platforms with hammocks for chilling, smoking and chatting to the other bungalow tenants, and everything constructed from natural resources. This is a place you could get stuck in.

Written 29th Nov 2002

Straight away we've chummed up with some Aussies, Mark, Kelly and Graham (Wiggo), and they'd only met an hour earlier. The first few days we didn't exactly rush about to see the sights, but rather planted ourselves socially within our little area of Pai, and everyone's travel stories became the entertainment. One night Kitty, myself, Mark and Kelly decided to give some opium a try (second or third night), scored the stuff and bombed it in rolling papers. That's about as much as I can remember of that night.

Kitty and me had already booked a yoga course for the following morning. How we made it I couldn't say. There we were, walking on eggshells through Pai, eyes fixed ahead and down, less chat the better, feeling like death but still going to yoga. Turned up and the madwoman that runs the course asks to make sure we haven't eaten that morning. Neither of us could even have looked at food without stirring unwanted bowel reactions. We got into it OK and managed the class without too much pain until just before the end of the two hour session, when the sickly oily shyte that had been gurgling in me guts finally said 'hello' and I had to spring for the curtained exit quick sharp. I didn't hurl, which I'm not sure was good or bad, but the madwoman just put it down to being my first time at yoga. 'You no worry, first time, you fine soon.' It gave me and Kitty a laugh for a moment, not too long a moment unfortunately.

We only had a four-hour break before the next two-and-a-half-hour session of yoga was upon us, and I was still fragile, as was Kitty. Our efforts didn't go unnoticed by the rest of our new family crew back at Jays restaurant, but their compliments on our achievement did nothing to quell the disquiet my digestive system was experiencing. After an uncomfortable time of pushing my fruit salad around the

41

bowl, busting in and out of hot and cold sweats, and recoiling bodily from the aroma of Kitty's veg soup, my decorum had evaporated and I was eyeing the surroundings for somewhere to throw up. I waited for Kitty to leave first because she wasn't feeling great either and, I'd say, neither of us wanted to witness the other spewing chunks in our tender state. My options seemed limited – not really on to vomit in the river which runs past the restaurant, didn't fancy projectiles within the place, so went for the cautious walk back to the bungalow. I made about ten yards into open area before the matter was taken unceremoniously out of my hands, big old gut surge and up it all came, right in front of an audience of laughing Thai farm labourers. After that I slept for a couple of hours, and the second yoga session was a sight more comfortable. Mental note, fuck bombing opium.

The Festival of Lights was on its way, and many people were heading to Chiang Mai for the big party, displays and processions. As a group we'd decided Pai was too chilled to leave so soon, and as they were having their own celebrations maybe we should join in. So there was hatched the idea between myself and Michl, a much-travelled German, to build a bamboo raft as our contribution to the big night. At this point we were just in the talking-about-it stage. Once Michl and myself had mentioned our idea to some of the others, including Jay the restaurant owner, we'd already painted ourselves into a metaphorical corner.

18th Nov 2002

While we were talking, Graeme was doing. He'd had a barby spit made by a Thai metal worker for 60 baht, he also bought three freshly slaughtered chooks for the family cook-up, and Jay supplied the rice and veggies. Another great night, fantastic food – the boy (Wiggo/Graeme) barbys a mean chook – plenty of drink and smoke after, and a bit of bongoing by Michl and Kitty, before me and Graeme took the stage and collapsed in a fit of giggles unable to continue.

The raft idea gained so much momentum that there was no getting out of it, even the Thais' had heard and were offering tools and supplies for the cause.

20th Nov 2002

The day came and we threw ourselves into it. One-diamond shaped bamboo raft on the way, most of the family were in on it, and others lent moral support. I was cutting, Mark was the tie-up master binding it all together, Michl was creating the tripod mast, and Orr (Young Touchwood, or Boy Blunder) was our apprentice along with Graeme. All made from bamboo, even the ties, and the girls bought flowers and candles to decorate it. I have to say, it did look the mutts nuts, we looked like some South American funeral cortege when we actually launched it, lots of pics and lots of fun.

Before our launch, we watched the festival procession. First off we thought we'd missed it, as everyone was heading in the opposite direction to us, so we parked our arses for a beer and rest, when lo and behold it goes right past our spot, good move. Lots of highly decorated 4 x 4 trucks with Thai pageant queens in and elaborately regaled villagers between, soldiers dancing through too, behind their band in a truck complete with singer, all in military uniform. I managed a combat photographer's roll in front of the procession at one point to get a shot looking up from centre, which gleaned some curious looks.

With the procession past we shot off to launch our pride and joy, the *Frat Flied Flog* which we had dedicated to the many ironed-out amphibians on the Thai roads. Kitty had designed a cool logo for the flag on the mast so it all looked

43

quite professional. What we hadn't realised until the actual night was that the elaborate floats were the trucks in the road parade, while the Thais just sent little banana leaf boats about the size of cupped hands down the river with their blessings aboard. Our vessel looked like the battleship *Bismarck* in comparison. Mark got in the river up to his waist to ease the launch and off she went like a dream, down the river at a furious pace. We watched from the bamboo bridge as our oversized baby disappeared around one of the many sharp bends in the river, before belting off ourselves to get to the main bridge downriver and see if it would make it. On its launch it was lit up like a Christmas tree there were so many candles on it, but when it hove into view before the main bridge, it had clearly met with obstacles, because only two were still alight, looking like car headlights as it came around the bend towards us. Fuelled by alcohol and excitement we cheered her on, a good 20 or so of us, from the campsite amidst the many indigenous villagers. Her mast was down and the flag underwater, but still going on nonetheless before finally snagging on some rocks after passing under the bridge and ending her brief but worthwhile journey.

After that we went on to the local school field where the party was in full swing with hundreds of stalls selling all kinds of wonderful foods, a kickboxing ring where the Thai boxing soldiers battered seven bells out of each other, and two stages set up for a variety of other performers. I got very caned and had a supremely chilled time of it. As with pretty much every night in Pai, we all finished up on our sheltered platform swapping bullshit.

Other than the festival fun, our days seemed to revolve around Jays restaurant, the Muslim bakery for chocolate croissants and coffee, the chilling shade platforms, swimming pool just outside town where we spent many lazy hours prior to 'beer o'clock', or exploring, good food and good fun basically. Graeme decided he wanted to stay longer in Pai so went out, bought a guitar, and made up his mind to learn to play it while still there. What a boy.

Sad farewells as Kitty left on the 23rd, big hugs and tearful girls. Mark, Kelly, Michl and Katja went off white water rafting and caving for the day. Me and Graeme went on our own trek into the jungle next to us on the 24th, and that night the remaining members got wasted watching one of the worst films in a long time, *Reign of Fire*, which had just one redeeming feature, the line, 'There's only one thing I hate more than dragons, and that's Americans.'

On the 25th me and Graeme helped Pak (the owner of the chalets me and Kitty were staying in), steer some bamboo rafts down the Pai river with two other travellers, a Dutch lad and girl, two-and-a-half hours of both sharp and easy bends, low bridges to either jump over or duck under, mini rapids, and general total coolness as we traversed our way back to the bamboo bridge outside Pak's restaurant and bungalows, where the rafts would be taken apart and used for building more chalets. Such a relaxing, enjoyable way to see the valley and mountains surrounding Pai as we took it in turns to steer with the bamboo punt poles, or lay back and chill.

<u>Pai time</u>

They're 'dead set classics' our Kelly and Mark,
Top mates as cool as a walk in the park.
They rocked up to Pai and soon as became mates
when grass and the opium sealed our fates.

The 'O' got us hammered and grass got us caned,
The Chiang which is brutal so oft had us brained.
A family grew from the few we first met –
I've not met a better lot travelling yet

45

Kitty and Katja, Michl and Orr, and
Graeme the 'doer', now he knew the score,
He had his own spit made and barbied some chook,
Bought a guitar and used Jay's music book

We all built a raft in traditional style, which
made all the Pai locals widen their smile
Embellished with candles and flowers and hair
Fresh cut from Mark, 'I'm me dad' he declared.

We ate and we drank and we lazed 'but', together
When Pai started crying they called it the weather,
The sadness it felt that all good things must end,
And saddest of all is the parting of friends.

But now I'll relax while my body repairs,
Less eating, less drinking, I'll try to be fair.
It's all been 'too easy' and 'cool as' right through,
As our lovely Thai waitress said, 'Khap Kuhn you too'.

One by one the family departed, and Pai, as we painfully
admitted, had been done. It had begun raining too so the
time was right. I eventually left with Mark and Kelly back
to Chiang Mai on the local bus. Not a straightforward
affair, the last few days of rain had contributed to a
healthy-sized landslip on one of the mountain roads, and
the bus driver lost his bottle after a couple of abortive
attempts to get it through.

As the bus slowed up on arrival, we could see some Thai
labourers and earth-moving machinery along with a queue
of 4 x 4 trucks looking on at mounds of wet and slushy
sand, strewn across the bend in the road. Our driver made
his first attempt as soon as his opportunity arose. Inside the
bus we watched with nervous interest as it went forward at
first, and then began to slide sideways as the wheels lost all

grip in the sea of sand. After a lot of shouting and furious waving of hands by the Thai workers, the driver stopped, and as he did, Mark and I jumped off, followed by other mildly concerned passengers. The drop from the edge of the road was considerable, and steep. After the rest of the passengers realised the wisdom of this move and followed suit, the driver rolled the bus back and took a run at it, with clouds of black exhaust fumes billowing out, sand flying everywhere, but still he was sliding almost to the very edge of the drop until he had to give up. With his elbows lent on his steering wheel, and his head buried into his hands, he didn't look a happy bunny.

Soon enough the bus was reversed back down the road and out of the way to let the pick-up trucks have a crack at it, mostly engulfing the area in plumes of dirty exhaust clouds as the thrashing engines coughed themselves hoarse, wheels spinning furiously and sliding all over the place while people tried to push them up around the bend. Having seen our bus abandoned, we opted to get our bags off its roof and try to hitch a lift. Mark, in true Aussie style, approached a Thai woman driver who didn't fancy taking on the slippery road, and she agreed to give us a lift to Chiang Mai if he could get her taxi truck through the mire. We'd watched with interest all the efforts to get through, and the best of the lot had been a full tilt run-up followed by a steady revving, not overcooking it. Mark did it faultlessly to our, and many others', cheers, and we had our ride sorted. Three and a half hours later and we're back in Chiang Mai once more. Our Thai lady driver asked for nothing for the ride either, but we had a whip-round to give her something towards petrol and she seemed well chuffed.

27th

Michl had his Pai photos burnt on to C.Ds for us all so we

each had a set, and then quite by chance Jason bumps into us, or, more accurately, he nearly mowed us down while paralytic on his 'chopaped', a confused motorbike that can't decide if it's a Lambretta or a Harley D. Jason's the brother of a mate back home. I hadn't known where to find him, but knew he was in Chiang Mai somewhere. Talk about weird, there I am with mates I've only known a couple of weeks, in the heart of a Thai city I don't really know at all, and we nearly get mown down by my mate's pissed-up brother from my home town. I don't know who was the most surprised. From that moment on it's been a case of eating and drinking too much (again) with various groups as one by one they all did the sensible thing and moved on. I've stayed rooted in the city while the clock ticks away. I think perhaps it's time for some action.

For two weeks I hung around Chiang Mai's old city area, getting to know Jason's mates and their bars, as well as the many entertainments the city has to offer, such as at the Tapai Gate, one of the entrances through the old city walls. Here *Tar Gor* tournaments are held at night – Thai football if you like, a game played with a ball made of basket weave, about 6 inches in diameter, with a net and court of volley-ball proportions. The players are as agile as any gymnast, often firing the ball back over the net with overhead scissor kicks from higher than the top of the net. The level of skill and agility make their fast, all-action games a truly incredible experience to witness. On the outskirts of this open concrete expanse are hordes of young Thais practising their skate boarding skills, and milling *farang* enjoying the whole spectacle.

There were some amusing nights spent around the Night Market district, often feeding at the outdoor Anusarn market where most Asian cooking styles are available, with the friendliest of service always. Bartering with the tiny Akha tribeswomen for knick-knacks we usually didn't want, wandering the extensive Night Market for which Chiang Mai is so famed, eating at restaurants showing the latest released films, where the background music is deafening, and the dialogue inaudible because the films are pirate recorded from the back of cinemas, hence the speed with which they reach the bar circuit. Not to mention the appalling subtitles they put on (English) which bear little resemblance to what's being said on screen, often with a comical result. It's the 9th now, and I'm not filling up my journal with a catalogue of piss-ups, so I intend my next entry to be from Laos.

CHIANG MAI TO CHANG KONG, CHANG KONG TO LUANG PRABANG, LAOS

15th Dec 2002

Written from Luang Prabang, arrived 14th. Now in Laos, but first a brief summary of the last few days in Chiang Mai. Met up with Irish boys Donny, Keith and Kelvis, and the Canadians (canidiots) Mark, Greg, Tara and McGregor, all through major benders involving Thai buckets, which mostly went through to nine or ten in the morning, and, other than minor internal pain and wallet damage, were a good laugh. Also Jessica, the sweet-looking American, 'Yeah, yeah, yeah', 'I hear you', 'I hear what you're saying', 'Right, right, right' – I felt compelled to ask her if her parents were psychiatrists.

Me throwing up by the pool during brekkie with the Irish boys and then returning to finish my fruit salad with yoghurt. Plenty late-night, early-morning, noisy 'Jenga' sessions. Jason and co. for live music in the Inter Bar at the top of Tapai Road (Tapai Gate end). Bingo's Bar, the Pink Flamingo, where much pool was played, and some very colourful, mainly European, characters resided or drank.

And excellent massages as regularly as possible, one hour for 100 baht (about £1.40).

On the morning I was to leave Chiang Mai, on a minibus up to the Chang Kong border crossing, I woke up with stomach cramps and the shits. Off to the chemist to get dosed up, then reclaim my room back for a couple of hours before the bus left. Doubled up foetus-style, with a hot water bag and towel that the guesthouse cleaning ladies gave me to ease the pain. Then a six-hour drive up to Chang Kong, many bog squirts on the way, and stayed at the Nam Kong guest house, which overlooks the **Mekong River** with **Huay Xai** in Laos on the other side. Got booked on the speed boat to Luang Prabang, six hours on that supposed 'hell ride', or two days on the slow boat. No contest in my condition.

Next morning, the view from the guest house up and down the Mekong was stunning as the early mists rose and fused with the rising sun. I took a photo using my sunglasses as a filter for my 'snappy' camera. After breakfast it's off to the border crossing and immigration, got a hefty shock there when asked for a 3,000 baht overstay charge; hadn't checked my immigration stamp properly, what a doughnut. Then, on the Laos side of the river, change up a $100 US and become a Kip millionaire, taking away your money in a holdall bag. The fine at the Thai border was made up for by the boat ride to Luang Prabang, a 16-foot long by 4 foot wide, flat-bottom, arrow-shaped boat with seating for six passengers plus luggage, and a car engine sat on the transom, it went like shit off a stick along the Mekong.

Armed with wax earplugs and a Diazepam, I sat back and revelled in the experience. The river itself is an angry, unpredictable, seething mass of confusion. Full of huge whirlpools, rips, lethal shallows, white water crashing in upsurges against the many mid-river rock formations, and overlooked on both sides by mountains, silt banks and lush green vegetation. Even though, in crash helmets with visors and life jackets, and bolting along the water at over 30 knots, it's impossible not to appreciate the vastness and awesome beauty of the surrounding landscape.

For six hours I couldn't help feeling like I'd want to go straight back and do it again, bouncing and bumping along the Mekong with your knees under your chin, and the deafening roar of the immense engine, definitely one of the highlights of the trip. It's easy to see why the Asian continent has, thus far, failed to conquer the Mekong. In places the rock formations and bends combine to make the current turn around so it appears to be running both ways at once, leaving the surface bubbling as if it's boiling up.

LUANG PRABANG

On arrival we were greeted by Laotian children running all around us, trying to grab our bags and cop a tip for their efforts, then the same deal with the tuk-tuk drivers. Dropped in town then yomped around and found a cool guesthouse, Moukdavan for 30,000 kip a night (£2), huge wood-panelled room with double bed and fan, and real friendly people running the place.

Met up with the Irish lads I'd met at the Royal Guesthouse in Chiang Mai and went out for the evening with them, top lads (Donny, Keith and Kelvis). They told me of their slow-boat experience down the Mekong, which they said was uncomfortable, but not unbearable, and how at the night stop at Pak Beng, all the villagers were trying to push drugs onto them, nearly resulting in a fight at their guesthouse between locals over who gets to sell what to who. The lads are shooting off to Veng Vieng this morning so I may catch up with them in Vientiane possibly.

Luang Prabang town is a bit of a dustbowl, but not without charm. The architecture is mainly old French colonial, with tall, narrow, louvre-shuttered windows, and lots of bakeries. Rivers both sides of the town centre, the Mekong and the Nam Khan, with terraced crops leading down to the winding rivers edges, lush green in places, and fallow brown in others, but pleasing to the eye either way.

Tonight helped Si, one of the Laotian lads that runs the place, with his English. He's dead keen and pretty sharp. I reckon he'll be spot on in a year or so if he stays this keen.

16th Dec

Another lazy day, but at least in a new place with new things to see, the banana shakes are fantastic, as are the fruit pancakes. Most of the restaurants are French style, so the food's good, as you would expect from our Channel cousins. I wish I could have more time here, but I'll try to make the most of the time I do have.

Here they have what I can best describe as moped pram taxis, which have a two-seated sidecar, with sun hoods just like pram covers. Also a variety of half rickshaw, half tuk-tuk types, mini-vans turned into open but covered taxis, and all ranging in degrees of age and condition from spanking new to 'how does it still go', and mostly highly decorated in bright colours.

Played bingo with Si, his mate, and a Japanese traveller, Taku, in the guesthouse. Good practice for my Laos/Thai numbers, and still picking up more Laos words. Winner gets to flick the last winner's forehead, good laugh. During the day I wandered around by the rivers and took a few pics, went past the monks' residence, which was quite funny; they find the travellers as amusing and interesting as we do them.

They were laughing, pointing and joking with each other like kids in a school playground: 'Hallo mister, *sabaii dii*', and so happy-looking, you have to smile back, you can't help it. I love seeing them walking along in their orange robes with their black brollies for sun protection, creases me up.

17th

Luang Prabang southern bus terminal, 6.30 a.m. Feel like shyte, no sleep all night, then up at 5.30 and out the guest house 15 minutes later, some poor baby screaming all night long from over the road from my room, then I'm on the bus five minutes and there's another one two seats in front of me. Syrup coffee and *sep lai* (very tasty) omelette in station before I go.

The drive: just outside Luang Prabang and straight through to mountains and river valleys. Light, tall bullrushes like feather dusters. In the clouds, above the clouds, silken cotton wool carpets lying between the mountains, roosters, goats, ducks, cows, calves, pot-bellied pigs, dogs, homes all in or around the road in places, little Laotians often staring, smiling or waving. Lush green, white-headed roadside bush flowers, villages rising through the mist, looking like castles in the sky, winding valley rivers, blood-red poinsettias, 'bloody hell' roadslips, huge drops (sheer), Mekong?

VIENTIANE

Arrived 3.30 p.m.-ish, wandered around after taxi dropped us in Vientiane centre by the fountain. Made my way to the Stade Nationale and found digs at the Syrie Guesthouse, another old French colonial place with tall ceilings, long narrow windows, and wooden louvered shutters. Nice room with pukka shower room, and as always, friendly people. Didn't stray far that evening, knackered after the nine-hour drive.

18th Dec

Up at midday-ish and off for a survey of the locality. The national stadium not very big, with adjoining tennis club which was well used. Most of the town in a state of disrepair, especially the concrete drain covers which, when there at all, are generally cracked or half missing. Even saw a Laotian guy dangling a rod and line down into the sewer, fishing through one of the holes left by a vacant drain cover. Took a wander up to the promenade on the Mekong. More heavily French influenced architecture, good bread in the restaurants, buzzing moped taxis and mopeds. Didn't stay out too long, back to room, booked ticket for Bangkok as money almost gone, finished *Glue*, by Irvine Welsh and started again, wicked read.

Left Vientiane on coach 5.30 p.m., met up with a couple more Paddies (Tom and Owen) that had been staying with two English Asian lads I'd met in Chiang Mai. Had the *craic* with them on the way back, smoking crushed-up Diazepam reefers, and drinking Chiang beer. Through the Friendship Bridge border crossing, after paying the border guards' late-night overtime fee, from Laos into Thailand, and headed uneventfully **back to Bangkok**.

19th

Back again in the early hours, got in at the D&D Inn after kipping a couple of hours in the lobby, 4.30–6.30 a.m., got a room for 350 baht this time, bargain. Met up with Tom and Owen in the evening. Tom had to show me how to get money out of the ATM, my first time ever (5,000 baht).

Went for drinks at the Khao Sarn centre and Gullivers, both in the Khao San road.

20th

Up at midday and out into the hustle and bustle of Khao San road, same old story. Discovered last night that I've lost my South East Asia Lonely Planet guide book. Oh well, lighter rucksack. I hadn't really used it other than the map to see where I've been, or to see where I'm going is.

Emailed Donny to let him know I was back in Bangkok, and he turned up behind me while I was still in the internet café – he'd been on the net himself just down the road, and came looking as soon as he got my message. That evening we got a taxi boat down the **Nam Chao Praya** River to the sky train terminal and caught the super-fast space-age train to **Phram Pong** and on to an Irish boozer he'd discovered. Nice place and people, if a bit pricey, 135 baht for a pint of Heineken. I'd booked my ticket to **Koh Chang**, but we still got larruped even though I had to be up for 8 a.m.

LAEM NGOB

21st Dec

Up no probs and off for another bumpy minibus jaunt for six hours down to Laem Ngob. I think its shocks are on the way out, but the roads didn't help, otherwise uneventful. Ditched the Koh Chang idea because no boats go to Silhanoukville from there, plus blown all the 5,000 I'd got at Bangkok. It's gonna be touch and go from now on. I've booked another minibus to Silhanoukville, 1,000 baht. I was sold a bum steer in Bangkok: they told me I could get a boat from Koh Chang to Silhanoukville, but no. If I'd known that, I'd have booked all the way from Bangkok. Ah well, it's not a bad place. I'm writing this from a jetty restaurant, and the cool breeze is quite pleasant in my current sticky, clammy state. Koh Chang hogs the view across the water. They have a new pier which has just recently been completed, but not ready for use apparently; once again the tourist revolution is in evidence. Also new buildings flying up everywhere, my guesthouse looks 'arry spankers' too, blue mosaic tiled veranda right out on to the seashore, fantastic, shame I can't stay here a few days.

THAILAND INTO CAMBODIA

22nd

Left Laem Ngob this morning. The sea was as calm as a millpond looking out from the veranda; the water lapping up underneath the stilted bungalow has a very soothing effect. Off at 10.30 a.m., headed for the Thai–Cambodian border at **Laem Chem**, another uneventful journey bar the German guy with a powerful foot odour problem, which the Dutch bloke with us tells him to sort out! 1,100 baht for visa at the border crossing, supposed to be only 800, but when you're dealing with armed guards in an often lawless country, you pay. Then get on the back of our new Cambodian host's Wattana's moped, while the others in our border crossing group jumped into the pick-up truck, and head for an overnight stop in **Koh Kong town** at the Rets Mai Bon Tam guesthouse. Pissed Wattana off in disagreement over exchange rate (he can't count), but he wasn't (it seemed) trying to rip me off. I'm a bit annoyed with myself because he's a real friendly and helpful lad – just a misunderstanding, hopefully one I can put right with a few beers. Guesthouse pukka again, floor-to-ceiling tiles, quite new, big room with fan and own shower. (Found out later from Gerhard, an Austrian, that Wattana had indeed been ripping off the other travellers over exchange rates.)

KOH KONG TO SILHANOUKVILLE

23rd Dec

Minibus to Silhanoukville after eating and smoking with the guesthouse family the night before, also trying to learn more Cambodian words from them, mostly to fits of giggles, while they tried a bit of English. Bumpy old ride on the red gravel roads, (sort of), which had big ravines running through them in abundance where heavier rain often washes away the roads. Good way to see the country though, excellent untouched scenery, four ferry crossings along the way, rickety old buckets but effective. Picked up a rice and dark meat meal with herbs for 20 baht, cooked on the ferry/raft, top scoff. After six and a half hours of boneshaking, packed in like sardines, arrived in Silhanoukville and booked in to the Victory Guesthouse on Victory beach, $4 a night. OK place, fan, shower/toilet room, two beds, and a grey metal crate bolted to the wall, which would normally house a TV set. Beach really nice, may amble down there for a dip tomorrow. Took taxi bike to town for a wander, had a couple of jars in The Anchor, an English boozer, reasonable. Then internet, followed by coffee and veggie burger at Mike and Craigs, English-run but good food. After that, short wander down the main drag and then taxi bike back, 20 baht each way.

Back at guesthouse, smoked with the Austrian, Gerhard, whose grey metal crate actually had a TV set in it, and watched *Mission Impossible 8*, and *Gracelands 3000*, ridicu-

lously over the top but entertaining and, often unintention-
ally, funny. Bit caned, bye-byes. Just about to nod off and
it's absolutely hurling it down outside, tin roofs everywhere
so a tad noisy, what.

24th

Up at the crack of lunch, after a brief stretch and yoga, out
for brekkie (cheese omelette in baguette, 3000 Cambodian
Riels), then taxi bike (moto) to main drag for bank and
internet followed by a short and dull wander before
hopping on a moto back to the 'Victory'. Booked bus ticket
to Phnom Penh, then chilled down at the beach with a
scooby, quality beach and view. Slight Mediterranean feel
as you look out at the gentle ripples curling in peacefully to
the shore, harbour to the right but not a busy one.
   Up to Gerhard's room for pre-match scooby before
heading into town for a few sherbets. Met up with the Dutch
guy and his wife that I'd travelled down with from Laem
Ngob to Silhanoukville. Sunk a few then got on motos, and
the moto boys took us to *farang* 'bang' club, cool as.

25TH, SHITMAS DAY

Up at 10-ish, brief stretch, pack, and out for brek at Rosies
opposite Victory. Only my second day here and she's treating
me as if I'd been a while, 'Goodbye, come back soon, you be
safe', bless her cottons. Moto to bus station for 12.30 kick-off
and a decent bus to the capital, pukka road too.

PHNOM PENH

Phnom Penh's far more scary than Bangkok; what a mad,

crazy, non-stop exhilarating loony bin of a place. Thousands of motos with no rules at all as they weave in and out of the mayhem, cutting across the flow, driving on the wrong side while dodging the oncoming throng of swarms of other motos. All the time jaw-dropping at the contrast of lavish new, set amidst desperate poverty and filth. I thought Bangkok was mad at first; it barely gets close to this frenzy, I don't think I've ever seen so many motorbikes all at the same time, and it all seems to work.

My moto boy, Polly, snagged me as I got off the bus, and after following some German, looking for super-cheap digs, to a hideous shithole area, Polly said that 'By the river's (Mekong) better', anywhere had to be better than this dump I thought: 'Go on mate, lead the way.' Quality choice too, Gullivers Guesthouse, spitting distance from posh promenade on the river, and a nice room for only $3. Then he ran me around to sort out money and flight tickets with Silk Air, which was closed, so will be off there in the morning, Polly's coming round between 9 and 10 a.m., looks like I've been adopted. Tomorrow he's taking me to the Killing Fields and war museum.

Met a couple of students by the river, asking me to help with their pronunciation, chatted for a while, they said not to go out alone at night as it's not too clever. 'Lots of robbers, you have robbers in England?', 'We call them politicians', I told them.

26th

Not much of a sleep, but up early to meet with Polly and sort out the ticket situ with Silk Air at Micasa Hotel, huge new and expensive-looking gaff on the bank of the Mekong; this river's everywhere. Got a flight provisionally booked for the 28th out of Phnom Penh, as long as their London office OK's it, fingers crossed. After that, Polly took me out to the shooting range, miles away, and double what I'd been expecting it to cost but still cheap, I thought: 30 rounds out of an AK47 Kalashnikov semi-automatic machine gun for $20 (US), 25 hit the target too. All kinds of weaponry available; they casually dumped a grenade in front of me, but I couldn't afford it. It was tempting though, just to see it and hear it for real. The power of the AK wasn't too bad until it was swung into automatic, short bursts to fire off three rapid-fire shots, and I could feel the gun taking itself on a wander, cool as to find out the hands-on way.

I was forgetting: before the shooting gallery, Polly took me to 'S21', the Khmer Rouge prison, where the lunatics once ran the asylum. After watching a not-too-harrowing movie on the subject, I ambled round the site of this giant torture chamber, which had been the Tuol Svay Prey high school before Pol Pot and his nutters got to it. Numbness was all I could feel as I checked out the tiny cells with chains and small tin chamber pots, first-floor brick cells, second-floor hardwood slatted cells, and top floor mass detention cells, which were closed to the public. Torture rooms with photos of some of the victims (just tortured, or dead), and some of the tools of torture still there. Harrowing images of empty, glazed faces with number tags, paintings depicting some nasty-looking torture procedures, showcases full of some of the many victims' skulls, stacked on top of each other. Barbed wire fencing from all the balconies to prevent the prisoners committing suicide. I couldn't wait to get out of the place, mobbed by amputees as you leave, just chuck your spare change at them and fuck off quick, 'You want go Killing Fields now?' Polly asked me. 'No thanks mate, not after that.' Numb.

Sitting in a Vietnamese-run pizza restaurant in Cambodia, overlooking the sloping concrete banks of the Mekong past the broad promenade. Watching the river traffic glide past, it's all a bit reminiscent of the Nile in the film *Death on the*

Nile, quite classy-looking. Not quite so classy looking back, mind you.

27th Written in the Cambo/Italiano/Vietnamese eatery

Up at the crack of lunch again, and off to check the ticket situ; no luck, so then it's rush off to make an international call and organise another money transfer, just so that I can buy a new ticket out of here. Bingo, and job done after another mini sweat panic with dodgy phones and looming deadlines (banks and Silk Air offices closing). New moto boy today, older, so not quite as up on his English as Polly, but we got there after a little map searching, the *Naga* ship, rather like a huge floating hotel, moored on the banks of the Mekong, which has a Western Union office aboard for me to sort out my money transfer. Real plush, full of military uniformed staff, and metal detecting gates as you enter the ship. Super-friendly as always too, even though I looked like an eco-vagrant.

I bet these countries were the most beautiful places on earth before they got sold the western ways, and a lot more peaceful I reckon. Shitmas tree in the corner would defo go.

Back at Gullivers. I can't help it but these two just have to be written in. English (northern) bloke and bird (southern); every time I've seen him he's so sauced he can barely stand up. Tonight he's sporting two black eyes that he didn't have yesterday. She always appears to be sober, and I've only seen her drink Coke to his beers. She has to guide him everywhere like he's a cripple or a drunk, and he bitches every step of the way about not needing anyone's help, while she smiles and calls him a pisshead without so much as a hint of resentment. Thing is, she's quite reasonable to look at, no model but defo OK, and he's got bottle-bottom glasses, a face like a bulldog chewing stinging nettles, always appears to be looking for a fight, although with glasses that thick it's anybody's guess what he thinks he's looking at, and at the evidence in front of me, he's rarely sober. No accounting for taste.

28th Dec, Written at Changi Airport Singapore.

Drinking with some Taiwanese, businessmen and a film maker, last night, it sounds like that might be a cool place to visit and teach English, $25 an hour apparently. Taught them a bit of UK history, and they told me about Taiwan's General Lee, who destroyed 500 Japanese battle ships with only 15 of his own, but which were small, fast and manoeuvrable, sometime in the fifteenth or sixteenth century, must investigate, sounds cool.

Got a Moto to Phnom Penh airport after a sound brek, wicked homemade hash browns, and top beans, all-round quality. Half-hour ride to the airport, uneventful. Another fat woman with body odour issues next to me on the plane, but she's a friendly Cambodian so no biggy. Posh new plane with drop-down screens for information blurb which the air hostesses used to do.

Australia: Manly, Great Ocean Road, and Tasmania Journals, 29th Dec 2002 to 23rd Mar 2003

SYDNEY, AUSTRALIA

29th Dec 2002

Arrived early morning in Sydney, took a bus to the Darling Harbour ferry terminal and hopped onto one of their wonderful ferries up to Manly, out past the Opera House to the right, and the spectacular Sydney Harbour Bridge to the left, and then off across to Manly on the Northern Beaches, passing the Sydney Heads entrance on the way, not a trip you'd quickly tire of. Hiked around Manly to find Bower Street, where Si's staying, tatty-looking place but great position overlooking Shelley Beach and the Fairey Bower Point. Unfortunately Si and crew are away surfing at Crescent Heads up the coast, so me and my bags set off 'pack mule' style to get into a backpackers' until they return. Manly Wharf Backpackers, $24 a night, directly opposite the ferry terminal, sharing a room with three Paddies, two lads and a girl, good lot, hit it off straight away. Checked out the area, very lively, lots of fit-looking people, hugely busy beach. Heaps of coffee bars, decent-looking eateries and bars, not cheap but not expensive.

Four days at Manly Wharf Backpackers, good crowd, mainly Irish. Teamed up for a few sessions with them and stuck to wine (take-outs), while living off bread rolls and cheap ham. Si came back from their surf trip on the 31st, met up and arranged to move in to Bower Street on the

2nd, staying in the cupboard under the stairs, decent-sized cupboard mind, and only $50 Aus a week, too easy.

Got nicely wasted with Si on New Year's Eve, hard 'house' party on manly beach, charging around with fat smiles, finished drinking on New Year's Day, 10 a.m.-ish.

Usual process of getting to know the area, slow and slack, bang-up place, permanent decent surf, perfect view of the bay and all the surf spots. The overall area is known as the Northern Beaches, a well-to-do area with 59 Bower Street at the top of a millionaire's hill, overlooking the vistas below, total result. It's only a ten-minute walk down to the surf on Manly Beach, and this is a place for water sports junkies. Boogy boarding's what I've started on until I can suss it all out without killing myself.

Written Tues 28th Jan

Still at the Bower. Si's brother, Rick, went back home yesterday. Three weeks the Rickstar was with us, and during that time, me, him and Si, checked out the Northern Beaches almost daily, although for the last few days I've been unable to go in after making the mistake of going out on the boogy board without a wet suit, or rash vest, my chest is now red raw as a result of the board wax and sea salts combined efforts to tear up my skin.

Mark Knowles, of the Mark and Kelly that I met at Pai in Northern Thailand, was back on his home soil and invited us up for an insider's guided tour of his part of the world, and he took me and Rick around to all the best lookout spots he knows. Mark lives in **Lapstone**, a small town in the heart of the blue mountains, and after a youth spent exploring it all on dirt track bikes, he knows the place well. We saw the **Megalong Reservoir**, which supplies the drinking water for South Australia, and looks like the most amazing natural inland water paradise. Azure-blue water and golden sandy beaches, all still and unspoilt by man's unwelcome footmarks. Because of its importance as the water supply, the whole area is barred to all but water board employees. The shape of it is mesmerising too, with many small bays and dead-end tributaries shooting off from the main body of crystal-blue wet stuff.

We travelled as far north as **Katoomba** to see the lookout point there which has wicked views of the canyons and valleys up that neck of the woods, saw the **Three Sisters** (sticky-uppy rocky pinnacles), almost vertical cable car to drop those that wish, down into the throng of the eucalyptus forest below. And a disused but awesome-looking roller coaster which goes around the whole cable car complex and down into the brush and tree lines below. Apparently, when the ride was tested with a crash test dummy in it, the roller coaster came back with a headless dummy, so it's never been open to the public as a result (thus far at least).

Stopping at various out of the way barby stops, we saw packs of kangaroos, and cicada beetle shells which clung to the charcoal base of the recently burnt gum trees, an odd sight at first as you look at batches of motionless big fat insects, or rather, the recently evacuated exoskeleton of the cicada beetle.

Katoomba is a hippy town with an outwardly looking bohemian feel to it, full of veggo restaurants. We weren't very veggo in our selection of Roo burger to accompany the 'coldy', mind you. After checking out the lookout points all over the Blue Mountains, and having already been on the road for five or six hours, Mark decided he couldn't live with himself if he didn't take us to the point where he said the 'real' Australia begins along the **Great Dividing Range**, as the Blue Mountains come to an end, and the farming plains start. We drove to the spot he had in mind and walked out to an overhung rock stratum where the view below showed the clear valley plains and farmsteads. Green parrots were all about, and the only noise was of wind or wildlife, so cool. After a great day out, we went back to Mark's sister's place for a bit of booze and a couple of 'billies', I had a stagger on as Mark and his Sis dropped us off at the station, so the trip back to Manly passed in a blur, top day.

Written Mon 3rd

I surfed the Point for 2 hours, got nailed on a 3-wave dump slam and came in, had calf cramps for three days after!

The Bower
The Bower House overlooks the point (**Fairey Bower**) to the right, a peninsula of rocky cliff which swings around from the sheltered Shelley Beach, and produces the best waves for the least effort (paddling out). Carving out from the left around into the distance, can be seen **Manly, Freshwater and Curl Curl beaches**, which all work best on their own favourite conditions.

As you walk in the front door, the first sight, straight ahead, is the surfboard rack with nearly a dozen boards, a weights bench, grubby beige carpet, and to the right, a big, lived-in lounge, very reminiscent of my old place back home; not so sure about all the potted plants, mind you. To the left as you walk in, just after the weights bench, is the door to the cupboard under the stairs, my home for my first six-week spell at the Bower. A real backpackers' house-share, pit of a place, with four bedrooms holding 1, 2, 3 and 4, people. Jesse, the curly blonde Canadian, has the single room behind the kitchen, he works away during the week, grafting on roads, and keeps himself fit on the weights in between, always full of beans and cheer in abundance.

Sharing the four-bedder with Si (or Mon), are Jeff, the

tightwad, weight-lifting workaholic, Aaron (Double A), and Phil (Bam Bam), the shy boy Kiwis, both terrorised by Si and his overt campness towards them. Double A is as quiet as a mouse, and difficult to get a word out of. He also works in a photography lab and sorts us out with specialist black and white film for free, which is handy. Bam Bam, the younger bro, is a little more buoyant but always wary. He works in a T-shirt factory and sorts us out with freeby Grolsch shirts, it's all good. They both like a smoke, drink, surf and laugh, which seem to be pretty much prerequisites for the Bower House.

Ben and Katie have the two-bedder. He's an Aussie into his boogy boarding, and works in a video shop so we get heaps of free vids to watch each week. Katie, his English girlfriend, works in a veggie restaurant/takeaway just off the Manly Corso, and often brings back little veggie treats for us, which is nice.

The three-bedder is the girls' room, Ingrid, the voluptuous Brazilian 'schlamper', shares with health and fitness freak Doreen, and kick-boxer Danni, both German. Ingrid is bubbly, loud and in your face, but fun too, while health-conscious Doreen and Danni are more reserved, although they step it up for their weekend 'dance-athon' club sessions. They call Ingrid a 'schlamper' (slapper), because she gets through so many fellas, and they're always younger than her. It's a friendly jibe though because they go out together regularly and enjoy each others' company.

Steve, from Cambridgeshire in the UK, runs the show and does OK by it. He'd been running the Bower for someone else just for free rent until he decided to bypass the link between him and the owner. Now he makes a tidy buck from the house on top of his earnings as an apprentice plumber, which he does through a sponsorship scheme. He's another health dog with his careful diet, and no or low fat everything.

67

All the lads in the house surf, and a large wedge of the videos we get in, tend to reflect that interest – *Dog Town and the Z Boys*, *Big Wednesday*, *Point Break*, and *Endless Summer*, to name but a few that are regularly strewn about the floor in front of the TV.

We had a bit of a hygiene issue for a while, with rats scurrying around the kitchen in the early hours. If you needed to get in there at night, it was recommended to make a bit of noise and then reach around the door to flick the light on, and hopefully scare the not so wee rodents off. I walked in and witnessed three rats scurrying off the worktops at about three in the morning one time. They'd also occasionally venture into the bedrooms and crawl over the sleeping bodies. Plenty of big, fat, cockroaches too, to encourage screams from the girls now and then, and usually at least a week's worth of the combined household's mess around the sink, just to keep the hungry vermin happy. I penned this effort and posted it over the sink:

Bower Kitchen ode

Keep me clean you filthy pigs, and
Don't encourage rats in digs, for
I am kitchen, lounge and shower,
Number 59 at Bower. Wash
Your cups, and pans, and plates, and
Don't rely on your housemates, they're
Not your skivvies for your shyte. Remember
Dirt comes after bite, and crap
Won't put itself in bins, so stash
Those finished cans and tins, and
Plastic, glass, and boxes too. Now
come on people, this means
YOU.

68

After almost six weeks of surfing, drinking, smoking, barbequing and generally living a very relaxed life, it was time to hit the road. Si and Nat were heading down to Tasmania, via the Great Ocean Road in their van, and they had room for me, which I liked.

Depart Monday 10th Feb

FIRST STOP KIAMA

With thick heads after another heavy night at the Steyne (a Manly pub) with the Bower crew, the three of us packed our bits into the combi and headed south down the Princes Highway. Manly was flat as we left, so no surf to make us upset about leaving, and Sydney was falling under a heavy storm, so our timing appeared to be spot on. Using our combination of road atlas, Lonely Planet, and an Australian surfing atlas, we made our first stop at Kiama, where they have a blowhole as a tourist attraction, and fine-looking beaches next door in Bombo, and the Bone Yard, which weren't working, unfortunately; classy looking waves but just too small, and with no swell to speak of.

The blowhole is situated in one of Australia's many rocky peninsulas, and blows up to 100 feet on a big swell. The whole place looks 'mean as' even on a quiet day. Behind the steps and barriers which surround the main attraction, is an impossibly clean-looking white lighthouse. Kiama, much like so many towns we've passed on the road, looks like a perfect little toy town, with its mixture of old English architecture, and 1960s 'new town' styles. Just behind the caravan park is a little fishing port, with its obligatory Fish, Bait and Tackle Shop, and a café with a variety of exotic birds flapping around outside, looking for a free meal:

lorikeets, pelicans, fantailed peahens (I think), and of course, seagulls, of which curiously, many were one-legged, and hopping about awkwardly after the scraps.

Our first night on the road we played cards and dice, 'Golf', '30 down', and 'Chicken Shit', accompanied by plenty of wine, and some home-grown leaf from the Bower.

DALMENY POINT

Tues 11th

Natalie cooked us up some brekkie as we decamped before setting off on the road again in The Roo (Nat's name for the van). A few hours down the road and the surfer's atlas took us to Depot Beach for a pit stop, off the beaten track on a rattle-the-van-to-bits road surface, through thick, untamed gum tree forest. Nice view, kangaroos and seals, but no surf so off we hopped again down the Princes Highway to Dalmeny Point, and what a place, caravan site right on the beach front, long sandy beaches with enough swell to have fun with the boogy board, or body surf; we did both. Friendly neighbours too, including the aged hippy Fred, the bushy-bearded painter, who befriended us straight away and ended up getting caned and pissed with us first night, causing him to be late for work next day.

Wed 12th

We stayed an extra day so Fred could show us where to find oysters from the seawater inlet running along behind the beach. He also showed us how to prepare them, and 'Oysters Kilpatrick' was our entrée for that evening, which he and Si cooked (oyster, cheese and bacon), while Nats knocked us up steak, pasta and veg, all washed down with a cask of vino collapso under the southern hemisphere night sky. Fred kept us amused with his tales of Oz travel, family religious connections (his mum a church official, so he got to paint the church), his wife torching their house, not forgetting his smackhead stories. He said he was 49 but looked more like 60, minimum. Sound bloke, though, and full of tips about good spots to check out on the trip.

LAKES ENTRANCE

Thurs 13th Feb

Up to a cloudy start and on the road heading down to Lakes Entrance, with a stop on the way at Eden to break the journey up. Eden once had a huge whaling fleet in the early nineteenth century, and now has a museum, and various places dedicated to making its history a tourist attraction. The star of which is Old Tom, the skeletal remains of a killer whale which led a pack to round up whales into the bay, where the whaling crews would harpoon the hapless victims, and bring them in.

Throughout the drive, the cost of one of Australia's longest droughts was evident in the landscape, with barely a blade of green grass to be seen, and many rivers completely dried out. As we came across the state line into Victoria, the green began to appear more in the colour scheme, and many parts were not unlike English countryside, even down to the dividing flint walls and farmhouses in a few cases. For the most part, the towns we passed still retain the mixture of Victorian and 1960s prefab architectural style, with lively colours and always fresh and clean-looking. Si let me take the wheel for the last 60k just to get the feel of the van; uneventful, but worthwhile. So here we are at Lakes

Entrance in Victoria for a couple of days, away from any surf, so 'chillin'' is the word, and perhaps a little rod and line action in the pipeline.

As it turned out, there was a surf beach ten minutes from our site. We hadn't spotted it because of the lake between us and the beach. We crossed a wooden footbridge, then through some sand dunes to check it out, and saw a few boogy boarders out there. The beach has a steep dip on entrance, which is protected by a hefty sand bar 20 yards out that the waves break apart over. We returned with our boards, and my new wetsuit bought that morning from a surf shop sale ($111 Aus), dived into the deep gully, and paddled over to the sand bar, then up and through the ankle-deep stuff and out through the pounders to some messy, but fun sets. Great for me on the boogy board, picking up some good speed, while Si caught a few on his surfboard, pumping it up as always as I could see him bouncing up and down from behind the waves as I waited for my own to catch.

The camp – Sunnyside Caravan Site – was a friendly place; we got on right away with the neighbours around us, Noel and Annabel, a Kiwi and an ex-Pom, were 1970s disco-style, music-loving travellers, with their tunes always kept wound right up.

14th

Stayed an extra day at the Lakes, because the surf was fun, and to relax before the big push on to Melbourne on the 15th. Two sessions this day on the water: more fun but not so great for Si. Nat's happy as, with lots of surf shop sales, and 'red-spot specials' at Safeway. I've never been shopping so much in all my life, since Natalie arrived; I'd swear we've been shopping every single day, sometimes twice in a day. Si cooked a Thai-style chicken fried rice which was wicked; I didn't eat this well at home, not forgetting the cooked breakfasts each morning. Natalie sticks to her gluten-free diet, yoghurt and fruit in mornings, and various wheat-free meals in the evening. Me and Si almost at the end of the leaf we cropped from the Bower, so nail-biters could be in the post.

15th

Off to **Melbourne** early(ish), and pulled up at the Hobsons Bay Campsite at **'Williamstown' in Port Phillip Bay**, south-west from the city. Bit grubby compared to the other places we've been, no surf at all here, so took a trip into the city for a look-see. Train in from North Williamstown, change at Newport for Melbourne central and Flinders St Station, old Victorian style stations, with modern trains and automated ticket gates. City under construction, cranes everywhere, just another city, but not as big, or busy as most. On return from the city we scored some weed, courtesy of some friendly locals that me and Si had played pool against at the pub by our home station. This pub had more 'pokies' (fruit machines) than I've ever seen in a boozer. Sick.

18th

Decamp once more and off to the **Great Ocean Road**, heading south to **Bells Beach** and some of the best surf spots in the world. Pulled up off Torquay Beach and set up shop, messy surf and late arriving, so no go on the 'getting wet' front. Lamb chops and mash with veg for dinner, plus the obligatory vino and scoobies.

19th Feb

Up early for a long stretch session before Si cooked a full

English (quality), then motor down to Bells Beach, which wasn't working, but to the left is **Winky Pop**, a reef break, which was chucking a few clean ones out. We suited up, took the hike down the wooden stairs, climbed across the little boulders to the water, before a long, ankle- to knee-deep approach to the waves over an uneven slab of reef, jump in and paddle out furiously. Peachy first wave, and fairly big for me, real hot surfers out there too. Got dumped on by a big one which slammed me star shape and feet first into the reef. Nearly broke my ankle I'd swear. Tried to paddle it off, caught a couple more straight bouncers, once wiping out another surfer, before calling it a day there. After a coffee in the van, me and Nats went down to get a few pics of Si surfing until he finished, then dry off and scooby on.

Stood with Si, looking at the locals ripping it up, when this guy walks up to me, almost nose to nose, and it's none other than Niall, the lad I'd met on Koh Tao and Koh Phangan, in Thailand. He'd just arrived from Western Australia the day before, what are the odds!. He's got himself a girlfriend that lives over here (Victoria) for university, so we got their number and hopefully we'll meet up tonight. Got back to the campsite and Torquay Beach was working, so we dived in for a second, much easier session, great for me on the boogy board. Flies here are a nightmare, all over you, wind strong, and nippy as, we're walking around in fleece jackets and woolly hats when out of the sun, and defo night time.

20th

Up late after a late night, stretching as usual after I wake, and get invited for tea and toast by a nice old couple, Betty and Vin. She took pity on me, seeing that I'm nearly always up before Si and Nat, and limbering up while I wait for them to waken. Friendly old couple, with a lovely black dog called Toby, which just lays on her back as soon as you're near, waiting to be pampered. Natalie knocked us up some scrambled eggs with chopped-up bacon and tomato in it, on toast.

After feeding, Si and I headed off to Bells Beach and Winki Pop, while Nats went out for some retail therapy at some of the many surf factory outlets here, which have some amazing deals on surfwear. Bells Beach not working when we got there, but Winki seemed OK so we went in, messy close-outs at first, but cleaned up soon enough and we caught some fun waves, also not too busy, which we like. No one in when we arrived, but word travels fast with surfies, and soon enough we were queuing up for the sets. Plenty there for everyone though, and the water wasn't a bad temperature. Later on we dived in at Torquay Beach after returning from Bells, and had a good long session in small but clean and easy waves. Chopped up spicy, gluten-free sausages, with veg and pasta (also gluten-free), cooked by Natalie in the evening, then early night for all.

21st

Pissed down with rain all night and my tent leaked like a bitch, so yours truly got a soaking, while the Victorians cheered the long overdue wet stuff. Shopping day at the surf factory outlets of Rip Curl, Billabong and Quicksilver, super-cheap, and quality cloth. Also picked up a dirt-cheap, second-hand, full-length wet suit from a surf school for $25 Aus (£9). Back to the van, and out for some afternoon waves on Torquay Beach for a couple of hours. Enjoyable bit of fun, but not that big. Rained pretty much all day, but fairly warm nonetheless. Went out for a couple in the evening, but main pub charging $5 entry, so short night, had a couple of beers elsewhere and went back.

Sat 22nd

Up early-ish to pack up and offski. No gas so no brekkie, then Betty invites us all for a cuppa with her and Vin, and before we know it she's piling home-made cakes, biscuits and toast under our faces, gratefully received too. They're both 80, have five boys, and 27 grandchildren. Top couple.

Mobile again and on the Great Ocean Road, headed for Apollo Bay, amazing and rugged coastline all the way, in places very much like English countryside on the one side, while the waves pound the mad 'rockscape' beaches. Weather still damp so another moist night in the tent on the cards. Si and I went in to catch a few waves in the mess of sea which rolls powerfully into the bay. Much bigger than it looks, once you're out there. Not too difficult to paddle out after walking through the early dumpers, and some surprisingly good waves were out there for the taking. I caught a fair few, and carved across a decent amount, me and Si even carving the same wave alongside each other, laughing as we bolted along, great couple of hours, at least, maybe even three. The water's cold down this neck of the woods, but the full suit does its job so no worries. Barbied chicken and veg on kebab sticks for dinner, very tasty.

23rd Feb

Up early for fried egg sandwich, pack up and push off again, passing through the **Otway National Park** on our way to **Port Campbell**, and to see the **Twelve Apostles**. Otway National Park is basically a forest with awesome-looking trees, the 'ghost gums', fittingly named, with their haunting silvery look, and the road strewn with peeled bark all over, hanging ready to fall from the trunks of the many varied eucalyptus trees lining the road. Huge tracts of woodland felled for logging here and there, and amazingly

76

green ferns and meadows. Stopped to see the Twelve Apostles and take some pics of the outstanding view from the huge sandstone cliffs. Si went down the **Gibsons Steps**, which take you down from the cliff's edge to the water, and in for a surf. I didn't fancy trudging all the way down there suited up and with a board. Opted instead to go for a paddle and watch; there were some shit-hot surfers out already tearing up the waves and looking impressive. Unfortunately, this is a place where you need to be on top of your game, and Si struggled in what, in fairness, weren't the greatest conditions for a good surf.

Port Campbell is an inlet amongst steep cliffs, and even has a small surf break to the left of the harbour entrance, filled with young Grommets on boogy boards among the plentiful belts of seaweed, the water is freezing too, so a full wetsuit is a must. The campsite is a short walk back from the harbour inlet, cloaked by trees all around, and with a gentle river alongside for some relaxing (if unproductive) fishing conditions. Si kicked back with rod and line while I snapped away at the wildlife and landscape. Barbecue chicken and veg, with sweet potato, and mash patties for dinner. Walked around the port before an early night. The place is Smallsville with a capital 'S', so no nightlife but quite scenic.

24th

Hit the road early, heading back towards Melbourne on the Great Ocean road. Came across a 3 to 4 foot long snake lying in the middle of the road, just past the Twelve Apostles; or rather, Si felt sure he'd run a snake over, so we turned round and drove back to check. When we got to the spot, a tour bus had already stopped there and the driver/ guide was investigating the situation, keenly watched by his passengers. He told us it was a tiger snake, apparently one of the deadlier varieties of snake, and aggressive, so not to be approached; he had to scream at one of his passengers as she tried to get in close to take a picture of the injured reptile. Luckily for her, Si had been correct in his assumption, and closer inspection showed the beast to have been run over with a wound some 8 inches back from its head. The guide decided it was best to put the snake out of its misery, but not before his coach full of sightseers had crowded round to take a picture of its last hurrah, I seized the irresistible opportunity to take a picture of them as they snapped away.

As we came into ultra-scenic **Lorne**, set in one of the many gum forest-clad bays on the Great Ocean Road, we detoured inland to see the **Erskine Falls**, an allegedly unmissable sight. Not so while we were there, very tame without much spilling from it, but a healthy walk down and up the steps to it. No swell, so just had a play on the boogy board in the tiny waves breaking onshore, another beautiful golden sandy beach with crystal-blue water. Campsite crowded with noisy cockatiels in the canopies of the gum trees around us, cool- looking but earache at sun-up and sundown. Big brown bitey flies too, as with the last few places down here (Victoria), nasty shits they are. Aubergine bake for dinner, tomatoes for sauce, and courgettes, other veg, and melted cheese topping, oh yes. Early night.

Tues 25th

Giant mushrooms on toast for brek, like a mushroom steak, I expect the old bod is rounding up, but with food this good, who cares. Making tracks again, this time to **Barwon Heads** outside Melbourne, stopped at Bells Beach. Bells and Winki were working intermittently, and both over head-height on the big sets but unpredictable and jacking up too quick and steep before closing out, I got caught inside just after getting out and got pounded by three of the biggest waves of the morning, crawled in with barely a breath in me. Si didn't have much better luck as the waves came hard, high, steep and awkward; even the good surfers were struggling this time. The tide was out a long way, exposing a lot of reef, so an extra 30 yards' walk across the craggy surface to the water, and my ensuing hydro beating, then drive on in search of **Thirteenth Beach** outside Barwon Heads. We'd been informed of the 13th by some of the surfers at Winki. 'You've godda try it out, mate', they'd told us. Not much in the way of surf when we got there, so we established camp and are in hope of better waves tomorrow.

Wed 26th Feb

Up at 9 a.m.-ish, beans on toast after my stretches, wander up the sand dune cliffs behind us to the lookout spots, see dirty surf along the Thirteenth Beach in one direction, and tide pouring in across Port Phillip Bay in the other. Si's up for a surf, but Thirteenth is a good half-hour walk, and no way am I traipsing that distance with board, wetsuit and fins even if the surf's good, which from what I saw, is doubtful. Natalie went with him to keep him company for the walk before heading off for her fix of retail. I've taken the opportunity to grab some peace and get into a football violence book called *The Naughty Nineties* by Martin King and Martin Knight, I'm always sceptical of these types of books because I grew up in the so-called 'thug era', albeit only with Brighton, but there was no shortage of action there in the 1970s and 1980s. I haven't come across any really bang-on accounts of the old Saturday afternoon rituals yet; however, Irvine Welsh gives it a worthy intro, so with that in mind I'm getting in to it, as much as you can while your own memories and experiences are rekindled by the book's evocations (maybe a good sign?)

Went for a stroll around the locality mid-afternoon, nice, quiet, relaxed feel to the place. Plenty of charming little coffee shops, mini art galleries in people's houses (something I've discovered is fairly common in Oz), and bait and tackle shops (they love their fishing too). Watching the extensive Port Phillip Bay fill itself with the incoming tide is an interesting diversion to meditate over, changing the look of the bay bit by bit as tidal rips and swells create waves in some unexpected places, some almost in the middle of the bay.

27th

Pack up and offski, check out Thirteenth on the way; big, shitty close-outs, not for me. Si went in and got slammed, then caught inside by dumpers, pretty big stuff, powerful and dirty, he soon came in. Off to Melbourne city to pick up the ferry to Tasmania on a night crossing, nice lumpy ride over the Bass Strait on the *Spirit of Tasmania*, electric storms, and plenty of beer, also a rather classy cabin. Met a northern Billy Bullshit that span me and Si his crap lines before he quit annoying us. Comfy sleep in cosy cabin bed.

TASMANIA

28th

Arrived early morning, off the boat at **Devonport** after quarantine check for fruit flies – no fruit allowed to be brought over from mainland Oz. Booked in at Bluff campsite on the Head, set up camp, then off to Coles for supplies, after which Si cooked a full English.

Bloody cold weather, so well wrapped up. Small-town feel, with quaint old-style buildings. Got a tarp from a camping shop for my leaky tent. After a long look around our first Tasmanian town, we stopped for a 6-buck Guinness, then lager and pool at the Elimatta' bookies pub. Madness. In you walk, and there are tellers' cages, and screens all over showing races from the dogs, horses or harness racing, betting slips, and booths too, all as part of the pub. Can't help thinking what a bookies' dream situation this must be: the locals come in with their wages, get a few beers down their neck, then start to make alcohol-fuelled decisions on the possible outcome of a collection of animals running around a track quickest. Bizarre.

Sat 1st March

I already knew it had been a cold night in my tent, but having crawled gratefully out to be greeted by the early morning sun, I was welcomed by the old boy in the camper next to us with the words, 'We thought of you in your tent last night', acknowledging the hardiness of this crazy Pom. It just hadn't really occurred to me how much colder it would be in Tasmania, especially the nights, fortunately the mornings quickly warm up and you soon forget any previous discomfort.

A long haul driving for Si, through rugged dry country-side, full of dry creeks, and barren-looking land just dying for a little rainfall. Shit-loads of roadkill, including possums, wallabies, roos and Tasmanian Devils. Burnt-out gum trees, more English-looking farmland, and winding up and down roads, past river valleys undernourished through drought, and great names (Break Me Neck Hill), we finally pulled in at a 'Big Four' campsite in **Swansea**, a quiet fishing town with not much going on, but really pretty. Making big of their heritage, dates stamped everywhere on the buildings, and plaques describing origins and suchlike. Good camp with a big aviary filled with a variety of multicoloured parrots in full song, a games room where me and Si played table tennis for a good hour. Bloody cold winds blowing fresh off the sea 30 yards behind us.

HOBART

2nd

Left Swansea and headed south for Hobart to meet Si's mate from the TAFE college in Sydney, Rohan, and his girlfriend Claire. Nice couple with a cool place near the city centre. Booked in at Sandy Bay campsite 3k out from the main drag, then went to Ro and Claire's for curry, beer and chat. Walked around town for a couple of hours in the afternoon, nice old 'proper' pub, Knopwoods, very English.

Mon 3rd March

Si and Nat with thick heads after previous night, me and Si yomped to Coles supermarket for provisions, poached egg for brek. I hiked into the city on my own for a couple of hours, nice. Fly fishing off **Nutgrove Beach** on the **Derwent River** with the gang, Si and Ro up to their waists in the water, flicking their lines back and forth, the girls nattering, me writing. Barbie back at Ro and Claire's after, with the obligatory 'slab of piss', before retiring to camp.

Tues 4th Pancake day

Off to Rohan's parents' farm for a look around, going walkabout across their land, picking blackberries along the way. One of their dogs, Penny, a German Shepherd, came with us, chasing the cattle all over the place, and bolting full tilt everywhere. She also found a possum in a thicket, so we got a natural sighting as it looked out from the relative safety of its nest, with its big black eyes, and cuddly toy face.

All the land was arid, having been starved of water for so long. That of course was about to change with my arrival. Rohan pointed out the various bits and pieces of interest as we yomped along past quarries for gravel, a prison farm, dry creeks, bull ant nests (Jumping Jacks), and witchetty grubs, before coming full circle to the field being ploughed, ready for planting, and Rohans dad chasing off some tatty, rogue, 'feral' sheep in his 4 x 4 Ute, with another of their dogs in the back, happy just to watch, a black cross-breed collie no less. Then back to the farmhouse with our rather lame collection of blackberries – we'd eaten more than we picked, and Rohan's mum fed us fat rolls full of home grown beet, toms, lettuce, and some damn tasty cheese and ham. After our fine feed, and a squawk with the kitchen pet, an African ring-necked parrot, we headed out to one of their crop fields to load up with giant courgettes (zucchinis), carrots, Dutch cream and Red-eye spuds, silver beet, and even more berries. We were like kids in a sweetshop, hardly able to believe our good fortune. Next to the field runs a rivulet, nicely secluded by woodland, which we cast rod and line into for a while.

Rohan had to leave for cricket net practice up at **New Norfolk**, so I asked if I could tag along and join in, leaving Si and Nats in peace together for a bit. New Norfolk Cricket Club have a nice ground set just below surrounding hills on three sides, with the sounds of screeching cockatiels noisily announcing imminent rain, according to Snowy, the club captain. Only three of their team turned up for nets. Their nets were decidedly ropey, but the lads knew their onions alright. Rohan looked very comfortable with the bat, obviously taught well from early on. Snowy, as their opening bowler, reminded me a lot of my old team mate from Shoreham, Macca, with his dry, caustic wit, and ability with the ball. We had a good hour-and-a-half session, in which I did well not to embarrass myself too much. 'Whaddya do?' they asked, 'Natural number eleven, and last resort bowler,' I told them. A good laugh was had regardless. Back at his Ps' farmhouse afterwards to meet back up with Si and Nat, collect all the lovely, fresh-picked fruit and veggies, swig a Boags' coldie, say our thank-yous, and offski. All of us tired enough after the enjoyable exertions of the day, after a couple more slurps of course.

Wed 5th

Up early-ish and stretch, pack up tent, beans on toast for brek, before upping sticks for Hobart centre, to check out the 'reggo' situ for the van, which was supposedly cheaper and easier in Tasmania. Once done, set off for **Port Arthur**, only 100k away, and worth the trip. Stopped at **Tessellated Pavement** on the way, next to **Eagle Hawk Neck**, to check the surf. T.P. not working, flat as, E.H.N. looked absolutely peachy, but too small unfortunately; must check on the way back. Booked in at Port Arthur, then drove out to check out **Roaring Beach**, outside **Nubeena**, a 7k dirt track out of Nubeena, then a 500-yard yomp through timeless sand dunes and seawater inlets, to a quite awesome display of surf power. With almost no swell, these mighty, deafening pounders just roared in on top of each other ceaselessly, hard to imagine what it might be like with a couple of metres' swell. It felt a bit like we were stood in a place where nothing had changed since the time of dinosaurs, with the sea relentlessly smashing against the fierce-looking cliffs to our right, brown, almost treeless, hills down to the shore on our left, and the ever-evolving sand dunes behind us. The weirdest thing, though, was that beyond the 200 yards of mean and turbulent frothing white water which continually rushed in, was a flat calm sea. It was as if the swell had to be coming from underneath. Unsurfable, but quite an incredible sight and sound.

Back to set up camp at Port Arthur's only campsite, and what a beauty it is, real green, scenic, and out of the way, peachy. Great variety of birds here, but they won't stop still for the camera. Got a fire going in the evening for a barbie, and cooked up, using the produce from Rohan's farm, plus a hefty rainbow trout that Rohan's Ma gave us, fantastic feeding, and healthy as. Kept the fire going late into the night, and had bandicoots running around our ankles. Natalie took umpteen photos, so we should have at least a couple of decent shots. Wallabies and rabbits also about, 'cool as' night, toasties by the fire.

6th

Up early again with the 'alarm back' gipping me as ever, stretched it off, then did the night befores washing up. More really weird dreams during sleep, got blisters from making light trails with burning stick by the fire, then dreamt some crazy animal was trying to bite the hand off. Wash day, and the machine ruined all the clothes, with heavy brown stains on all the best gear, can't be moved, better off not having bothered.

Lovely clear, dry, sunny day, first hot day since arriving in Tas, nice easy relaxing time, swinging in Si's hammock, chucking a frisbee around, and doing a little skipping with my new rope. Tried to get a few shots of the wildlife, but not sure how successful they'll prove to be. Bought 4 kilos of logs for the evening, Si and Nat picked up beer, wine and assorted meats for the evening meal. Now relaxing in front of the fire, awaiting feed time, and firing a few cold ones down the hatch. Went to scavenge for kindling earlier at the water's edge, life's rosy. Meatballs, spud and veg for dinner by fire, early night.

7th

Off to Hobart again, sorted the van's seatbelt at a breakers yard on the way. Couldn't get in at Sandy Bay campsite, so had to go back across the Derwent River, and around to Seven Mile beach campsite. Only 20 bucks a night, and good facilities – mind you, all the sites in Oz pretty much blow you away, so well geared for the travellers. Rained most of the night and the morning.

Port Arthur to Hobart
On the road 7th March 2003

Love my music
On the road
Somewhere new
Life's good
Easy to please
Look at the trees
It's the journey
Roadkill sightseers
Bird feed
Dream states
Take me away
Too easy
Turn me neck
Window gaze
Love my music
On the road.

Sat 8th

Woken by back, and screeching cockatiels, upped sticks late, and made our way to Boyer, outside New Norfolk, to watch Rohan and his team in their cricket play-off game. They won an all-action fixture with three balls to spare. Beer at the clubhouse after, and then over to Rohans Ps' farm for plenty more drink and a big old barbecue, plus his Ma's speciality potato and vegetable bakes, wicked all round, and thick head. We were given our own rooms for the night in their plush guest accommodation, shower, kitchen, lounge and two double bedroom unit, royal treatment. Back says 'thank you' Jon and Vi (Rohan's Ma and Pa).

Sun 9th

Up by afternoon, time for a long stretch and shower before Ro and Claire whisk us off to Claire's Ps', Phil and Diane, to be treated again. More fine home cooking, coq au vin and beef stroganoff, plus nearly cleaning out poor old Phil's wine cellar. Wizard home-made coffee choc cake for pud. More thick heads, but excellent night, and they insisted on putting us up too, so more extreme comfort to enjoy. Beaut house on **Mount Nelson**, high up above Hobart, with wood-planked flooring, glass-panelled frontage, decking outside with stainless steel guardrails, and the biggest TV I've ever seen in a house.

Mon 10th March

Ro and Claire took us out for the day to **Mount Field National Park**, with its eerie prehistoric forests, huge trees, both fallen and living, giant table waterfalls, and wildlife. Plenty of dry and barren Tasmanian countryside on the way owing to the extended drought they've been suffering, but still cool to see, maybe because of that. They took us up to the **Nelson Signal Station**, overlooking Hobarts Derwent river estuary from the top of Mount Nelson. What a great view. Many stories linked with this place, including Russian whalers, Japanese warships and submarines in World War

87

Two, but now just a great lookout. Picked up DVDs for the return, and another big dinner put on for us, curries, rainbow trout, and yet one more thoroughly enjoyable evening accompanied by vineyards'-worth of wine, depleting still further Phil's cellar stock. Lots of chat and laughter, and many pics taken, also met Claire's bro Chris and his girlfriend Taran, a wonderful family altogether. After being wined and dined like kings, we also got to stay the night in the palatial comfort of Phil and Di's spare rooms. Slept like a baby.

11th

Up at 9-ish, so had time for tea and a chat with Diane, lovely lady, and devoted to her family, also not short of anecdotal amusement. Nipped in to the city to get the van looked at. Bad news, they found a shitload wrong with it, so it'll be left undone and sold as it is on return to Sydney. After that we were back on the road, heading up the west coast, pitched up at a free campsite outside **Hamilton** on the road to Queenstown. Nice site amongst rolling hillsides next to a running stream, and a million mozzies. While we were in Hobart I bought a bag for my boogy board. Starting to look the part now.

Very quiet here other than the birds and insect life. Don't know what lays ahead, but looking forward to it, and glad to be on the move again. Dirty clouds coming our way; no surprises there, I am the Rain Man. Vegetable bake for dinner, early night for Si, me and Nat sat up and knocked a hole in the 'collapso' cask, poor thing got hammered and fell over a few times before turning in. Sore head for her in the post.

12th

Up nice and early, squawking birds, hot sun, and achy back

as per. Tried my hand at sketching the scenery here, but I don't think I'll be turning pro somehow, wrote a few lines for it, but hardly 'Wordsworth' reading, just something to pass the time and assist the old memory bank.

Hamilton 12th March 2003

Up at the crack with
me dodgy ole back,
On a fishing chair
Down by the stream

With brown thirsty hills
Rolling front, back, and side
And the crops below
Watered and green.

Stretched, packed the tent, washed the night before's dishes, then walked to the café and pie shop down the road for a sausage roll, apple pie and coffee. Come back and stretch a bit more; I suppose they'll wake up soon. Nightmare flies here, and it's F hot. Offski by midday-ish and into one hell of a journey through vast plains, rain forests, mountains, lakes and rivers, and some of the dodgiest, snakiest, steepest roads you could imagine, in a van that's falling to bits a little more each day. The brakes are iffy to say the least, and soon after setting off, the red battery light was on, so one more thing to worry about. The views on the way were outstanding, but tempered by the concern for the van's ability to make it.

QUEENSTOWN

Queenstown was once a major copper and tin mining town

from the early 1800s, and this industry clearly took its toll on the surrounding landscape, which has been decimated by the sulphur fumes which killed off all the vegetation, then, without the roots to hold the soil together, the elements stripped that away too, leaving a barren, desolate, moonscape. The town itself is like a museum devoted to its past, much like a lot of Tasmanian places, but here it's virtually the whole place given over to it, and a really cool restored railway, and sculptures depicting its copper and tin mining heritage.

Checked out the van, and isolated the problem as a broken lead from the alternator to the battery isolation unit, so hiked to a garage with battery in backpack and picked up a new terminal to fit, left the battery to be charged. Picked up a slab on the way back to celebrate what we hoped was a problem solved.

Thurs 13th March

Up early and stretch before hiking to the garage to pick up the freshly charged battery, only to find after fitting, that the battery light's still on. Dark moods swung over. Back into town with van, and ask the garage guys to give it the once-over for us, no probs they said. Turns out that the regulator for the alternator has blown, so the battery is over-charging, will have to be dealt with in Hobart. At least we now know. They advised us to drive with the lights on and anything else that would use up the extra juice to stop the battery cooking. Took a few pics of the interesting town, and off we went. This was to be the beginning of a fractious day and frayed tempers all around. Si seems to enjoy leaving his braking 'til the last minute, and taking 'foot to the floor' run-ups to every downhill, regardless, also steams past road signs at full tilt, giving little chance to recognise in time for the navigator, Natalie on this occasion.

90

The 'Big Red Pebble' – sunrise at Uluru (Ayers Rock).

Whale's Head, Uluru, Australia.

Uluru's 'Vertebrae'.

Bangkok's Big Buddha.

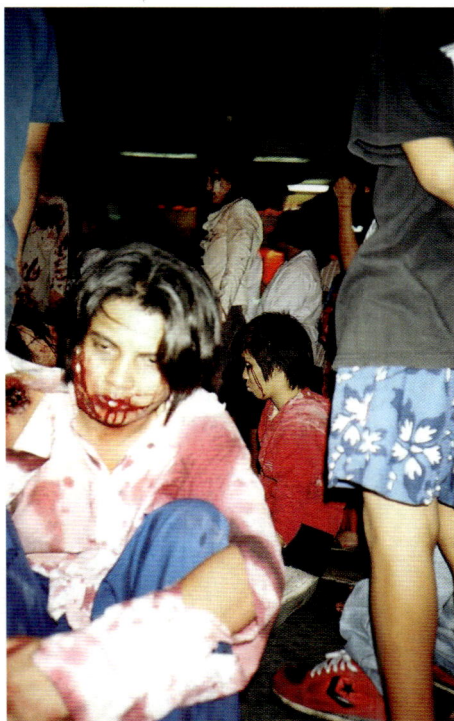

Koh Sarn Road, Bangkok, 31.10.02.

A windswept Cape Byron, Queensland, Australia.

Chiang Mai local, Northern Thailand.

Chiang Mai night market stall.

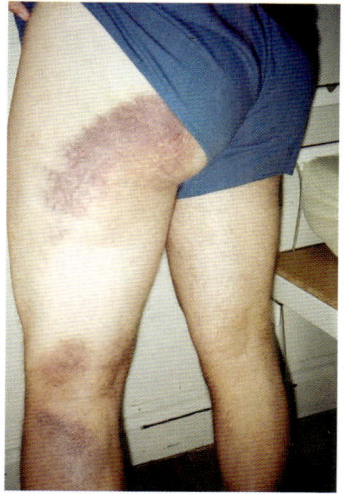

Ouch! Snowboarding bruise, Queenstown, New Zealand.

'Dead Animal Zoo', Fosters Bighorn, Rio Vista, California.

Matakimbal Creek, Fiji. Self far left.

Roadside Galahs, Australia.

Woken by surf 'thunder' outside Kalbarri, Western Australia.

L A dude, Venice Beach, California.

Early bird emus at Lake Hart, Australia.

Luang Prabang monk, Laos.

Sunset at Monkey Mia, Western Australia.

Glen's friendly 'Kookies', Mission Beach, Queensland, Australia.

Self 'n Scoob on the road, Western Australia.

Then when we stop, having backtracked a few k for the second time, I speak to a local café owner, who informs us our planned route may not be that wise for the poor old van.

SHEFFIELD

Arrived in Sheffield and set up tent quick, then off for a walk and some peace, plus to get some pics of this 'mural town'. Great murals, and so many, but sleepy town which goes to bed early, or to the Retired Servicemen's League club. Back at the van we're running the CD full tilt to drain the battery a little. Yesterday's left-over carbonara heated up for dinner, and with wok-cooked veggies, v. nice. Beer, wine and cards after, while listening to Madonna's greatest hits back to back 'cos we couldn't be bothered to lean over or get out to change the CD. Went to call Ma and Pa at 11 p.m.-ish, but no one in, tried twice.

Fri 14th

Up early, stretch, then hoof off to call the Ps again, engaged this time (for half hour). Back to shower and ready to offski, everybody relaxed, and day before unmentioned. Bacon sarnie for brek, next stop Hobart, van willing; after bump starting the Roo, we'd obviously drained the battery a little too well. Nice easy drive with no dramas, got into Hobart and sought out a place to get the van repaired, Auto electric specialists in Liverpool Street. Over to Rohan and Claire's place and out for a few beers after internet. Had an email from Kitty, the Canadian I went to Pai with, also a newsletter from Kelly and Mark, also of Pai and Chiang Mai. Kitty's cold in Canada, while Mark and Kelly are in the Himalayas, where they're so close to the snow-

91

capped mountains, that they can see the snow blowing off its surface. Finally got through to the Ps, everybody's well at home.

Evening beers at Ro and Claire's place after the pub, everyone nicely sauced. Me, Ro and his mate Wardy were driven by Claire on a schoolboy mission, to snag some weed from a bush outside Wardy's old place. Comical effort as we ran quietly (we thought) through alleyways, to the flower bed with the goodies. Giggling like school kids as we plucked a heap of heads, we all but raped the poor plant before scuttling back to microwave dry our booty, and get lamping. Long-awaited herb soon being smoked by grateful recipients, me and Si especially. Much quoting of 'Python', and *Young Guns*, keeping us amused. Claire's bro Chris and his girlfriend Taran were there, plus a friend of Claire's, everybody in good spirits and well lubricated. I did my usual, and snuck off, having been laid waste by the bassett, but only after having had a great night.

15th March

Slept on Ro and Claire's lounge sofa last night, shot off to the corner café for eggs Benedict on toast, and weak washy tea, nice café though, and a chilled-out start to the day. After a few beers and pool at the Prince of Wales pub just around the corner from Battery Point, we made our way to Sandy Bay Beach, where Si and Ro are now fishing for the salmon, which are running at the mo. Si's landed a good few with the lure, while Ro isn't having quite so much luck fly fishing, though it's cool to watch as he flicks the line back and forth. Chris joined us after an hour or so, and he's fly fishing too, strange but interesting to see them in a line, 20 yards or so apart from each other, waist-deep in the water, hoiking their lines out, pulling in the salmon, then unhooking the slippery fellas before returning them to the river. It's a curiously relaxing spectator sport. The view's pretty good too, with Hobart Bridge over to the left of the bay, rolling hills across the other side of the river Derwent, Mount Wellington wrapped in still and peaceful clouds behind and to the left, and sat on a fine sandy beach with dry grass and green bushes behind me, serious boot chillin'.

Sun 16th

Back for poached eggs on toast at Mummy's' Café over from Ro and Claire's place, then all out to watch Ro's bro, Hayden, steal the show for their cricket 'two's', as they romped home by 100 runs in their play-off semi-final. Poor oppo, mind you, and an early finish. Said our goodbyes to all the New Norfolk CC lads, and wished them luck in their respective looming finals before heading off for yet another night of comfort at the plush home of Diane and Phil, not forgetting 'that' TV. Brought all my washing round, which brought a smile to Diane's face, clean clothes at last. Good food and company as usual. Bit of friction between Claire and her mum, girl thing. Stayed up with Si and Nats, chatting to Di after the others had gone.

Mon 17th

Up mid-morning, cuppa, sit down, stretch, stick on *Human Traffic* DVD. More stretches, then shower, pack up, and take photos of the gaff. Still around early arvo for Diane and Chris to catch up with us. Amazing really, we've only known them five minutes, and they happily leave us alone in their palatial premises, such is their generous hospitality, can't say enough about the friendliness bestowed upon us. Headed back into town to eat, and so I could sort out a visa extension, also checked out Hobart's Tasmanian museum, full of British history. Over to Hayes farm,

Rohans Ps' place, for an evening barbie followed by some night shooting on the back of a Ute, with Rohan's dad, John, driving us all around their land in search of possums, rabbits, Roos, wallabies, bandicoots, and anything else not endangered, owned, or 'cute'! Si got a roo with his first shot of the night. We'd stopped, as did the roo, it looked at us for just a second or two, enough time for Si to take aim with the 20-gauge, then as the gun cracked, the roo collapsed like a puppet with its strings cut, Wardy got a rabbit, which was probably the shot of the night, and I shot the dust up a possum's backside, like something out of a film comedy. There it was, caught in the spotlights, running side to side, everyone shouting at me to get the shot off as I followed the possum's path down the barrel of the 20-gauge gun, not even sure about shooting, then *bang*, for a split second everything seemed to happen in slow motion as the possum stopped, side on, and a cloud of dust sprayed up from a fraction behind it, illuminated perfectly by the spotlights, and while we were all laughing at the comedy of the moment, Sarah, the fat black Labrador with us, had jumped out of the Ute, and was off after the wee beast with a speed and agility which utterly belied her physical stature. Back she came with her trophy hanging from her chops, funniest sight to see, she's so fat she has to be lifted into the pick-up, without relinquishing her catch. Three or four times she literally leapt out in chase of game, like a two-year-old greyhound, every time needing to be lifted back in afterwards. Rohan, during all this time, shot off six rounds with the twelve gauge, threatening only the greenery, and giving warning to the rest of the wildlife that as long as the gun's in his hands, they're safe.

Me and Si taught them how to play conkers for our part. they have good-sized conker trees here, but no one knew about the game; they do now. We gave it up after threatening the windows once too often, as usual everybody drifted, leaving me and Si to cane the rest of the wine, plus our beer reserve in the van, and a good few bassets prior to another pleasurable nights kippage in their classy guest accommodation.

Tues 18th

Starting to feel a little sad at the thought of leaving Tasmania, Ro's Ps once again making us all feel at home, real old farm country style, with raw wit and plain talk. John's a funny man, guaranteed to amuse, and pretty much always smiling. Bade farewell to John and all the dogs by midday, and made for Hobart for one last time before heading back up north to Devonport for the ferry on Wednesday. Got my visa extended after satisfying their immigration criteria, so just my flight times to get adjusted next, should be no hassle.

I shall miss the nice easy pace of Tasmania, the relaxed mood of the people, and of course their friendliness. I expect we'll get drunk again tonight, I'm sure I could do with a little less of that. Si cooked a Thai-style green curry with chicken at Ro and Claire's place, v. hot and tasty. A few doobs with a cask of vino and plenty of bullshit waffled through the evening, nice.

Wed 19th March

Up in time to scrub up and go out for lunch with Claire's Ma, Diane; she wanted to treat us all and say goodbye. She even turned up with presents for us, an engagement present for Si and Nats, announced the night previous after Nats had seen a ring she liked. Three nights earlier she'd been telling whoever was listening how she wouldn't get engaged, as it's a 'waste of time and money'. I got a present too, as Diane put it, 'I couldn't leave you out', bless her cottons.

She gave me a photographic book of Tasmania, classy effort too. She took us to a Hobart Marina restaurant, and we had some fine tucker, creamy mushroom and onion soup with fresh bread rolls for me, lovely, and then after that, to Sticky Fingers, where Diane insisted on treating us to ice cream. I was starting to feel like a little kid.

After our goodbyes to Diane, we packed up our kit from Ro and Claire's, said goodbye to Ro for the last time, and were back on the road once more. Just an easy ride up the A1 to Launceston and the Treasure Island campsite, rain on and off at the mo, but Tasmania needs it so bring it on. Pitched up and had a couple of scoobies as we played cards. Beans on toast for dinner, which was all me and Si wanted after the banquets of the last few days, and just the one beer each, for more or less the same reason. Early night.

Thurs 20th Launceston to Devonport

Here we are on the last day, poached eggs on toast for brek, early morning scoob, and pack up for the off. Stopped in town to look around first, lots of similar style architecture to Brighton, UK, quite Georgian on the whole, with a little Art Deco/R.K.O radio styles circa 1920s to 1940s back home, cool and weird at the same time. Snapped away for the record anyway. After our dekko of Launceston, we motored off up the A7, West Tamar highway, then left on the B71, and off back to Devonport, past the now familiar, rugged and beautiful mixture of countryside, lakes, rivers, gum tree forests, and plenty more. Checked out the Bluff aboriginal museum of art and carvings, and the lighthouse, had a couple of scoobies whilst overlooking the headland from the car park, with a bit of 'bang' on the CD. Head to town for last couple of Boags, and some pool before making for the ferry, 'bang' on as we queue. Get me on that ferry.

Fri 21st

Writing now from Holbrook in NSW, on the M3 Hume Highway. A nice quiet town in plains country, with wild roos hopping around, and flocks of Galas swooping about the place noisily. Fairly new campsite, with quality facilities, and a nice little pool, which me and Si had to ourselves with the frisbee for a good bit of arvo relaxation. The trip over on the *Spirit of Tasmania* ferry was ok, with high winds and choppy seas to liven it up, leaning into the wind on the top deck as the power of the howling wind and sea spray kept me from falling while at near on 45 degrees. It felt like I was being shot blasted. We still have some bassett, so lamped some scoobies for the night, and smoked them all on the top deck outside. Got taught 'Aussie Snap' by a Kiwi, Barry: deal out the pack, then lay your cards alternately, and if a bullet (ace) shows you smack your head, for a king, slap your right shoulder, for a queen, punch whoever's next to you, and for a jack, bang the table. It didn't take long to work out it's a painful game, returned to the cabin bruised.

The town we're in now is named after some ex-pom that won the VC during a war involving Turkey, Dardanelles, while commanding a submarine, so they have a full-sized submarine stuck in the ground, as a tourist attraction, no water for miles.

Sat 22nd

After an early night before, up early a.m. to make for Mittagong, 100k outside Sydney, everything getting greener as we get closer. Bit of a nothing day really, me and Si played conkers after setting up camp, smoked the last of the bassett, and had another early one. Got directions to a phone box, mid afternoon, only to find emptiness where the phone box was supposed to be. After politely telling the guy at reception that he must've given me dodgy info, he informs me 'it must have been stolen again', as if this were perfectly normal, then he tells me how it's become something of a game locally, 'they back a Ute up to it, knock it over, then drag it away, that's the third one this year', it's only March now. Somehow, I think this caper has more to do with humour than desperation.

Sun 23rd March

Up early again with the alarm back on overtime, stretched it out, did the washing up, packed up, and waited for the off back up to Sydney. Stopped at the airport to try and sort out my flight tickets, no luck, systems down. Arrived back at the Bower and everyone shot out for a wave, I couldn't be bothered, and went for a pie instead. Good to see everyone again, but no Bassett around, already thinking about moving on, no room at the Bower, but I can stay on the couch until I sort something out. Trouble, I'm in one of those annoying 'lost interest' phases, don't know what it's going to take to get me excited. Juicy clean, but small waves across Manly on our arrival, absolutely perfect for me on the boogy board, but no, just can't get interested, maybe tomorrow.

All change, struck a deal with Steve, sleeping on a mattress on the lounge floor for 50 bucks a week, and we all got pissed in the evening.

More Manly (Sydney) and East Coast Oz Journals, 24th March 2003 to 15th June 2003

24th March

Up early, and seven of us hoofed it up to Curl Curl Beach after checking out the Northern Beaches. I couldn't get past the breakers, despite all my efforts, a real strong rip kept dragging me miles down the beach, so I was doing laps, paddling in, getting nowhere except sideways, then getting out and running back to try again. Four times I attempted to make it out the back, through the pounding white water swell, often so close before a biggun would come in and wash me back still further. The other lads actually finished their surf without me ever making it out there, good exercise mind you.

Back to the Bower for a chilled afternoon, and a surf at Manly in the late arvo. Cool, small, clean waves, water temp warm, real refreshing, surfed until dark. Weather overcast all day, with a fair amount of rain, but who cares!? Nats hiked all over Sydney, posting 'For sale' notices for the van, and Si got a call of interest before she even got home; they're coming over to check it out in the evening, two (UK) West Country blokes, just arrived in from Thailand. They turned up while me and Si were out scoring bassett over at Brucie's. First appearance, opium fiends! Vacant as, and keen to get out of Sydney first opp. They left a deposit that night, saying they'd be back next day with the rest. Celebratory drink and scoobies after.

Tues 25th

Up early to work on the van before hand over, I put the new carpet in, while Si finished off the paintwork, and Brucie sorted out the brakes by bleeding them through. All done by one o'clock, had a few scoobs at Brucie's and checked internet. Spaceheads didn't show, but phoned to say they'd be up at 9 p.m. Si went surfing, but I was caned already so carried on, watching vids and drinking. Cane heads arrived and bought the van, everyone happy, them included. Bower now rammed with me, Si, Nat and Geoff fighting over the lounge floor space, 16 people staying in the house at the mo.

Wed 26th

Up at 8-ish for a stretch and yoga, hiked down to the beach to catch a few waves, small but clean, and uncrowded. Back by 11, everyone moving now, going surfing as I come back, good timing. Ended up getting caned for the rest of the day, lounge shift-around to accommodate Si and Nats in the view corner behind the chairs, and I've got the sofa. Fred the Brazilian has my old 'Gimp room' under the stairs, and Steve's even upped its rent to 75 bucks! Jason is a local waiting for a Bower space to open up, but meanwhile he's more or less a fixture here anyway, always up for a wave, and motivating those around to join him either side of his chef shifts. Cheese and biscuits night with collapso and bassett.

Thurs 27th

Jason arrived 9-ish to get us up for a surf, so we motored down to Queenscliff for some small but clean stuff, me body boarding, J on his Malibu, and Si on his Gun, easy couple of hours. Back for beans on toast before heading for the city to get my flights put back, all dealt with quick and painless. No sightseeing or coffee breaks, so back early arvo for chill and vids. Boris and Danni, the Kraut fitness chicks, came back from their Fiji holiday, but there's no room at the inn! for a while though the lounge was filled with all the Bower crew from the night we said goodbye seven weeks ago. Si cooked curry beef with pitta bread, v. nice.

Fri 28th

Jason did us proud again and got us up at 10-ish to go for a surf at Curl Curl, where we had a good two to three hours in crystal conditions, with small and medium clean waves, some perfect, others sucking out too quick on the low tide and closing out, but a good day if you choose your waves well. Heaps of surfers and body boarders in the water but plenty to go round, great way to start a day! Back to the Bower after for some nosebag, Si knocked up cheese, tomato and mushroom omelette on toast. Nats, bless her heart, has cleaned the whole place spik 'n' span, rarely has this squatters den looked so tidy, but for how long? Scoobies and vids for the arvo and early eve, Fred and J bringing a slab each to get things going, as everyone's up for a night out, I took the opportunity for a quiet one in, and some rare Bower peace.

Sat 29th March

Early stretch, yoga and scrub up. Everybody suffering after the excesses of the previous night, so what better than a surf to blow off the cobwebs, three cars and off we set to Curl Curl Beach, nine of us, and some more clean, decent-sized wave action: Jess and Emma, Bam Bam, Double A, Stevo, Si, Gunny, Fred the Brazilian, and yours truly. Overcast day, warm water, waves ranging from, over-head height and dumping, to small, clean, peeling and peachy. Got pitched in and over a couple of times, undertow so strong after the wave, even on a not too rough day the rips there are ridiculous. Nearly took out Stevo on one wave, he wasn't happy, I was laughing, poetic justice! Little ripples of excitement at the prospect of the Point going off sometime soon, it's on our doorstep, and on its day it's one of the best waves on the Northern beaches. Another lazy afternoon and eve of smoke, beer and vids – courtesy of Ben as always.

Mon 31st

Up at 10-ish, and the Point's looking OK, so after a stretch, and poached eggs on toast for brek, me, Si and Ben headed out to catch some waves. Good size, if a little infrequent, very shallow in places with rocks sucked dry on occasions as a wave jacks up around it, not a good time to fall into the pit. Stayed out for a couple of hours and caught a few nice ones before the sets began coming further and further apart, and the wait for the waves became too long. Ben carried on on his body board for a while longer, and Si persevered for longer still, while I kicked back for another lazy afternoon in front of the box. Jess has been rained off, and Bam Bam's chucked a sicky. Pissing down with rain most of the day, but who cares. Now watching *The Game* with Michael Douglas, tuned out pretty soon, shit film. Uneventful evening.

Tues 1st April

Flat day, no swell around. Brief stretch routine, watch a black and white Edward G. Robinson movie. Weetabix brek. Wandered into Manly in the afternoon, met Chris Barnes, of the Shoreham boys out here, also Sophie Pratt strolled up while Chris and I were talking, halfway around the world and I'm bumping into mates from back home. Apparently there are heaps more Shorehamites out here right now, so we've arranged to meet up for a drink at the Steyne pub tomorrow. I grabbed some Woodstocks and returned to the Bower for another lazy one. New blood moved in, a Canadian chick called Alex, she's just come from Thailand, having a blast on all the party islands by the sounds of it, good to talk about Asia again. Stayed up late talking about travelling. Off the lounge floor and in for my first night in the room with Bam Bam, Double A and Arnie the Deutsch boy.

Wed 2nd

More flatness! May have to hike down to Queenscliff in search of a wave. Me and Freddie surfed Queens and then paddled across to the Point – minimum mile! – just for the *craic*. Last night Jess noticed that our 'pet deadly' redback spider has spawned a shitload of mini deadlies. The cockroach they put in with them has survived three nights in their plastic prison so far. They may have to be ditched soon.

3rd

Ingrid (the pet deadly) gone from the mantle piece, Arnie taped up its container and binned it with all its offspring, somewhere in Manly. Cruisey day for me, no surfing. Had a few drinks in, during the evening, before a moment of madness swept through the house, inspired by Helena the Kiwi girl, taxi through the monsoon rains to town and got trashed at the Shark Bar. Came back to the Bower in the early hours, and made lots of noise and commotion apparently, Si running around naked trying to hug, sleep with, and basically annoy all of the lads in the place, camping it up to the max as usual.

Fri 4th

Up midday and feeling fine unlike the others! The stories of our noisy arrival, and Si's behaviour from the night before coming out now. Bam Bam slept at the bottom of Si and Nats, so Si stripped him and took photos, he also tried to snuggle up naked next to Jason, the Aussie on the lounge floor, who decided he'd get more peace at home, so left. Then Si's attention turned to our room, so he came in to cuddle Double A, kick me until I had to boot him back to fuck him off, and generally wake up and irritate whoever he could in the early hours. Next came Jesse's turn in the back room, but even in a semi-comatose state, Si knows to be wary of properly upsetting Jess, a strong, fit and far too muscular proposition, just the light-switch flick for him, otherwise Si may have spent the rest of the night on his back unconscious on the kitchen floor.

Took Alex the new girl down to the beach to try out body boarding, she enjoyed it but had to stop because of earache, wax plugs for next time. Some bastard has swiped one of me fins which is a pain, so although the point was peachy I didn't go out. Steve pissed off about the night before, but got a bit over-shirty and says any more like that and I can fuck off. He must have had a bad day, threats should be a last resort rather than a first. Wait and see if the dust settles.

Quiet night in for most of us, Ben got a heap of new vids in, Katie chored some bog roll from the public toilets, and we had a film night, alcohol- and ganja-free, *Vanilla Sky*, *Fast and the Furious*, and *The Sixth Sense*.

Sat 5th

Down to Manly to buy me own set of fins, and then out for some clean waves off from North Steyne on Manly Beach.

Sun 6th April

Everybody up early as the Point's pumping with a 2-metre swell, and all of its breaks are crawling with surfers and body boarders, me and Si counted 60 from the Head which overlooks the Fairey Bower, took pics then headed down to Manly for some wicked and large, clean sets, some, way over double head height, which I scooted down on like a bullet, bouncing off the surface, such was the speed, and manoeuvring around the oncoming surfers that were paddling out as I was steaming towards them! Great two or three hours. Everyone at the house stoked about the day's waves, and more to come tomorrow according to the weather reports, so we're all considering an early night to make the best of the next day.

Mon 7th

Swell not so hot today, but still good enough for some Point action and far less crowded now everyone's back at work. Nice-sized waves coming through every now and then for some good long rides around the Fairey Bower. Two sessions today, nearly nailed myself on the rocks at **Dead Man's** after Ben talked me into trying it out. Lucky escape and won't be back there in a hurry! Poor old Ben was paddling all over the place, shouting up to the spectators on the cliff, to see if I was OK. 'Fucken idiots just waved back', he laughed later on. Me and Si went round to Al and Brucie's in the eve for a smoke and beers, kipped on their couches.

Wed 16th April

Jesse left this morning, everyone feeling weak from the night before and sad to see him go. Quiet day of watching films while the heavens opened up outside. Saw *Almost Famous*, *Harry Potter and the Chamber of Secrets*, and *Planet of the Apes*. Kate's parents arrived yesterday, so her and Ben are showing them around. Are they ready for the Bower house though?!

17th–24th April

Plenty of surf as the Point has been working for a while with 2–3 metre swells. I went out on the big day, only to find once I'm out there, that no one else from the house was going in; they all watched from the Head. Lots of good surfers out there, too good for me to compete and get many waves, probably for the best given the size of them!

Si and Nat left at 11.30 this morning (24th), the 'crew' were there to see them off, tears from Nat, lots of luggage, and now the house feels a little empty without the big fella around. Big clean-up once they've gone, the place has never looked so good.

Mak (Makoto), a Japanese lad, has moved in to the room with me, Bam Bam and Double A, seems pretty cool although we don't see much of him. He surfs so should fit in fine. Time to start thinking about making plans for my next move up the coast. No swell and no waves in Manly today so time on my hands.

Fri 25th

Surfed Curl Curl in the morning with Jason, Ben, Steve, Double A and Freddie, messy and unpredictable.

Bam Bam talking about his imagined chances with Alex the Canadian chick, and how he should sleep naked with a sign pointing to his 'snake' saying, 'Tug to wake up, if no luck just keep tugging'! What a charmer.

Sat 26th

Bam and Double A off to Queenscliff, Gareth and Baz from England moved in, Baz is from Shoreham and drinks at the Waterside! Gareth's from Maidstone – they know all the Shoreham lads at Pittwater Street. Surf no good, blown out.

Sun 27th

No surf, still blown out. Out for coffee, chat, and backgammon with Caroline, nice.

Eve smoke and crap films (*Jaws 2*, and *Speed*!!!). House so quiet, all the characters have left.

28th

Went surfing with Fred off the Corso, nice and clean, then checked out the Point, not so good today. Good ole stretch and yoga after, back 'stiff as' today, so mucho limber uppo needo.

Phoned Ma about my card, in the post so sweat for a couple of days.

Wed 30th April

Out to the Steyne for my birthday, and Max's (Shoreham) seeing off drink, good night. Max cosy with Caroline, lucky lad. Nice clean surf, but got rammed by surfboard in the ribcage, put a hole through the wetsuit, and now have a juicy fat bruise and scrape down my left side. Still went in for a second session late on mind you. Also spoke to Tim Ellman, telling me about his new job at a place that makes vodka jelly, and how he's managed to get 35 litres of the stuff away. Me and Steve went round to their place at

Pittwater Street to pick some up, and filled our fridge with jelly bowls.

Wed 7th May

No surfing from 1st to 6th May, to allow healing of wound, nice bruise! Back in on the 7th and what a peach of a day, went in with Jason and Caroline, perfect waves and nice size, good to be back in again.

As I got out after surfing off the Corso, Taku came along, he was just going in. Got talking, and he tells me he's driving up the east coast in a week. 'No kidding,' I said, as I'd intended to book a coach ticket that week too. So there it was, a chance meeting on the beach, I've got a ride up the coast, and he's got someone to split the costs with, plus a navigator and English speaking co-driver, everybody happy. Also heard from Chris, Speck, and Hannah on the internet, they've just arrived in Oz from India, they're heading for Byron after buying a van, so I'll be hooking up with them hopefully.

8th

Me and Freddy went in at the Corso again, small but fun, chores after, laundry, internet, and Coles (shopping). Internet down again so lost my diatribe to North! Not a happy bunny!!! Bought Baileys flavour Haagen Daas to cheer myself up, mmmmmmmm.

Fri 9th to Mon 12th

Bleary eyed weekend, flat Manly so no surf. Went with Mak, Taku, and Freddie, looking for waves but nothing going off. Maks car died up at Narrabeen, he called out the NRMA man, who got it to start with two clouts of his hammer on the starter motor casing, $200 for the privilege! 'A hundred bucks a tap,' we laughed.

Helena's fella, Terry, dumped for playing away. 'All men are bastards,' came the cry. 'Yep!', we all agreed.

LEAVING SYDNEY WITH TAKU

May 14th

On a tropically wet day, we packed all our stuff into Tak's station wagon as rivers ran down the Bower, even mini waterfalls cascading down the steps from the house, helped by the torrents pouring off the gutterless roof. It's a dilapidated old house but I'll miss it a little.

Had a few sherbets with Fred, Steve, and Caroline at the Steyne last night, not too many mind, goodbye hugs and handshakes after.

Fred and Mak saw us off in the morning, Ben said goodbye earlier, and we set off. It pissed down virtually the entire six and a half hrs we were on the road, we rolled in to Crescent Head Campsite at 7 p.m.-ish and pitched Tak's big tent without too much bother under the security light next to the washrooms. Went for a look around the town and got saturated, had beers and pool at nearby surfers boozer before early kippage.

CRESCENT HEAD

Thurs 15th

Up early and check out surf. Dirty, raining, and cold, not for me! Taku wanted to go in but said no because I wasn't. Being hit with guilt trips first thing's no good. I couldn't

109

convince him to go in on his own, so we packed away the tent and pushed off, without having to pay because their reception was closed both on our arrival and departure, free night as a bonus. So now we're back heading north on the Pacific highway, and it's still dirty wet weather and no sign of a 'kangaloo' for Taku, he hasn't seen one yet.

Crescent Head on a good day is probably a peach of a wave, a small peninsula jutting out and creating the point break right-hander to its left as you look out to sea, and on its right are mean-looking heavy fat waves pounding into unforgiving rocks. I don't regret not going in, I'd just rather it had been nice enough conditions for me to want to go in.

Got a chicken burger at the petrol station that beats any I've had at home, and for only $4.80. Food in Oz is so much better and cheaper than at home, too easy. Broken Head Beach, outside Byron, great name! Arrived Byron at 1 p.m.-ish, still monsoon conditions, found the Arts Factory but can't book in until 4 p.m. Taku keen to surf so we headed to Cape Byron, he went in, I couldn't be arsed with it, waves not that great, and overall conditions dogshit.

BYRON BAY

Fri 16th

Got a two-person canvas wagon at the Arts Factory with Taku, 30 bucks each and well comfy, all on wood stilts with wood slat gangways over the pond beneath, amid all sorts of tropical trees, well cool.

NIMBIN

Taku bust his board while surfing yesterday, so repairs while we're in Nimbin for a smoke-up, 'Cheech and Chong' style! Big brekkie this morning, so ready for anything now. Mosquitoes biting hard and plenty. Monsoon conditions abated, and now nice and sunny, let's hope it stays that way for a while. Picked up some weed in town at Nimbin, what a very strange place indeed, just one street really, with a large drug-dealing community prowling the pavements, encouraging you to sample their produce. Got a $20 deal and some booze, and me and Taku retired to camp to play cards and get wasted. Job done.

Sat 17th

Up early and packed, ready for the off, with a last look at the wicked scenery around the campsite. Stopped at a few places on the way back to Byron, so that Taku could ask about work, he dropped me at the Arts Factory and I felt bad for him, he drove me all over the place and got nothing for his troubles but split bills. He would have driven me all the way to Noosa if I'd wanted and looked sad to say goodbye. Good bloke, hope he gets on OK.

Pitched tent at the Factory, got bitten to death by mozzies in the process. Set off to find Jim, Hannah, and Chris, quickly done. Caught a couple of small waves at the beach, had a pie, then got pie-eyed on beer and bassett after. Zig zaggered to the Factory pick-up point, and made it back to the mozzie farm and my tent. Lights out.

Sun 18th

Up tent and drag all my kit to reception for check out and move over to Speck and Co's site. Pitched tent and went for waves with my new 'rashy'. Beaut day but tiny, slow, fat waves, but fun anyway. Chris body surfed and had a go on the boogy board, got slammed a couple of times and he still loved it. Got a slab that night, sunk a few, then signed up for surf lessons with Chris on the morrow, some fit chick dishing out the flyers signed us up.

Mon 19th May

Late sleep, pie for brekkie, and out for body surf and frisbee before surf lessons. Typical Ozzie Crocodile Dundee/Jeff Daniels (*Dumb & Dumber*) lookalike, off his trolley, aged dude. Repeatedly bangin' on about wetsuits lost out the back of his van en route, how bad the English are at all sports, and general Pom-bashing, as well as the usual spiel about the indigenous wildlife and its environment, another Bush tucker man/Steve Irwin/Croc Dundee composite. During all this we're getting bitten to death by mozzies as we stood under his carport while he faffed about trying to sort out the wetsuits, sounded like he was on the wrong side of a cone-punching session, funny as fuck really. After an age, we set off in their two vans, which had clearly seen better days, and made our way to Ballina for some small and clean perfect learner waves. After suiting up and carrying our 'ocean liner' surfboards to the shoreline, we listened studiously as the Ozwit sailed through his well-rehearsed patter, 'Best day of your lives, mate' (repeated regularly throughout the duration). Five minutes later we were in the dark brown water, 'No worries, that's just the silt and leaf pigment, washed off the mainland after a heavy dose of rain, innit luv', he explained in his Dick Van Dyke English accent. Soon enough, with all of us in the water, the 'lesson' descended further into chaos as Dick Van Dundee tried to grab whoever he could, and push them into waves, while the rest just went it alone all over the place. I stood up on my first wave, and was already thinking about my first 6-foot toothpick surfboard, and joining the pro circuit around the world. Second wave I pitched nose-first, and somersaulted into the wash; maybe the toothpick can wait! Me and Chris cheered each other on as we kept on trying wave after wave on our surf ships, all around us were children, effortlessly carving and ripping up the waves, and thus downgrading our achievements. Time on water, one hour, lesson sold as four hours, unhappy bunnies as far as rip-off, but amusing time nonetheless. Bitten to bits again afterwards as we changed by the vans and DVD blessed us with more adages of Pommie shortcomings, and insectorial anecdotes in his appalling attempt at a cockney accent, 29 bucks well spent! Out that evening for a movie at the cinema next to Woolies, saw *Matrix 2*, OK action flick.

Tues 20th

Me and Chris headed out to Clarkes Beach for the day, catching point break small stuff, smoking herb, and chucking the frisbee around, all good stuff. Out for beers in the evening with a few other travellers, met another Shoreham girl in the Great Northern Hotel, Sarah, she knew me from home and Manly. I didn't know her from Adam, but do now. Home early and drunk.

Wed 21st

Saw Sarah early on, she's opposite us on the campsite! But leaving today for Manly, how small is this world. The four of us (Speck, Hannah, me and Chris) set out for Lennox Head today, (where I am as I write), and what a good move, nice waves and empty beach. Long slow waves and quite easy to get out the back, but not so easy to catch, fun as always though. Jim (Speck) suffering rectal problems so not playing in the water today. Went to Cape Byron after to check out the lighthouse and sunset view, pretty cool vista one has to say. The most eastern point of Oz, and a passing

113

point for migrating humpback whales, we yomped one and a half k along the path skirting the coastline, all the time stopping to take in the gorgeous wild and rugged surroundings, until we reached the lighthouse and its panoramic photo opportunities. Chris blistered all over the place from step one, as he chased around for his ideal pictures until he ran out of film, same time as Jim. I didn't even have a camera! No whales or dolphins this time, but a very serene experience anyway. Quiet night of booze and bassett, and listen to some of Chris's travelling tales, including, 'rivers of shit', and Gav's near thing with a married, gay Indian, and general madness of India.

NOOSA HEADS

Thurs 22nd

Packed and off for Noosa, uneventful trip, arrived at Tewantin Caravan Park and set up. My tent failed, so using Jim and Hannah's, nice site, full of palm trees, and ever more mozzies. Contacted Muz and Debs at Sunshine Beach, then the four of us went round and cleared out their beer supplies, chatting about travels and stuff. Stopped for pizza on the way back.

Fri 23rd May

Chris's birthday, so off for big breakfast while Jim and Hannah slept in. Well fed and then off out to hire a 'putt-putt' so the four of us could chug up the Noosa River with beers and vodka, Kahlua and milk mixer. Took down the awning and chilled as we gently traversed the Noosa waterways, stopping for scoobies as we went. Checked out Hastings street for night life, but so desperate we came back without even having the one beer. Drinker-wise, Noosa is a desert of worthy boozers.

Sat 24th

Up for swim and shower, then off for some par 3 golf for the day, nice relaxed day, beer-free and healthy. Home and asleep well early, having shopped for BBQ gear, only to grab last-minute cooked chook from the deli, slept before any barbecue food was even warm.

Sun 25th

Up for swim again while the rest slept, Chris joined soon after, good way to wake up. Nice pool at this place, so cool, and decent length. The four of us hoofed it around the National Park to the right of Noosa main beach, nice walk with cool trees, plant life, rocks, and rugged coastline. Stopped at headlands for a scooby, and photo ops for Chris and a heron, easy day all in all. Picked up cheapo pizza on the way back to camp, played cards, smoked bassett, slept.

Mon 26th

It's all slipping by very fast with not very much happening, lucky we have a pool at this site. J and H content to do zero but laze, Chris keen to break records in the 'doing stuff' league, while I just want to go and catch waves. Maybe something has to give in this odd situ. Swim in the pool as usual in the morning, pack up and head to the beach for swim and frisbee as no swell to speak of. Chris getting irritable through boredom, I'm starting to feel like a 'third wheel', if that's the right term. Great weather mind you, but not the liveliest place to visit, more of a couples, or rich people's rest ground! Loaded up with meats and booze in preparation for barby at Muz and Debs, only to find they're expecting us Tuesday and not today. Plan B (spur-of-the-moment decision), drive down to Brisbane instead, so that J and H can pick up the reggo documents for the van, and we can have a night out in the city. Fun and games navigating our way down and around the city centre, fortunately Chris has been here before, so takes over directions, while me and Hannah sit in the back giggling as Jim gets irate with the traffic. Booked in at the Newmarket Garden campsite, got caned, and sunk half the booze on the site before crashing.

BRISBANE

Tues 27th

Troubles at camp, money at the centre, Chris thinking of going home 'cos (a) bored, (b) skint (not really as he has a grand at home). J and H having trouble teasing dues out of him. See how things progress from here, another fine day weather-wise. Went into the city to sort out J and H's reggo stuff, and for Chris to ask about flight details. Another very clean metropolis, as usual in Oz. Chris snapping away, always looking for the next great shot. Checked out the Brisbane Museum and Art Gallery, really cool water features inside and out, life-size whales suspended from the entrance hall ceilings, with whale calls emanating from within. Water spouts shooting green, blue and red liquid from one disc to another in short spurts, making arcs before disappearing, all set in a large rectangular pond of 8-inch deep, light green water gently rippling, and polished pebbles at the bottom, soothing and captivating. Lots of flora and fauna, past and present, beautiful birds, butterflies and much else.

Back at camp we played '1,2,3', a drinking game, to

prepare for the night out in the city, much amusement! Taxi in for the harsh realities of Oz night life, or lack of it more accurately, bleaksville. Ended up at a fully backpackers' bar, got well pissed and made the most of it.

Wed 28th May

Chris decided to go home today, so dramas as he tried packing his tent away in the deluge that had been upon us since the early hours. Couldn't find the bag for the tent, so stuck it in a couple of carrier bags, everything soaked.

Went for last brekkie, had blow-out mixed grill each, Chris discovers his trainers not in van, so barefoot boy, everyone laughing at his continuing misfortune. dropped him at the airport with his mess of bags, stick and tent, wearing hiking boots and woolly hat. Sorry to see the ole kiddy going, good convos as always with him, good lad, should go far, (providing he can lay off the weed long enough)!

Made our way back to Grant and Deb's place, had some tea and biscuits, nattered for ages, and drank. Scored some weed from Grant's mate, nice. Deb cooked spag bol with garlic bread, good being sat at a table to eat, and swapping stories of travels and our youth, his wedding, where he looked around during his speech, and saw Stig and Shoddy laying back fast asleep, plastered, and Stig telling a racist joke while chatting up a black girl! Good night of drinking, talking, smoking, and laughing, followed by a good nights sleep.

TOWN OF 1770

Thurs 29th

Good kip on a proper bed, up at 9-ish to get ready for the next move up the coast, to a place called 'Town of 1770'

117

because that's the date that a certain James Cook rocked up and set foot on QLD for the first time; he was a lieutenant at the time, he certainly got around, the ole kiddy. Campsite at shoreline, but set back and protected from the main sea by sand bars, quite idyllic, with World Heritage National Park all around, and nice blue seawater inlets. Dusty campsite with good facilities, and a nice array of exotic trees everywhere. Cooked up all our meat on the BBQ so it wouldn't go off, and had a blow-out feed, washed down with beer and bassett. Played cards for the evening, crib and rummy, Hannah kicked our asses. Turned in, caned, at 11-ish.

Fri 30th

9 a.m. rise and out to check the beaches, no accessible surf here, but possibly up the coast at Agnes Water, which has a designated surf beach, I'll check later. Saw the spot where James Cook was reported to have laid his grubby size 8's, they have a pyramid of stones with a bronze plaque inset commemorating the date. J and H cleaning the van out and reorganising.

Shot out for brekkie, and see the local sights, such as Agnes Water surf beach, and Workman's Beach with its shark-infested point breaks (apparently), waves long, fat and slow, but easy, all long boarders, bar one boogy boarder who didn't look too happy (a Pom). Cool coves with loads of mad rockscapes, as per usual, with small exotic-looking fish in various seawater rock pools, mostly black and white striped and differing shapes, not out of place in a flash aquarium. Up to Round Hill Head for chance of seeing dolphins, sharks or turtles, not this day unfortunately; bit rough, maybe they're seasick! Fantastic views nonetheless, raw ocean power, trees bent to stoop, through continual sharp wind cutting across the peninsula, good ops for the camera. I drove for the last part of the day, nice and easy van to drive, saw two roos on site when we returned, mum and nipper hopping about, fairly unbothered by the human contingent around. Evenings up here warm, when not too windy, days hot and blowy, all good!

Bought power leads and light for the van, so nicely illuminated tonight, making cards a little easier. Last night laughing as J and H lurched forward into the dim battery lights every time after I laid my cards down, straining their eyes to see what I'd laid, all the more amusing when you're caned. Right now Speck's having 'ideas', he's constantly looking for ways to improve our surrounding space with awnings and windbreaks, it's entertaining watching him experiment, with renewed vigour each time as he dispenses with the last idea and embarks on a new one. I'd offer to assist if I thought it would do any good, but let's be fair, I never was a Boy Scout, and it's more fun watching him in action anyway, mumbling away as he goes. Hannah smiles through all!! Another cards night, trying more new games, all good, polished off the 'abbo's pillow' with bassett.

EMU PARK (CAPRICORN COAST)

Sat 31st May

Up early to pack up and move on, I drove today, which was cool, up the Bruce Highway through QLD to Emu Park, on the Capricorn Coast, near Yeppoon. Nice easy drive in good weather, past plenty of farmland, woodlands and rainforest, cool rivers and creeks, not as spectacular as some Oz coastlines, but good to see anyway. This is the beginning of crocodile country, so beware where we camp! Slight rain after setting up camp, but tarp awnings do the job, and the new strip light keeps us well lit for the evening. Picked up a cask and some Woodies for tonight, booze, bassett and cards'll be this evening's entertainment, or 'Pass the Pigs' !?? both as it turned out, and 'Jenga' too.

Sun 1st June

Up and around by 9-ish, poached egg on toast in the camp kitchen, sort out the awnings, and off to see the town, plus shop. Went out on the lake in a putt-putt for an hour, dropped lines, and Jim caught a white and yellow-bellied mud flathead fish, shaped a bit like the bullfish we used to see around the breakwaters at low tide on Shoreham beach, but bigger – Jim's catch was about 8–10 inches long, and after a good inspection, we put it back. No one thought to take a picture!

Great scenery all about as usual, mangroves, golden sand, distant misty hills, tranquil with the engine off.

Back to the site and prepare for evening meal, mushroom steaklets and onions in garlic mushroom sauce, with home-made potato salad and tuna sauce, once again making the most of the camp kitchen. Polished off the 'pillow' with cards during the night.

Mon 2nd

Packed up, washed, and revived with a cuppa, out of the site before 10 a.m.! Mozzies still on form, with keen aim. Didn't see any emus, but loads of wild turkeys, noisy kookaburras, and plenty of other diverse-looking birds. Met a young family that had been opposite us on site at 1770, chatted and find they run a surf school at Byron, and they know the Dick Van Dundee 1960s space cadet refugee that took me and Chris for our surf lesson. 'He's out there,' they said about him. 'You ain't kidding', I told them as I recounted

the humorous details of my experience being DVD's pupil
on the waves, 'Best day of your lives.' They're off to Keppel
Island today, but may bump into them up the coast
sometime – these things DO happen!

MACKAY

After another long drive, we're at Mackay, one of the larger
towns up here, but very small-town feel. Abbos and cards,
highlight of evening, when a frog climbed the awning pole
with the strip light on, and snatched a fat moth! Frog still
there, funny as. Hannah's first long drive today, she did
good, smooth, and no dramas.

Tues 3rd

Up early and took a walk out on the vast sandy beach on
our doorstep, a good 15-minute yomp from high tide to low
tide shorelines. Cool little round blue crabs with white side-
markings, scurrying about in herds, and burying themselves
as I came close. Sand ripples channelling the last of the
outgoing water, and small jellyfish strewn all over on dry
ground, deserted by the sea, a good reminder of why it's
wiser not to swim these waters! Jim still has a bee in his
bonnet regarding the tarp situation, so it's off into Mackay
in search of bigger and better things. Ended up at a bargain
centre out of town, where we all left with something cheap
and worthwhile (nice big tarp for Jim!!)

Late arvo, rigged up new tarp (Jim did while I disappeared), big improvement! Cards and bassett, saw an as yet
unidentified, local rodent on our fence, and some bright
green frogs seem to have become attracted to our new strip
light, and the insect life it draws in, some of the moths are
so fat that they even look good to me! Hannah cooked

dinner for us, a pasta dish, and nice. More cards and bassett, before heading for town and beer, bit quiet, but nice-looking pubs, not too many pints, and no go to take-outs, so dry end to evening. Now being entertained by the circus of insect life surrounding the light, and the frogs feeding off them. Peacocks strutting all over the site, wild as you like, crap light for pictures unfortunately, maybe tomorrow.

Wed 4th June

Up early and hiked across the sand again, smiling at the scurrying armies of little blue crabs charging up and down the 4-inch high sand bars which carve across the low tide surface. As I come closer, the wee perishers start burying themselves to hide from the giants feet pounding towards them, it all puts me in mind of the animated Pooliverse crabs, in the cartoon strip 'The Perishers'. Had a good last look, and lay in the sun, as the low tide turned, and began closing out my space to encourage me to turn back. Packed up and pushed off for the short drive up to Airlie Beach, and some sailing action, hopefully.

AIRLIE BEACH

Well here we are at last, the gateway to the WhitSundays! And well worth the trip on first impressions. Really beautiful part of the world, with turquoise water, yachts everywhere, and a good mix of backpackers, yachties, palm trees and golden sands. Tasty-looking social scene here too, hedonism must be the byword for this place. Should be here a while, so will try to make the most of it, hopefully booking a sailing trip soon too.

Booked our sailing trip for Sunday! Now enjoying the

area with yet more 'R&R' until then. Cards and grog with a little basswana to finish the evening.

Thurs 5th

Tried out the cheap rackets and shuttlecock we'd bought in Mackay, not all that, so retired to the pool – very nice! – surrounded by exotic trees, parasols and perfect weather, it's all still good! Went into town for stuff and beers, eyes stinging like a bitch, too much chlorine in the site pool, got eye drops, but no effect, so crying like a baby, and temporary blindness, making a comical sight as I blunder around, hands out and wet face! Beers and live music at a bar on the main strip, lots of sailor types around, nice female viewage swanning past all the time, yum, yum!!

Fri 6th

Woke up groggy, so hit the pool straight off for revival, we all went out last night for Hannah's birthday, and got a little pie-eyed. My chef efforts seemed to work OK, broccoli and courgettes, chopped and boiled, onion and mushrooms, chopped and fried in margarine, chicken fillet and sausages, chopped and fried, packet sauce powder in the water which cooked the veg, and a splurt of tomato sauce, put everything in with the sauce and mix it all up, didn't taste too bad either!!

That set us up for going out, Hannah asked us not to smoke bassett, didn't want us caned too early, we obliged. Good night out on Airlie Beach's main drag, small, but better than most of Oz night life, Jim being mistaken for a dealer, as smokers homed in on the dreadlock boy, 'Know where I can score some gear, mate?' All of us back pissed and happy.

Hannah has a thick head today, so suffering, hangover style, throbbing pounders, and a need to stay in the shade, quite right too! – a birthday, if celebrated properly, should be followed up with a 'just let me die', death's doorstep experience. Cooked up a scrambled omelette, with onion, ham, cheese and tomato, not bad. More splash and frisbee with Speck, then head to town for briefing about the sailing trip on a Maxi yacht, called *Samurai*. Given free meal vouchers, so no need to buy food today. Back to camp, in for a swim, play a bit of 'half-court' tennis with J and H, more swimming, check out the 4.30 p.m. bird feeding bonanza, as heaps of parrots swarm around the campsite bird table, while the resident gardener gives out feed trays to the gathering audience, who subsequently become engulfed by hungry, or curious, multicoloured, tropical beauties. I had them on me, with their high-pitched screeches in my ears, and upside-down beaks peering from under the rim of my camouflage bushman's hat. I watched in awe as the whole flock suddenly bolted in a flash, while we all stood, rooted to the spot, while this noisy green blur swept under us, over us, and past the sides of us, with what felt like a warm-air protective shield, created by the mass of wing power flying past.

Sat 7th

Lazy day of not much but doss, had a few cones with our site neighbours, Mike and Linco, in their converted bus, taught them some card games, and sunk a few in the process. They both come from Adelaide, where, apparently, the herb is both cheaper, and better, mental note – must get there! Retired caned.

WHITSUNDAYS

HOOK ISLAND

Sun 8th June

Woken up by howling winds blowing everything about, so we packed up all the kit and headed for town, bummed around passing the time 'til the 4 p.m. meet to go sailing from Abel Point Marina. Speck mentioned, before we knew who we'd be sailing with, 'Hope we don't get stuck with a load of Yanks.' Well, guess what?! Nice crisp sail to Hook Island, and a sheltered bay, where the drinking began, or continued, in earnest. Guess who got messy! – giving out foot massages, and forgetting names almost as soon as I'd been introduced.

Mon 9th

No thick head this morning, headed out to the lee (sheltered from the wind) of the island because it's blowing a hooley, right on the nose around the other side. Just the genoa (big foresail) up, and the donkey (engine), on, but pleasant enough to be at sea, and with fairly good scenery to pass too. Made it to Luncheon Bay in a couple of hours, where we hit the beach, and kitted up for a dive; nice corals, and multicoloured fish in various shapes and sizes, down for about half-hour or so, at between 0 and 10 metres, all good. Snorkelling just a few metres from the shoreline and plenty of life to see, quite an amazing place. Spent the afternoon on the boat sunbathing after lunch, which was more than we could eat, and tasty. Americans, Dutch, Germans and more Poms as passengers, with Karl, the Kiwi dive instructor, Trevor, the Canadian cook, Adam, the Pom skivvy, and Bluey, the very red-headed, and humorous, Oz skipper, no bad apples. Cards, drinking games in the evening, quickly reduced the mob to a mess, and much amusement.

Tues 10th

Up v. early today, and rewarded with the sight of a minki whale breaking the surface, only 6 feet or so, at a guess, but quietly impressive nonetheless as it gracefully swept past us. Saw the crumpled genoa move, and a head appeared from under it, belonging to Karl the D.I, keen to see the aquatic show too, nice way to sleep and rise. After the cereal breakfast and tea, it was cards again as everyone tried to work out whether they were hungover, seasick or just plain tired. Slipped anchor and made for home, nice brisk conditions for another good sail, Speck even got to steer the beast, which made him very happy. Great sail back, on its ear all the way, everybody loving it, with no complaints from the novice sailors.

Back to camp, set up, then rest after a swim, shit, shave and shower. Great shower, much appreciated, stayed under for ages. All the boat mob meeting up at Magnums (main drag boozer) later for fun and games, should be just so! And it was! The 'Septics', Dave and JR, on fine form, Adam, the boat skivvy, won us beer jugs for his efforts, and eventually won the best prize, in the shape of the lovely Rachel, the blonde sweetheart from our trip. The American girls turned up smashed already, after a heavy afternoon session, and soon faded out from their explosive start. Great night with the whole crew of our days on the water, all in party mood, and spread all over. Karl the DI thrown out of a club, having been caught shagging his missus in the toilets, Dave and JR banged Annie, the dumpy English girl, and some weirdo crazy Aussie bird, in the 'Sperm Bank', or 'Gene Pool', as Airlie Beach's man-made lagoon is referred to, because of the nocturnal sexual encounters going on there. I bailed at 3 a.m.-ish, feeling wiped out.

TOWNSVILLE

Wed 11th

Up rudely early, had a wake-up swim, and shower, before packing the tent away ready for the next stage up the coast to Townsville. Jim and Hannah feeling a little washed out after last night's fun. Picked up the Dutch girl, Marije, who's joining us for a while as she's heading the same way. Had a tyre explode on the van, just short of Townsville, which made us all jump a bit. Jim and I changed it, while heaps of motorist morons steamed past, hooting and getting close, we responded with appropriate gesticulations to the fuckwits. Bought a tasty melon from a roadside stall, and we slurped it back at our 'revive and survive' stop, nice.

Got into Townsville, and went to sort out my visa extension at the immigration centre, sent Da his Father's Day card, shopped for food, and decided to have a night off the grog after so long on it! No weed, and not bothered either, so de-tox on the cards for a bit.

Booked in at Rowes Bay Caravan Park, on the beach front opposite Magnetic Island, tarp and tents soon up, then started cooking a stir-fry of chicken, mushrooms, peppers, courgettes, toms and rice, and damn fine it was too! Jim cooked, the girls prepared, and I washed up – teamwork. Discussed the next few weeks' travel plans, its destinations, and hoped-for arrival times. Played cards, wrote in journal, kippage.

Wicked trees at this place, with mad roots which drop from the canopy, and look weird. (banyan trees).

MISSION BEACH

Thurs 12th

Up early again for a swim, shower, and pack up the tent. Cooked giant mushrooms on toast, which I loved eating, but was rather messy cooking, Marije had one, despite her reservations over mushrooms, she ate it, and didn't seem to mind. Jim and Hannah said they liked it, but may be just being polite! Cleaned up, packed up, and headed out for some new tyres for the van, good place recommended to us by locals, $138 for two retreads, fitted, and old ones taken for disposal. My turn for driving today, off up the Bruce Highway to Mission Beach, nice easy saunter, with no troubles. Lots of signs, as we approached our destination, warning the motorists about the cassowary birds, an aggressive flightless bird by all accounts, stands 2 metres full height, and armed with a disembowelling middle talon to rip your chest open.

Beautiful place on arrival, got in to a cheap-as-chips campsite, set in the coastline rainforest, Mission Beach Caravan Park, 14 bucks between the four of us! Internet and shopped for the evening's grub, Jim cooked dog rolls, then we played cards 'til kippage. Walked, late, into village for look around, late turn-in, woken soon after by wind which picked up the van's awning in the pissing rain. Speck and I got damp sorting it out, but not too bad. Slept like a baby after.

Fri 13th

Slept 'til gone eleven, then up for brekkie, dog roll with egg and lettuce. Spoke to the old boy across from us, Glen, he's lived at this site for eight years, and has his own uncaged pets, a group of fine-looking kookaburras, that hover on or around his caravan in expectation of a feed. Got some cool photos, and some excellently dirty looks from the Kooks.

128

Glen's a lovely old boy, looking a bit weathered, but only on the outside. He has family in Perth that he's hoping to see at Shitmas. I got the impression he thinks this maybe his last chance to see them all together. I hope he makes it, got his picture, about which I'm glad, so cool with his pets!

We all set off for a trek through the rainforest, from Mission Beach to Kennedy Bay, more amazing beaches and scenery, just like you might imagine a desert island dreamscape, with all sorts of green palms and mad mangroves with their wicked root systems, more great photo ops as ever.

Passed Tam O'Shanter lookout point, where we saw a turtle break the surface of the sea, and disappear again. No cassowarys yet, but we live in hope. Kennedy Bay was the turn-back point of the trek, real deserted and unspoilt, with a rough and rugged beauty of dead trees, and branches strewn about, and shoreline debris cast along the coast.

Cooking up in the evening, we introduced ourselves to our neighbour in the bus next door, Andrew, an Indian Aussie snake charmer and entertainer who travels plying his trade around the country with his python, Olivier. He showed us a few tricks, we showed him a few card games, he gave us some cooking tips, and we all swapped travel stories.

Last two cards match: tear a group of five cards in half, then count back one-half, and get someone else to hold the other half, then give it the old, 'me–you' routine for each letter, to put one half to the bottom, at the end of each word, put the top card of each hand on the table – top trick, but I sussed him, the only one I did!

CAIRNS

Sat 14th

Everyone up early to pack for the trip to Cairns, said our

goodbyes to Glen and Andrew, then set off. Drove past amazing tropical coastline roads, banana plantations, sugar cane fields, and rich green country for the short trip. Tried to sort out my visa, but the DIMA closed 'til Monday, so checked out the city, had a few beers, and sorted out a dive trip for me and Marije on the outer reef of the Great Barrier Reef for tomorrow, only $110 each for two dives and a day out! We all went to watch England (15) v. New Zealand (13) rugby union at a pub, and came back for beans on toast after. Cairns looks a fair place even though it's a bit like a British suburb, with so many Poms here, but very warm, and very tropical. Looking forward to tomorrow. Played cards in the evening.

Sun 15th June

Up extra early again to go diving on the reef, me and Marije all set for the day ahead. Lumpy journey to the outer reef, about three hours, two dives, with lots more exotic and odd fish of hugely varying sizes, shapes and colours, not that much different from Koh Tao in Thailand though, maybe even not as good, but huge value at 110 bucks, and a great day out! Back to camp, for scoff, drink and cards with the gang.

Start of the big journey West tomorrow.

Oz Crossing East to West, West Coast and South-West Australia Journals, 16th June 2003 to 22nd Aug 2003

CHARTERS TOWERS

May 16th June

Up well early to get the laundry done, pack up, then into the city, me to sort out bank and visa, Jim and Hannah to book flights home for Huw's wedding. All done by 1 p.m., then hit the road back to Townsville and drop Marije off at the ferry terminal for Magnetic Island, more sad goodbyes. Then on the road to Charters Towers, 140k inland, on our way to Ayers Rock/Uluru, the start of our trip across the country from east to west.

After a long drive, we stopped at the Aussie Outback Oasis campsite, vans transmission died on arrival, luckily J and H joined the RACQ today, so we'll call them out in the morning. I bought some sale CDs in Cairns this morning, Simon and Garfunkel's *Definitive Collection*, Bill Withers *Best of*, and Van Morrison *Best of*, good to have new tunes for the trip, 31 bucks for the lot! Hammered down with rain first thing, sporadic bursts after, then fine for the drive, arrived 8 p.m.-ish. Set up, and cooked pasta curry and bacon, then played cards until too cold to carry on. 'F' cold now. Phoned Ma while still in Cairns, Da's Father's Day card not yet arrived, should be soon. Wait for RACQ man tomorrow to hopefully sort van, then head for Mount Isa. Freezing presently, so quick smoke and vino, then crawl into the tent, try to get warm, and sleep!!

Tues 17th

Early rise, stretch, boil up and wait. Worst news poss. – engine blown up beyond repair, second-hand one being ordered, two days for delivery and fit, 1,600 bucks layout for J and H, just two days short of Speck's birthday!, and just a day after they've laid out 2000 bucks each for their flight tickets home. They're taking it insanely well, but what can you do?!! Van runs sickly, but enough to get us in to town, and on to the wreckers yard, which will be our home for the next day or two until the work's done. Not your quintessential backpackers' destination, but nicely different, and plenty of cool photo ops with the dead cars, vans and engine bits, disused mines, and, as always up here, palm trees. Easy day while they take the engine out of Big Kev (J and H's name for it!), presently waiting for the sunset, with cameras loaded and wine cups filled. Friendly mutt Bernard has adopted us it seems, especially Speck. Beautiful sunset, watching the changing colours of the clouds, from soft pinks through to blood red, with Massive Attack soothing our ears, and dusk patrol flocks of birds swooping across our horizon, before disappearing into the tree canopy's edge-of-the-outback visual delights. J and H take their disasters with amazing grace, and smiles, when many others might chuck in the towel. Played cards 'til late, talking of all the good things that outweigh all else, quite a spirit! Van Morrison sees the evening out for us.

Wed 18th

Early rise, stretch in the morning sun, no news on engine availability, so set off for town to email and nose around. Lovely day's weather for a good hike, but more bad news on return – wrong engine sent for van, followed by even worse news, as this van had two different engine sizes for its type, making our situ a nightmare roller coaster of downs, and further downs, with tiny ups in between instantly washed away by disastrously worse news coming up behind. Mechanics doing all they can to sort it out, but being thwarted at every turn by lousy luck. Latest is poss recon engine to come from either Darwin, Melbourne or Brisbane! Poss five day wait, all up in the air at the mo. Sent my longest ever email, to put all my contacts in the picture regarding my last month's travels. Hope I didn't bore everyone. Being allowed to stay here at the wreckers yard for free helps a little, they know we're in the mire, and trying to ease our strife.

Jims birthday tomorrow, so we'll put all the bad stuff behind us for a day and make it a happy one no matter what, I hope. This place is road train central, with the monster trucks and their cargos (cattle mainly) steaming past continually. Bought myself a CD Walkman today, so now able to play all our music without jumps. Cold night and clear sky, so stars quite bright, and beautiful to see, especially with Pink Floyd playing. Western Australia seems a distant possibility at present, but we remain optimistic, as ever. Friendly pit bull terrier seems to have taken a shine to us, he's soft as shyte, jumping in our laps at every opportunity. Fingers crossed for good news tomorrow, J and H deserve some! May be some fruit picking in the pipeline to ease the situation.

Thurs 19th

Woken up by the sun cooking the tent, had a good stretch, and a bit of yoga. J and H up soon after, and Speck's getting into his presents, first up, his eagerly awaited 'new release' Radiohead CD, which went straight on, for the first of many times! Also a bottle of his beloved Glennfiddich scotch, which he got into right away, also filling his Thai-

133

bought hip flask, for handy access nips later on. Soon enough the Irish coffee idea is put forward, so after a hike to the shops for some double cream, I'm in action, having borrowed glasses from Bill, the owner of the yard. After a couple of those, the wine came out and drinking games commenced. Pretty soon we were bleary eyed in the afternoon sun, and feeling a little more kindly disposed to our situation.

An Israeli couple arrived late afternoon, with carburettor problems, pitched up next to us, and chatted for a while, before me, J and H set off to town for a birthday dinner. Got a lift from Bill in his pride and joy Holden Minaro, and he gave us a tour of the town before dropping us at the Chinese restaurant where, bizarrely, we had a blow-out smorgasbord, as much as we could eat for 9 bucks each.

Fri 20th June

Usual morning stretch, chat to Gal about his time as a tank commander while in the Israeli army, three days' 'dry' training (no shooting, no sleep), wet training, shooting lasers to mark persons or tanks hit, people cheating, 'Bit like children not taking their shots in the playground,' I said, but I'm not sure he understood what I meant. Mital, his wife, or girlfriend, told us extensively she loved NZ, hated the sandflies, which are only bad in one place apparently, and not to camp at that place (can't remember the name).

Bill's son showed us his photos of the feral pigs him and his mates killed, and talked with pride of his wrestling the pigs, and small cows, to the ground, prior to battering them to death with a baseball bat, axe or any other suitable implement close at hand. We're in real hillbilly country here, but they're being kind to us, and I enjoy hearing it all, it's another world altogether.

Gal and Mital's van got sorted; now they're off to Darwin. It was nice to have extra company for a bit. More huge cattle trains roll past the rail lines behind the yard, we seem to be the epicentre of the Australian cattle freight line here.

Invited to barby with Bill, wife and friends this evening, amusing roughneck mob, huge slab of steak that they carved up for consumption, lovely sausages, and other nibbles, fantastic feed, plus another 'pillow' emptied. Lots of ribbing coming our way over our country's ineptitude at sport, but told them we weren't into sport anyway (biting my tongue). Plenty of rude, sick, racist jokes being bandied about, real hillbilly stuff.

Sat 21st

Good news day, after my stretch, and a reviving shower, we saw what looked suspiciously like an engine, being delivered. Yes! We're in action, and they're working on it already. I took another hike into town to soak up some time, and check out a bit of their gold mining memorabilia, which seems to be everywhere, like the town itself is one big museum, dedicated to its past. Buildings very much the same as those all over Tasmania, and all with the dates of construction embossed into the rendering. Cool stories from the gold rush era of the mid- to late nineteenth century, its pioneers (Mosman, etc), whorehouses (called dance houses then), skulduggery, diggers (where I presume the Aussie term originates), and my personal favourite, the 'Convincing corner', where bar room disputes would be settled on Sunday mornings, in front of eager audiences! Also rags to riches to rags stories, all being part of this sleepy hollow's colourful past. On return, Bill's son Liam and mate Nick are recounting more of their outback experiences, generally culminating in some unpleasant end for the local wildlife.

Nick drove us to the Bottlo for the evening's stock, a half-empty bottle of rum on the dashboard tempting him all the way. We came back and got 'on it' as we watched, on Bill's loaned TV, England turn over Australia at rugby union, much to their disgust and our amusement – 25–14, the first win in Oz for 40 years.

Nick getting more excited by the minute, as he tells us his barbarous tales of their quest to wipe out all things animal-wise, not on their 'OK' list: pigs mainly, Abbos occasionally. PC doesn't exist up here; poor Hannah doesn't enjoy hearing any of it.

Tomorrow, Liam and Nick are off to de-ball and de-horn a bull. I've bagged a seat to go along and take pictures, can't wait for it. Bill and his mates had another barby, and sent some steaks and sausages over to us Poms, which were greatly appreciated and tasted damn fine; more first-class Australian hospitality. The boys have headed off to a party, I declined their offer to join them.

Sun 22nd

Woken rather early by a voice outside the tent, Nick getting this Pom up for the cattle-knackering action. Got my cameras ready, and off we go for a slightly different backpackers' experience, involving bolt croppers, a scalpel, and a liberal but not excessive amount of claret, spurting or dripping from the dissected areas. Four calf bulls to de-horn, two of them to be castrated, and one of those to have a curious spiked ring put through its nose to stop it suckling any more. After a good deal of shouting and arm-raising in the pen, they've segregated the biggest calf, and herded him into the stall, closing the gate on his neck, while Nick grabs the tail and yanks it forward over its back, at the same time as ramming himself, rather indelicately, up against its backside to hold it steady for the de-horning with a set of

136

bolt croppers, a quick and, seemingly, painless affair, followed by small jets of blood shooting from the hollow left at the base. Then the next one's up, but this one's getting his nuts chopped, a disturbingly quick and simple operation, over in seconds, with the 'testies' laying in the dirt for their poodle to sniff, then lick, and finally march off with to consume, me chasing all about, trying to get a decent shot of this 'prairie oyster' hanging from his chops. Between all this, they're talking of the best way to prepare bulls' balls for consumption, soaked in salt water, then lightly fried with basil! Bit like calamari in taste, apparently. An eventful morning, if slightly uncomfortable for Nick and Liam, who'd been at a party 'til the early hours, and were feeling decidedly below par as a result, on return to the yard, Nick kept me amused with his bush stories involving pigging, cattle herding on horseback, his grandad that could shoot the head of a matchstick at 30 yards, and the general colour of his distinctly Aussie style of speech. He's only 18, but has chased, slaughtered, or maimed, more varied types of animal, often at the expense of (eagerly recounted) personal injury, than someone his age might reasonably be expected to have done.

Then Bill sidles up for a chat, and we're treated to some of his, even more colourful encounters with parts of the world's natural habitat, plus allusions to his bodily wounds, which include three gunshot wounds, and a nasty-looking scar on his wrist (through both sides!). As with so many ex-servicemen with war wounds, the 'Won't talk about it' makes you wonder why they mentioned it in the first place. Him and Scum, his mate, used to dive for the police, to retrieve bodies from a local waterfall sink pool, until they came up with the idea to plug the hole that had been sucking the unsuspecting bodies to their soggy end after diving in from the rocks. Many stories involving them being trashed while boating, pigging, or anything really – all their activities, in fact, seem to be something they fit around drinking! Just about the only thing they haven't shot, or tried to eat, in this barren outpost, seems to be the Aborigines, and to listen to this lot talk, you could be forgiven for thinking it's only a matter of time on that score!

Mon 23rd

Hoping today's the day for the engine fit to be completed, and for us to get away, took a last trot into the 'city', for bits, and a look around.

Bad luck again with the van, probs with the fan which cools the engine, new cover needed, typical, just after I've packed up my tent and kit for the journey! Bill says I'm the Jonah. After re-pitching my tent, minus the rain cover, 'Wrong time of year, won't rain now' (dry season), we got into cards, before Bill came to sit with us a while, and bless us with a few more stories of his, thus far, eventful life. How they used to flog each other with tentacles, ripped from jellyfish, and then more sombre story of retrieving dead mates from a wreck, while tiger shark still on the scene. Luckily there were three of them, and each got a shot off with their harpoon guns to kill it. Hugely interesting life he's had, and by some quirk of fate we've been privileged to hear about some of it.

FLINDERS HIGHWAY HEADING WEST

Tues 24th June (woken by rain)

Finally!!! Last snags fixed and we're on the road, and what a road, so much of it, and so relentlessly the same, but not, if you know what I mean. At a glance it looks all the same, but look again and it seems to change, depending on the light and cloud cover. At last I saw a free-roaming wild creature along this vast expanse, an emu, and a good 6-footer at least. I was beginning to think the only wildlife I'd get to see would be laying by the roadside, or ironed into it. There's been plenty of that in the shape of rather large roos liberally spread along the Flinders Highway. Fork lightning and sporadic downpours from the unseasonally moody skies above kept us cool through the journey, as we chased the sunset until it finally disappeared under the horizon, only after visually delighting us with its continually changing hues. Hopefully the photos will reflect this. Quiet evening at **Julia Creek** caravan park, except for the insect life, which is in an irritating abundance, until we ditch the strip-light that's always so popular with the flying contingent. So many different varieties of each species, especially ants. I never thought about it before, but you can't fail to notice, with them being just about everywhere, tiny ants, huge ants, orange ants, green ants, red ants, black ants, green front and back with orange middle ants, I can't keep up, there are so many, as with so much of Australia's life forms. And some wicked shapes and colour schemes. You see, even the dust is worth looking at in this country – what looks so barren, is often bursting with life, a sort of entomologist's Jurassic Park.

Wed 25th

Early rise for early off, my turn to drive, can't wait. Plain and flat scrubland first, termite hills appearing soon after, galahs swarm over a tree like lots of pink kites, swooping and circling. Free-roaming cattle by the roadside, calf makes a bolt across to them, luckily I'd spotted him already. Plenty of roadkill. Roos being feasted upon by rooks or hawks. Termite hills really cool to look at. Hawks, ravens, and even an eagle, feeding on the carrion left for them.

Crossed the border from Queensland into the Northern Territory, and instantly get the feel you've passed from the edge of nowhere to the middle of it, huge empty panorama, totally encircling the van. Jim drove from Mount Isa, so we did about 400k each for the day, and I got to enjoy the view as we once more headed into the setting sun, no clouds this time, so no amazing colours, but bloody awkward driving for Speck. Made it to this rest area just in the nick. Glorious star-filled sky at night, but not much idea of the names. Ground too hard for the tent pegs, so my first night kipping in the van, toasties! (Nights out here F cold.)

BARKLEY HIGHWAY

Thurs 26th

Up with the sunrise, brew for tea before early set-off, Hannah driving first shift. Bit of a cheery chat with Aussie cattle people, then on the road. Stopped at Barkley Homestead for fuel, 117 cents per litre! Bit of a shock, but no choice out here, plus I guess for that very reason out here, not cheap for it to be delivered. Brewed up again, then got back on it, waving back at the cheery smiling faces passing in the opposite direction. Virtually all of them wave too! Some more enthusiastically than others, so we find ourselves becoming overly exuberant in our 'advance responses' (well, just me actually, J and H smile and wave, I decided to make a game of it, it is a long drive after all). Saw some huge roadkills yesterday, notably two big, bloated and absolutely stinking, yet curiously unpecked, brown cows. Usually a carcase is attended by ravens, hawks or occasionally eagles – perhaps the roos are more to their taste. Another thing just struck me as we passed a sign, advertising the town of Tennants Creek, pop. 3,600: out here it's like the old western movies, where the camera plays on the town's name as the cowboy rides in, 'Dry Gulch, pop. 253', often with a line through it a few times, signifying that it's a place not to stay too long, unless of course you're starring in that particular film. Camooweal had a population of 360, two petrol stations, a small pub with lots of framed pictures, and certificates of racehorses on its walls, and some mighty road trains, full of cattle, parked on the road.

Reached Threeways at the end of the Barkley Highway, now headed south, down the Stuart Highway, on our way to Alice Springs, barring any more calamities. 1 p.m. sharp as Hannah pulls in so I can take the wheel. We're only on the road a short while before we've spotted a place called Devil's Marbles, and just have to check it out. A mad-looking place, with huge round, oval, and even doughnut-shaped sandstone rocks, sat all over the place, as if they'd been dropped out of a giant bag. After a quick photo session, we got back on the way again. Plenty more hawks and eagles feeding on the roadkill.

Up this way seems to be more Abbo country than anywhere else I've been so far, by quite a way, mainly under trees, or other shelter, shouting a language I can't make out to each other. Since the last few ks up to Threeways, and down the Stuart Highway, the terrain we're passing has changed from ceaselessly flat to hilly with bendy roads, a pleasant deviation. After the Devil's Marbles, we came upon some deep red, flat-top hills, which looked as if they belonged somewhere in Colorado, again, more than a touch of the TV western feel. I could almost hear the massed Indians bansheeing, before the much deserved slaughtering of the white invaders, as they swarm down from the high ground.

141

We've already discovered a new problem with the van, a full tank is giving us a 100k less than it has been previous, and we have a 'gloopy' substance dripping from the gear box casing. Will try to get it checked out in Alice Springs tomorrow.

ULURU/AYERS ROCK

Fri 27th

Not a great deal of luck yet, got up absurdly early (6.30 a.m.), and drove the last 100k to Alice, to find a garage, all booked up, provisional booking for Monday, so now making for Uluru/Ayers Rock. Saw a few camels roaming, got out to take photos, then a few more k down the road and we saw a herd of nearly 30, one-humped beasts, ambling through the wilderness; more photos.

Turned off the highway, headed for Uluru, and it's all red, the soil that is, deep and rich with burnt-trunked tree and shrub life sticking out of it. Heavy cloud cover, spots of rain, and very windy, but all good, just another world!

Found the Uluru money-making facility, checked in for two nights, everything available to buy here, but at quite an inflated price. Too cloudy for spectacular Rock views, but hope for better tomorrow. More rain early evening, but only light. Had much-needed shower, then cards with J and H before heading out to check this rather unreal place's night life, 'Barry Bishops' country-cum-'cover rock' lame musical extravaganza at the Pioneer Lodge bar, music to make you want to kill to escape from hearing. And they seem to love it! I'm lost here, but they're all so happy, I can't help smiling amid their obvious joy. I don't think I've gone mad, but who can tell!

Sat 28th

Up before the birds to get to the Rock in time for sunrise. Popular time, with hordes in position to get their shots of the Red Pebble as it's intermittently illuminated by the sun, when it shines, through the letter-box gaps that the cloud layers leave. I can't say I was massively impressed initially, but it was early yet, and the size of the thing surprised me somewhat, I hadn't given any thought to that aspect. After a walk around the Aboriginal Cultural Centre, we were going to leave, because the overcast sky didn't seem to make for good pictures, then the heavens opened and it pissed down, all of a sudden the rock was full of waterfalls, and it glistened, everywhere changing hues by the second as the light varied. We'd hit pay dirt. Parked the van up, and went for the 9.2k hike around this big red pebble. I was constantly drawn to any part with the channels of water cascading down, and the fine mists of spray given off by them, but also, close up to this mammoth geological phenomenon, the textures, time and weather erosion, fault splits, indentations and general magnitude made it difficult for my opinion of it not to become inflated a tad. The more I walked around the thing, the more pleased I became that I'm here. This dwindled, I'm sorry to say, in the last half-hour, as my poor old left knee began to signify its displeasure, I hobbled the last part on the road, with no interest but to get sat down and rest. Crap really as it's not a huge walk, and all flat, but there you go. Also kicking myself for not having a wide-angled lens. A good day though, and with luck some good shots – I live in hope. We were, at the very least, blessed to be there on such a day; rain doesn't come often here, especially at this time of year. I'd love to see it when it really hammers it down. I would just say, though, it wasn't an inspiring moment overall, and I didn't experience any 'oneness' with the Mother Earth, or any

143

other daft inclinations to which I'd had the misfortune to be a witness. It's a cool rock, and I'm glad to have seen it, that's all.

That evening, an Aussie called Jamie rolled up next to our plot, and, as with so many of his compatriots, he came straight over to say hello and get chatting. He's been over the west coast with his partner and newborn. Telling us all about the good places over there, and also his time in England a few years back, also about his cousin that married Johnny Vaughan. Jamie nearly denied entry at Heathrow because he'd overstayed his visa by two years on his first visit, they let him in when he showed them his wedding invitation for his cousin's marriage to Johnny V, which he was on his way to, ''ere geeze, this bloke's on his way to Johnny Vaughan's wedding! Through ya go, mate', Jamie mimicked in a sound cockney accent.

KAJA TUTU

Sat 29th

Slept like a baby and up before 6 a.m. to get out to Kaja Tutu for sunrise, time for a brew up once we got there. Nice view of both Kaja Tutu and Uluru, then off for the hike around the Ananga, (local Aboriginal tribe) male sacred site, Kaja Tutu. Better than Uluru, with passes running through the huge domes of red rocks, and plentiful life within its spaces. Climbing up and down the solid rock paths, occasionally looking up to see the clouds vaulting past the crisp summit lines. Wild flowers and birds of type and colour I'd not seen elsewhere in Oz, made me feel as if this place was its own self-contained sanctuary, or oasis, and easy to see why the Aborigines hold it in such high regard.

I'd been unsure if I'd be able to do the walk, but once I got started, I had no intention of turning back, and soon forgot about the knee. I was captivated, just hadn't expected anything like it, so full of life all the way through the place. $16.25 for a three-day pass is an absolute bargain, I wish we'd had the time to go and see the King's Canyon. I even had a couple of rock wallabies bouncing along above me at one point while on my own.

After Kaja Tutu, we stopped off at the Yulara resort to fill up, get provisions, and have a shower before hitting the road again. Found a free rest area off the Stuart Highway on the way back to Alice Springs, going there tomorrow to get the van checked out, suspected oil leak from the gear box, (well, actual leak, but not sure of what), and no more dramas needed with the long drive ahead to Perth in the next few days. J and H's finances almost dry now, so making every cent count, though the ice creams, choc bars and baccy still seem to appear after one of their 'budget control' meetings. A constant source of amusement for me – not their situation, just the comical way they deal with it all. One small example: at the Cultural centre after the Uluru walk, I'm sitting eating potato wedges with mayo dip in the Centre's café, J and H come and sit with me, and pass a glance at my food, I said to 'take one 'cos they're nice', which they did, and agreed, so I suggested they get some, and they exchanged looks, which betrayed their desire, and then said, no, they couldn't afford it – we're only talking three bucks here. So I order another lot anyway, and they demolish them like they hadn't fed for a week, and are appreciably grateful, but here's the thing, half-hour later at the resort shopping centre, I come round the corner, and they're gleefully walking towards me with double ice cream cones each from the posh restaurant, 5 bucks apiece. They quite literally don't have enough money for the petrol to get to Western Australia, Hannah had her card refused today, and between them they have $125, we have 2,500 or more ks to travel, and possible work on the van at Alice Springs, and how do they deal with it? Ice creams! It's fuckin' hilarious, honestly, and that's just one example. Also to listen to them discuss anything is funny enough; Hannah is quite a nervous girl, and as Chris so aptly put it, 'She's frightened of, well (pause to think), everything actually', and she often spits out her words in a low, rapid fire, just about impossible to understand until you tune in, usually I can make out one word from a sentence, often nothing. Jim on the other hand, mumbles incoherently through his pursed lips, so you can only imagine what on earth they're saying. I try not to most of the time, it's easier that way, but what entertainment!!! If Paul Whitehouse was here in my stead, he'd have a whole new series on his hands.

Right now it's pissing down, and has been since we arrived, it's early hours of the morning, and basically, rain rattling on the tent persistently, not conducive to sleep pour moi.

Mon 30th

STILL RAINING!!!

Got wet packing up, left the free rest area, and my turn to drive, 200k back to Alice Springs. The garage mechanic said the fuel pump's shot, $220 to supply and fit, but it has to be ordered. Luckily they've put it in an 'airbag' so it can be flown in overnight, and they can get started in the morning, J and H borrowing from me to get it done, and we're parking on the garage forecourt to save money and be there when it arrives. I took a walk around the town, sorted internet then had a nose about. Nice library, learned a bit about John Batman, one of the founding fathers of Melbourne, son of a convict, and a blacksmith's apprentice (who got hanged on his evidence!). He left Van Dieman's

Land (Tasmania) to look for more fertile farmland on the 'big' island, came across the Yarra, and said, 'This looks like a good place to build a village!'

I also noticed a small plaque outside the info centre, dedicated to Satours Camp, a former site of the town's largest Afghan community. Cameleers from Peshawar and Afghanistan were brought out here under contract in 1900, and paid £2 a month. Their old mosque was knocked down during World War Two for military deployments, they built a new Islamic centre in October '93, and called it the Afghan Mosque.

Alice Springs retail centre bears a disturbing resemblance to Crawley in Sussex, and as all us southerners know, that is not a compliment. In all fairness, it isn't as bad, and has quite a mixed-culture feel, with several European elements (restaurants especially), as well as the liberally spread Aboriginal art shops and galleries. It's also surrounded by wild parks, dried-out rivers and creeks, all of them with groups of Aboriginals dotted about under trees or bridges. Cloudy all day, with spots of rain here and there since arriving.

Tues July 1st

Good nights kip with all three of us in the van. Fuel pump arrived 9-ish, so we shot into town for a last look around while the mechanics got on with the work. Got Jim his winner's prize of a Red Rooster meal as this week's cards champ, then set back to get the van, pay and hit the road down to Coober Pedy in Southern Australia. $248 to pay, J and H are skint, so they'll repay me when they return from Huw's wedding back home, plus whatever else they'll owe me before they leave, i.e. petrol etcetera. Northern Territories seems to harbour a large amount of ZZ Top fans, with long starched beards, or shaven heads, bushy goatees, wife-beater vests, and the obligatory mean looks! Also,

147

mullets aplenty out here. Uneventful day's driving for J and H, crossed into South Australia from Northern Territories with little for me to do but watch the central Australian landscapes zip past, some as yet unidentified ranges, and flat-top hills left and right occasionally breaking up the vast flat plains of spinifex and scrubland. Road trains steaming past in the opposite direction, rocking the van about, such is their size and speed, also looming large in the rear view before we slow to encourage them past (not that they need encouraging!). No eagles or hawks today, but a couple of roos roadside, mercifully hopping away from, rather than onto!

CADNEY HOMESTEAD!!

Hove into to Cadney Homestead for some free camping and a decent shower and washing-up facilities, much appreciated out here. Also a friendly and welcoming bar, where I'm sat now with a cold stubby of VB, all good! J and H retired early for a sharp start in the morning. ATM here is down because they took a direct hit from lightning last night, so only the one for me tonight, but that'll do me.

Waddya know, went to the bar with $2.20 in shrapnel, and the barmaid Cassie puts up the extra to help this poor struggling drifter afford his next stubby of VB! What a nation of people they are. So here I am, enjoying the liquid pleasures of subsidised beer. On top of that, she poured me a cocktail and we got chatting, also Paul, the barman, was your usual top, friendly Aussie. Both of them into their 'bang' dance music. He brought his mini disc player out, and before I knew it I was back home in the Escape, or the Zap in Brighton, or an Ollie gig, real class bang. Once they heard I was from Brighton, that was it, couldn't put a foot wrong. At this point it occurred to me how surreal the whole situation was – I mean, here I am at a roadhouse miles from anywhere, in the top end of Southern Australia, with an Aboriginal family on the pool table, a few ZZ Top truckies by the bar, and the bar staff are into their 'bang', sorting me out for drinks, and bloody good company too.

As the bar thinned out a little, Cassie took me to her room for a scooby, and gave me some to take away too, returned to the bar caned. We filled the juke box with dance tunes, chatted and laughed until turning in, and guess who got lucky! She's twenty, reasonably fit, funny, and keen as, explored each other with vigour, and for once, I both spotted a situation, and acted on it. What a night, what a girl! Crawled back to my tent by 6 a.m., freezing but happy, up 20 mins later, packing up to hit the road again.

Only a few ks down the road, and we saw a flock of cockatoos by the roadside, which took off then swooped alongside us, and then four huge wedge-tailed eagles, two taking off, and two just sat on the roadside trees branches, one aside, minimum 2 foot high standing.

COOBER PEDY

Got to Coober Pedy and looked for a café, fat chance as nothing open 'til noon, eventually found the Underground Café, just opening for us, but not cheap (food good though).

Did some 'noodling', which is basically grubbing around in the dirt, in the forlorn hope of finding opals. Looked over the town, but soon realised we should have overlooked it, and driven right on, which we soon did. Got my head down for the journey, and caught up on some much needed kip before we pulled into Lake Hart rest area, just in time for sunset. Jim cooked omelette in toast sandwich, very nice. Cards and kip.

Thurs 3rd

Up early again, packed up tent, baked beans on toast for brekkie, then wash up, take pics, and get back on the road. First stop. Pimba, for fuel. Took over the driving at Iron Knob, and although the roads were clear and straight, while the fields to our side were the greenest I've seen since I left home, we had the petrol light flashing at just 260ks, no good, also noticed original leak back under the gear box housing. J and H, understandably, not happy. Filled up and set off for rest area 44k east of Ceduna. Had a small fire for the evening to warm our feet, first time we've had a whole site to ourselves too.

Nullabor tomorrow.

NULLABOR PLAIN/EYRE HIGHWAY

Fri 4th July

After packing up, and a fine omelette and sausage toasted sarnie, cooked by Jim, we once more set off, also got some good shots of galahs in trees and in flight. Nice easy drive along South Australia's relentlessly straight roads, keeping the speed and revs down to economise on petrol. Stopped at Nundroo motel to get coffee and feed, got chatting to road train driver Jim, who turns out to be a mechanic, and gives the van a once-over for us. Sound bloke, explained a few things to us about how to check the transmission oil level (when the engine's running), and where to fill from (through the dipstick pipe). He also gave us the name of a good mechanic, in Wangarra outside Perth, to go to. Jim's road train is apparently just a baby at 425 horse power and a 14-litre engine! 'That's all.' Transmission oil now topped up, and we're once more chasing the sunset, with Speck at the wheel this time. Driving along, through the Nullabor's treeless scrubland, and you notice after a while that you're travelling parallel to cliffs overlooking the Great Australian Bight, and Southern Ocean, where whales (apparently), are to be spotted between June and October; no sign yet though.

Found a good rest area with shelter from scrub trees, and got a small fire going to warm the toes while we played cards 'til kip time.

Sat 5th

Many dreams night, with Billy and Michelle (very pregnant), Ade Thompson, all in Brighton pubs, herb, and much else, very surreal (obviously, but more so). Great night's sleep, woke up feeling fresh as a daisy, full of vim, vigour and vitality. Now on the road again, with Jim on the morning shift, Hannah driving afternoon, and my day off in the back. Just remembered – also saw Lee Murphy in the dreams, in a pub, then a garage (very small), and asked about work, which is funny because he lives in Perth, and that's where we're off to. Also saw, and spoke to, Neil Gilmour, that I worked with at Maidenbower, and his wife Sue and son Alex. Even though it was a dream, it was so good to see them after so many years. Strange but nice, as we keep driving, the dream seems to be reawakening in me, like real memories of actual events.

Seen a couple of awesome eagles this morning, feeding on roadkill, huge fat legs, and impressive wingspans as they took off, going too fast to stop for pictures unfortunately. Nullabor here just looks like a piece of neglected council wasteland back home, but strangely hypnotic and subduing in its sameness. Dull greens, dark greens, grey-greens, blue-green, sandy, stormy, bushy, grassy, *dry*, still waving, road trains thundering by. Pack of red roos springing up through the scrub; a dozen or so stop as we go by, only the head,

151

shoulders and arms visible, just after the end of the 90-mile straight stretch.

Stopped at one, for me to make the toasted omelette sarnie, 'à la Jim', my first, and a success! Storm clouds above make the wispy, deathlike, prehistoric murderscape of trees look even meaner. Stop at Balledonia to fill up. The clouds are ejecting their loads and it's belting it down now (2.07 p.m.). This whole route looks as if it were never meant to be tamed, and probably never will be (by man at least). Truly wicked, I love it!

COOLGARLIE/ESPERANCE HIGHWAY

As the skies cleared and brightened, we arrived at the Norseman junction, where we swung right, towards Kalgoorlie, and pulled into a rest area with, hopefully, just one more day's driving ahead of us, and maybe a shower and some clean clothes at the end of it. Driving all day then sleeping at 'freeby' stops is all very fine, but gets a little grubby, and with the journey so close to completion, the novelty, for the moment at least, is all but dead. It *has* been a feel-good day though, just a little tired now.

Sun 6th

Another early start, cold crisp morning, and Hannah on first shift at the wheel. Semi-overcast day blowing hot and cold as the sun comes and goes. Filled up at Bullabulling, driving conditions OK, dry and not too windy. Never thought Western Australia would be this chilly during daytime, and the sun's out! This is like an autumnal afternoon in England. My shift started just after 1 p.m. Surprised, as we approached Perth through Northam, at just how hilly it all was, and very green, all quite like the

152

Sussex Downs, but much wider to drive through. Van struggled up the longer, steeper hills, but managed all the same. Seemed a little weird coming back again after 14 years, and the closer we got, the stranger I was feeling, as if it were all yesterday, and they'd just seen me off at the airport. There's definitely something very odd going on with me, but I can't quite put my finger on it, define it – one minute, super-confident, the next, a waste of space, looking forward, then retrospective, at peace, then on fire, mostly happy, but occasionally desolate, all with no rhyme or reason as to the timing.

Here at Jim and Leonie's place now, having been fed, chatted and played 'Scrabble', Leonie whooped us without breaking sweat. Clean! So good. Sleep, warm!

SAFETY BAY, WA

Mon 7th July

Arose to the clinking of china as Jim and Leonie set the table for breakfast, tea from a pot, no bags, Weetabix cereal, scrambled eggs, and chat about travel stuff in general. J and H shot into Perth to sort tickets home, while Jim, Leonie and myself went for a walk. They gave me the 'dime' tour of Safety Bay, nice place. Drove into Rockingham for big shop-ups and me to sort out phone cards, had a coffee, sos roll, and caught up on home news from international paper. Afternoon tea in the winter sunshine, with profiteroles, read some of Uncle Jim's stories and scripts. Visit library for internet, bit slow, but free, so all good. Got in contact with Comfy Dad re money owed, he's on it already, spoke on Speck's phone, so hopefully that'll be in the account by the end of the week, and peace of mind for a little while longer.

Nice roast dinner cooked by Leonie, all sat at the table, very civilised. Leonie and I play 'Scrabble' 'til late.

Tues 8th

After breakfast I nicked off to the library for my latest marathon email. May have been a tad boring, but hey, they don't have to read it I guess, eh!

YALLINGUP

Mon 14th

Writers' group with Jim midday, then off to Craig's at Yallingup, easy drive, 2 and a half hours. Met up with Craig on the road, he was going in the opposite direction, on his way to deliver a gas bottle to one of his customers. We dropped my van off and I became his 'trolley boy'. Afterwards we got drinking at his local, then back to his place to finish us off with a bit of weed.

Tues 15th

Thick head early on, went on the rounds with Craig on his gas delivery job. Great way to see the area, and what a fantastic part of the country this is, right on the coast, great surf and scenery. Very green everywhere because of the heavy rainfall they've been having here, and still are.

I was trolley boy, loading and unloading bottles of gas for Craig to hook up the house supplies, loads of great-looking houses, set in wicked countryside. Good day chatting, past, present and future stuff, Craig glad to be out of chipping, and enjoying his new job, I can see why too.

Saw all sorts of different birds on our travels today,

including some big black cockatoos. Drink and bassett in the evening.

Wed 16th July

Another day on the rounds with Craig around Yallingup, Dunsborough, and surrounding lush countryside. Getting an education on the wildlife in this neck of the woods, jarra trees for best timber, silver-topped blackboys, more birds, roos in the paddocks – a huge mob of them early evening (30 or 40), just outside their place, so cool, and some of them boxing! Many quality places newly built, with all sorts of differing designs. Checked out the local surf spots, Indijup especially. Met Craig's wife Annie, and the kids, Emma and James, in the evening, quiet night.

Thurs 17th

Up at the crack, and out shifting them bottles asap, so we could get an afternoon surf in. Saw some more cool birds while out, black cockatoos (red and white tails), a curious yellow-chested (golden whistler) bird, and plenty of virgin bush too.

Surfed **Super-Tubes at Smith's Beach**, small and clean, felt bad 'cos Craig should be in the big stuff alongside, but he's babysitting his Pommie cousin in foreign waters. Some dolphins swam past us only a few yards away, which was great. Out for an hour and a half, bit chilly towards the end, but good fun.

Great stories from Craig during the day too. (1) 'The kangaroo's balls against the windscreen', as he and his mate, plus a 16-year-old sweetheart, driving, braking, swerving, to avoid the inevitable collision, the girl saying, 'D'ya see his balls?' Craig replies, 'Hard not to, darlen'!' (2) Rocking up to **Three Bears at Cape Naturaliste** without his wetsuit, and the surf's ripping, spots the world's number 10, Jake Patterson, they chat about how smoking it looks, Craig asks if he's got a spare wetty, 'No worries, mate', says Patto, and off they go. Craig drops the suit round Patto's place, with a couple of stubbies as a thank-you. Many 'long walks for surf', stories, I have my own after todays hike to the water, all made worthwhile when those dolphins turned up close by, checking us out.

Fri 18th July

Bit of a lie-in day, with 8.30 rise time, then hit it and get those bottles out. We shifted 46 of the 85 kilo beasts, and I'm starting to feel fit again. Saw a huge mob of the dark-backed roos, got in amongst them and took some, hopefully, good pics. Checked out some wicked local surf, and got some great photos of that too, great day all in all.

Little squeaky-voiced darlin' at the bakery, keeps me smiling, must get a picture, she's as sweet as cherry pie!! Few 'midis' at Caves Bar, before home for scoff, maybe a couple at the boozer later. Fun and games with Emma and James in the evening, then bedtime for them, and beer time for us! Me and Craig got a couple of late ones in at the Caves, before the night was dead.

Sat 19th

Nice lay in, in the van, then up for a fine farmhouse breakfast with duck eggs (yum!). Trip to the tip, then deliver nine bottles of gas, checked out the surf after, big swell, and cranking waves in full cry, as Craig put it. Early finish, and a family afternoon with James and Emma, filling in holes in the driveway, then collecting logs for the evening.

Sun 20th

Day out, driving to the sights with the family. Climbed to the top of the **Cape Leewin lighthouse** with the children and Craig, V. windy at the summit, but great view of the South Western tip of Oz, overlooking where the Indian Ocean meets the Southern Ocean, and from where whales and dolphins are often to be seen – needless to say, not this day. Awesome waves and swell action at **Margaret River**, not much of a river, but a hell of a stretch of big wave power boomin' in, messy today but still impressive. Heaps of roos mobbed up in the paddocks, and a few emus too.

Checked out a winery and its lush grounds, Craig and Emma save a green butterfly/moth from the pond, then release it, only to witness a yellow, black and white bird swoop down and swallow it up mid-flight, right in front of Emma's mesmerised eyes. Before anyone can come up with a good reason, which this four-year-old would believe, as to why the recently devoured green moth would have vanished in such a manner, 'Magic', she proudly shouts, and looks sternly at us as she follows straight on with, 'of course'. A real *Simpsons* moment.

Out of beer back at the house, much to Craig's horror, so a quiet end to the weekend.

Mon 21st

Out with Craig for my last gas run in the morning, then work out a route for me to take around the region, and see some of the best sights. Checked the transmission fluid, and oil levels before the off, then trundled gently through the countryside forests, which were glistening nicely in the fresh rain that's once again keeping me company. Parked up (unwittingly) at the **Diamond Tree Lookout**, and stayed the night. I'd made a mental note, when Craig told me about

157

this tree, to make a point of not finding it (don't like heights). It was dark when I pulled up, and I had no idea where I was at the time.

Tues 22nd July

Up with the pitter patter of raindrops on the van roof, gutted to see where I'd parked, then out to see if I could take on the climb up the damned lookout tree. Yeah right! 60-odd metres high, with spikes spiralling up it for footholds, Craig had said I wouldn't be able to resist it, hmmmm. Yellow to the core, I tried, but it was a pathetic effort. Bear in mind it's wire caged for safety, but all that goes out the window once the fear kicks in. I made it about 10 metres at the absolute most. I felt acute embarrassment at my lack of bottle, even though I was the only being around. Shuffled off, tail between legs, one more challenge chickened out of, I'd never have made an explorer!

Moved on and made my way down to **Beedelup Falls** in **Beedelup National Park**, and the **Cascade Falls** further on in **Gloucester National Park**, winding country and forest roads all the way in lush green colour, and huge, straight trees forming tall avenues along the verges. Karri and jarra are the prominent trees down here, with the karri being the giants, which tomorrow I'll walk amongst, on the tree-top walk they have outside **Nornalup** in the **Valley of the Giants.** Pitched the van up, next to the tree-top walk national park for the night, had a mini scoob and a Woody, then turned in with just wildlife noises around.

Wed 23rd

Pumpkin soup for brekkie, plenty of twittering and cheeping birds, supplying the dawn chorus among the regrowth trees, either side of me, in their military lines, north to south. Six

158

bucks for the walk among the Valley of the Giants, quite impressive, but a little less than I'd expected, worth a visit all the same. Tall Red Tingle and karri trees are the main attraction here, but the birds remain elusive around the 600 metres of steel-structured pathway through the forest canopy. As always, staff are hyper-friendly and helpful, loaded me up with 'things to do' and 'places to see' leaflets for the area, then off I drove, ready for it all. Took the scenic route down the Valley of the Giants road on my way to **Denmark**, and saw some more outstandingly lush countryside, grazing land, burnt and new forest, and generally not too shabby viewage. Arrived at **Ocean Beach** in Denmark and, as Craig would say, 'it was crankin', just perfect, easy 2 and a half metre swell, offshore, peeling a treat, and a beach point break, so no dramas getting in. Time to be gutted! Feeling chuffed to be there when the conditions will rarely be so perfect for me, open the back up, and there's a fuckin' wet spot where the board used to be! I've left the bastard thing at Craig's place, complete with wet suit, fins and bag. What a dickhead!!! Crushed as I was, (*am*!), I got the camera out to record some of these waves, and the lucky bastard boogy boarders out there on them, just so I can torture myself by remembering what I missed out on.

Currently sitting in one more idyllic spot, by an inlet with all sorts of ornithological wildlife scooting about the water, or on the tree branches overhanging it, serene. Also, wicked river with moody overhung death trees, in and along its banks.

The drive up to **Wagin** had plenty of pic ops on the way, with life and death in the environment showing each other off, charcoal-blackened trees sprouting fresh green growth after the rain, silver trees, long since died, springing out the earth and water, without a leaf, twig or branch left on them. Stopped at **Cranbrook** for a sos roll, and to ask about

Robert's (cousin) firm. Turns out it's over the road, what are the chances, eh?! Door wide open, so in I wander, no one around, so I have a nose, find a phone and it works, so give Robert a call. Not a happy man that his workshop's left open, 'I'll shut it on my way out', I assured him. Five minutes out of town, and one of the weirder sights out here greets me, a dull grey-pink pool or lake, with a curtain of dead trees encompassing it, like a not-so-gentle hint to leave the water well alone. Wicked photo ops, and big camera runs out of film! Little 'snappy' camera takes over. 240ks from Denmark to Wagin, but by no means a dull drive. This must be sheep country, general sheep, wool and shearing stuff on walls everywhere. Old-style buildings with verandas, balustrades, and a look of a time when things were slower-paced.

Arrived in Wagin, got a beer in at the pub that Robert's staying at, and waited. He works all over South West Australia, miles from anywhere, sinking boreholes for water, for farmers usually. Soon enough he's here, and we're chatting, he's telling me all about the salt left in the strata in this area, from when it was an inland sea, how trees act like a pump, pulling it up to the surface, and poisoning them, and all the other plant life, Yates, and White Gum trees being the exceptions that deal with the salt. Also, beta carotin in the salt, causing the pink colour to these lakes. Mineral deposits within the salt too, black quartz, Palladiums, etc, he knows stuff about the earth that I'd only expect geologists to know.

Thurs 24th

Revived with a dump in the pub bog, followed by a livening coffee, am now making for **Lake Dumbleyung**, where Sir Donald Campbell achieved one of his speed over water records. Robert arranged for me to keep the van behind the pub while I'm up here. He's given me directions to where they're boreholing, and some other stuff to check out.

Lake Dumbleyung!!!! Oh my word! This place is amazing, a valley of death in the middle of lush green farmland. What was once a great lake (the largest semi-permanent wetland of inland South West Australia, 11k by 6k), and even still has a sign for a yacht club somewhere here, is now all but dried up, but resonates beauty, almost indescribable, in its shades of pink, yellow and beige. Just the sounds of the wind, birds and buzzing flies, so tranquil and peaceful, awesome.

Drove up to **Pussycat Hill Lookout**, which gives a panoramic view of the lake and its surrounding deathscape, and there's a plaque dedicated to Sir Donald, unveiled by his daughter on 31st December 1984, recognising his feat of the World Water Speed record of 276.3mph, here on 31st December 1964. Off to find the yacht club next. Ha! just a tin shack.

Moved on to try and find Robert's crew drilling, but seem to be blindfolded, found the routes no probs, just couldn't see past the trees. Took another look at the lake, scoobed on, and left, a little elevated. Driving around Bibikin Road, Sand Plains Road, and Sunters Road, was an enriching experience, as would be expected, with some great-looking blackboys, funny-looking grass plants which have a real look of character about them – these ones put me in mind of American Indians dancing around their campfires, stooping forward and back, with the war feathers sticking out, just great. Took plenty pics kemo sabe.

Fri 25th

Up at the crack, and off with Robert to see the crew in action. Drove through blankets of mist hanging over the paddocks, as Robert points out the white (ghost) gums, and

Yates trees. Parrot like 28s swoop before us, spread up, and out in front of us, like a Red Arrows air display team, in a flash of yellow and green. Lime-green budgies buzz us too, darting up and down above and beside us as Robert hoons it along the dirt roads in his jumbo-sized off-road vehicle. The 28s especially, seem to like racing alongside, same when I'm in the van.

Just had a go at water divining. It worked, all about magnetic fields apparently, water running past rock, creating the 'fields', also learning about mineral deposits. Andrew and Stuart, two of Robert's firm, had already drilled down 12 metres, pulling up loose clay, thick clay and water with double the salinity of sea water, all pumped up through the hollow drill tubes, connected at the surface to a rubber reinforced hose, which pumps the debris out through a curious cone-shaped chute, for the contents to be checked. Finished up early, and Robert took us through the red-gravel farm and country roads, to get some more shots of the 'Red Indian' blackboys out here. Dropped me off at my van after, and we said our goodbyes. Filled the van up, and off I went, out of **Woolarama Town** to **Arthur River** and over to **Bridgetown,** through all the country roads, passing fast-running rivers along the way, fuelled by the rain that's been in plentiful supply recently. Everything such a contrast to those death lakes, quite stunningly rich green pastures, and white foam on the rivers and streams as a result of all the extra rainfall. Night at Craig and Annie's.

Sat 26th July

Babysat James, while Annie took Emma to a MacD party, and Craig out delivering bottles. Craig soon returned, and James dropped off to sleep, to leave us free for a bit of land management on his property, pulling trees down with the 4 x 4 Ute, chainsaw action to chop them up, burning off the

dead wood, and beer and scoobs on the way, all good fun!!
Food, beer and fire, for the evening, watched the Perth
Eagles flog some side in the AFL (Aussie Rules Footy).

Sun 27th

Went over to Craig's accountant's house, to rehang some
ropey old doors, in a 'bodge it and leg it' manner, assisted
as always by stubbies. Easy job, then back for some more
'land management', and pyromania. Joe (accountant) joined
us for 'man stuff', and a bit of fun at table football in the
shed. Eve beer and scoobs with Craig again.

Mon 28th

Out on the rounds with Craig on the gas bottles again, all
done by 1 p.m. Got in one last surf (sort of), a 2- to 3-metre
swell of smokin' surf at Yallingup, or Yalls as the locals call
it. 200-yard walk across craggy reef, knee deep, in my fins,
to a drop-off into an inhospitable mess of turbulent, swell-
driven rip, breathing up and down at the reef's edge, raising
and lowering 2 or 3 feet, jump in when it breathes 'up', then
paddle like mad while getting dragged like a matchstick
sideways, into the al fresco washing machine. I persevered
for a bit, with all I had, before allowing the faithful yellow
streak to take over, gratefully catching the next mass of
white water back in over the reef and in towards shore and
safety. Craig battled on, in what looked like pretty hostile
conditions from where I stood, but returned defeated or so
he said. I have a feeling he may have just said that to make
me feel better about my own pitiful experience. Also some
other surfers that had watched us without moving from
their car bonnets, greeted us with smiles that said, 'rather
you than me'. Maybe I should never have gone out in the
first place! It all looks a whole lot bigger when you're under

163

it! At least we got wet, and I've now been for a surf with my Oz cuz twice now, so all worthwhile. Delivered a few more bottles late afternoon, before another fine feed, cooked by Annie, with choc pud and sauce, to complete a full day well fed. Last night of scoobs with Craig on the veranda.

Thurs 31st July

Breakfast, then we're out walking Leonies guide dog, Kulak. The dog across the road, Z, joins us as always, he's the most walked dog in WA, sits in his garden, and joins any dog in the street that's on its walk. Told J and L I'm off up the coast for a bit, left Safety Bay at 11 a.m.-ish, stopped at Bassendean to catch up with Liz and family, she also helped me sort out my email, which was a bonus. Saw the boys again, and Anne, Brett and baby April, left Liz with her hands full.

Off up the **Brand Highway** a couple of hundred k, and inland another 100k, arriving a couple of hours into darkness, parked in **Cervantes Town** at present, ready to go see the **Pinnacles** tomorrow.

Fri 1st August

Pinnacles OK, but probably not worth the 200k round trip off the Brand Highway to see them. Took a few pics, checked out the coastline to see the surf off the reef, then hit the road again. Farm country all the way, this is the wheat belt, and spring flowers are preparing to bloom. Arrived at **Geraldton** early afternoon, took the scenic drive around, and checked the beaches. No go for surf, as there's a reef half a mile out, breaking the swell up before it gets in, small 1-foot waves at most, maybe ok for learners.

Sand dunes and beaches of white sand, and much used by 4 x 4s. This is a port town, with a few old buildings, and the ropiest-looking palm trees down the centre of the main street, funniest sight. Lots of estate agents' hoardings, with the agent looking at you in his best. 'Trust me, your money's mine' look, as if they're local celebrities. I don't think the hoardings would last very long in Britain!!

Drove out and on towards Kalbarri, another 160k north, lots more of the 53-metre road trains up this way, huge wheat silos, and often, a great view below in the distance of the waves crashing in, in perfect sets onto the reef out at sea below.

Glorious 'half-rainbow' sunset, and a nightmare for a while, as the sun dropped, making vision almost non-existent for moments. Saw a roo in the road after dark, slowed down, but it just stood there, so I stopped. It looked at the van for a bit, then hopped off into the bush, tall as the van, easy. Drove on and kept the speed down to less than 80kph, through **Port Gregory**, and up to a rest area just outside **Kalbarri**, right next to the Port Gregory–Kalbarri road commemorative opening plaque, March 7th 1997.

Sat 2nd

Woken by the waves crashing against the fierce, jagged cliffs, like not-too-distant thunder. Off to investigate a little closer. Big swell, but dumping straight onto the rocks. Drove into Kalbarri town, a small coastal community, thriving on tourism, and especially fishing and boat trips. It's sheltered from the power of the sea swell by a natural reef bar across the river mouth. You can enjoy a view of the ocean's ferocity from the lawns or car parks along the river's edge. With the surf blown out, I decided to move on up the coast for **Monkey Mia**, stopped off at **Shell Beach** for a nose around, very white (shells), blue (sea), and quite still, like a lake. Arrived at MM about 4.30-ish, and relaxed. Had a look around the site, then early kippage.

Sun 3rd

Up early for shave and scrub-up, then down to the beach to see the wild dolphins swim inshore to be fed, many of them with bite marks from shark attacks. Very playful, flipping out of the water and chasing each other. Booked up for an afternoon boat trip, sailed for two and a half hrs around the **Shark Bay Marine Park** off Monkey Mia, on a 60-foot catamaran, *Shotover*, another former race yacht turned over to the leisure industry. A brisk day for a sail, but unfortunately not so good for viewing, which was the main purpose. Overcast with clouds, and winds blustering to stir up the sea, combined to make spotting species an awkward task. However, the dolphins in the area came and gave us an impressive show, a couple of pods of ten or so males in frisky mood, performed for us at the sides, front, back, and underneath of the boat, many of them with bits chewed out of their dorsal fins, and deep-seated scratches from past scrapes with sharks. Didn't get to see any dugongs, but it's not the best time of year, and visibility was poor anyway. Although we did get to see a weather-beaten old loggerhead turtle, with half of its forepaws missing, it dived down once we were almost alongside, so I couldn't get a decent shot. Worthwhile afternoon anyway, nice sail, and the dolphins were fun.

Pelicans roam the beach here, unbothered by the human contingent, and make good photographic subjects too, very graceful gliders as they circle to land, and very funny to watch as they walk, or rather waddle, along.

Mon 4th

Up early again, to go see the dolphins, in for their breakfast shift. All female dolphins, with the exception of their youthful offspring, staying inshore to avoid the amorous advances of the pods of males waiting away offshore for some action. Stood in the knee-deep water later on, and a mother and child dolphin came within a couple of feet, and turned on their sides, showing their stomachs as if to say 'Feed me'.

Strolled along the beach to take more pics of yet another idyllic spot. Cooked up another tasty toasted omelette sarnie, 'à la Speck', with the addition of a slice of cheese in it, top banana! Now sat enjoying the late afternoon sun, with just spiral palm trees on the green lawn, golden white sands, and electric-blue, swell-free sea, out to the horizon. One of the few parts of Western Australia where you look eastwards to the sea, with the sun setting to your left as you look out on Shark Bay.

Tues 5th

Up at 8-ish, and out for a final look at the dolphins before setting off; pelicans out too, also after their free feed. Hit the road joining back up with the **North West Highway**, quite a long slog of more relentlessly straight roads, and not a lot to stop for. Made a short 5k detour, and stopped at the **Hamelin Pool**, famous locally for its **stromatalites**, our life giving **cyanobacterial** comrades, responsible for creating enough oxygen in our atmos to allow us breathing creatures a chance to get started. They look a bit like a broken-up tarmac driveway in a foot of very salty water, not an earth-shattering view to behold, but it was kind of on the way, and a good excuse to break up the day's driving. Moving onwards again, to **Carnarvon** this time, not much to it really, a 1k jetty, some more ropey palm trees, plantations, and a road out, which I was on soon enough!

Western Australia's wildlife springing into action with rich purples, yellows, and lily-white wild flowers brightening up the roadside viewage as I trundled along. Feral goats, unbothered by the traffic, feeding by the road, plenty of roadkill, dried-out rivers, an eagle, and Carnarvon's L6 radio station keeping me company.

Pulled in to a rest area, 40k short of **Coral Bay**, just in time to see a large mob of roo's bounding off into the distance. Also, crossed the **Tropic of Capricorn** again today, quite different to the east coast version.

CORAL BAY, NINGALOO REEF

Wed 6th August

Up at 8-ish, brief stretch, and a welcome coffee made in the van. Quick look at the 8-foot tall monolith, which I had first thought was a termite mound, then offski for the last 30k or so to Coral Bay.

Amazing beaches, coral reef just yards from the shore's edge, and sea pounding the outer reef wall half a mile out. Booked in at a site, bought a mask and snorkel, went off to try them out. Lots of brightly coloured fish, many different species, but water a tad chilly, so only stayed in 20 to 25 minutes. Sat in the sun for a while, then back to camp for a read and relax. Evening beer and chat with a Kiwi couple, Glen and Jill, parked next to me, ex-New Zealand farmers, now retired, been in Oz travelling for seven years since. Nice couple.

Thurs 7th

Went out for a snorkel and swim, got talking to an English girl on the beach, proper sweetheart, turns out she's doing the same trip as me, but the opposite way round, swapped travel info. Few beers in the eve at the bar by the shore, live tribute band, not bad. Cool day. (Locked my keys in the van, Kiwi Glen sorted it out.)

Fri 8th

Saw Glen and Jill off, went for a walk along the beach, decided to head back to Perth as I'd had enough for a bit. Drove about 700k down the North West Coastal Highway, stopping en route to get pics of roadkill roos, feral goats, red dust roadsides, etcetera. Pulled up at a rest area for the night, and bugger me if Glen and Jill didn't pull in five minutes later, literally! Went over to speak, and we had a laugh about it all, they invited me over for rice, curry and beer, so we spent the evening gassing, and swapping yet more yarns. (1) Morris 1000 car, as a young couple, driving back from a party in NZ farm country, ended up in a ditch, on its side. (2) Coming back from a ball, to go straight out at 5 a.m. to sort out the cows. (3) Trips to England, and experiences there, (ABC = Another Bloody Church). (4) Bali trips, son Callum, and more. Blinding couple, and fun evening.

Sat 9th

Saw them off again first thing, they're off to Kalbarri, I'm off to Geraldton (maybe). Stopped at **Coronation Beach** for my omelette sarnie, 8k off the highway, nice and quiet, and v. sunny. Driving back to the highway, I saw a cool, fat, stumpy-tailed lizard on the road (found out later it was a 'Bob tailed Gink'), got some pics and carried on. Pulled in at another rest area for the night, 150k short of Perth.

Sun 10th

Up early and hoofed into Perth for a look around the beaches, **City Beach, Scarborough Beach**, etcetera turned up at Liz and Graham's place (**Bassendean**, suburb of Perth) just after midday. Had dinner with them, and stayed the night, chatting and drinking their wine. Was going to kip in the van outside, but they insisted I make use of their spare room, nice.

Mon 11th August

On the net first thing, looking for New Zealand info. Went into the city to book up a Kiwi Experience package with STA Travel, too easy. Kiwi Experience basically run tours which take you all around New Zealand, with all kinds of activities organised to choose from, and all run by people that know the country inside out, apparently. On return to the city car park, only to notice, some little shits have nicked the van's reg plates! Got back to L and G's place, and found some of the reg plates' nuts and bolts around where the van had been parked, so the fuckers had them away during the night while I was sleeping in comfort. I was rightly pissed off, wishing I'd been in the van at the time, but as Liz wisely pointed out, it was probably best, for any number of reasons, that I wasn't. Phoned the Old Bill, reported the plates stolen, got a crime number, stewed.

Tues 12th

Into Perth to confirm the Kiwi Experience trip, after downloading transport info regarding new reg plates for the van. Paid for the New Zealand trips, and went to watch a movie at IMAX, had the 75 by 100-foot cinema screen to myself for *Too Fast, Too Furious*. Lame action, fit chick, flick.

Wed 13th

Sorted van and kit, ready for leaving. Filled forms out for new reg plates, and got busy on the net. Anne and wee April came round for the arvo. Went to watch Thomas and

Matthew train for OzKick, that's junior Aussie Rules Footy, in the evening, then back, and out again with the family to a city food court, for a nice meal and beer, then walk about King's Park, and fun with them at the Whispering Wall War Memorial; nice night.

Thurs 14th

Made temporary reg plates for the van, out of plywood, and painted to look the real McCoy, in the afternoon. Easy evening.

Fri 15th

Easy day doing sweet FA. Phoned Ma, had a good chat.

Sat 16th August

Took Jim to hospital in the morning, bowel probs, all OK thankfully. Picked him up later, when sorted. Into Perth on the bus to finalise travel stuff for New Zealand. Back at J and L's place, hear Craig and his mob are on their way up, so the house is on 'red alert', battle stations on all decks! Leonie preparing for the welcome invasion of the little people, making cakes, clearing rooms, and general excitedness of expectant grandparents. Craig and Annie are coming up this way to check out a buggy for their horse, so Craig's stopping the night with Emma and James, cool. Good family night, me and Craig sunk a few later on, while swapping yet more yarns, ended up finishing the last beer in the van outside so we didn't keep the house awake!

Sun 17th

Woken by the sun, into the house to find James crying 'cos

Mum and Dad are gone. Soon managed to distract him from his tears, and then began a fun day of being a kid among the kids. Liz and Graham turned up later, with Thomas and Matthew, and I was besieged, loved every minute. Oh to be between the carefree age of two and ten again. Got a little flattened, tugged, prodded and abused by the miniature gang, bless 'em, but oh my word, what a lucky lad I am, and what wicked kids they are, little explosions of energy, with heaps of character, full of smiles and laughs all day long. Got the number plates fitted to the van, and all packed up, ready for the off.

Mon 18th

Dinner with the family, last emails, said goodbye to Thomas and Matthew after, chat and beers with Liz and Graham, before he drove me to the airport for my flight back to Sydney.

SYDNEY (AGAIN)

Tues 19th August

Arrived Sydney at 6 a.m. (lost two hours), took the train to **Circular Quay**, ferry to **Manly**, then taxi, to the **Bower House**. Saw Tim Ellman Brown, another home-town boy, in my old room when I arrived. Talked Western Australia surf, then went out to the **Fairey Bower Point** for a good couple of hours catching waves, really great to get back out there. Got a chunky steak pie at the Manly Corso Bakehouse after, mmmmmm those pies!!! Cold and blowy day.

Moved into what was the girls room, with Canadian girl Meg. The Bower 'rent man', Steve's, bird, Emily arrived back today too, just got in from LA. Saw Bam Bam and

Double A too, they both moved back in to the Bower a little while ago, had a smoke with them, my first in ages. Good to see Stevo again, and Kiwi Caroline.

Wed 20th

Good stretch, and then out for a surf with Dan and Daz off the **Corso** at Manly, two and half hrs of decent-size waves, and I even got my first barrel!!! Dan scored some weed for us, held out 'til the evening walk to the Shark Bar, and had one for the journey. Met up with Caroline for pool and beer, plenty of beer! Got quite sauced, and she even went skinny-dipping on the way back. Fuck that for a game of soldiers, its cold enough out there in a wet suit, so I watched as she stripped on the Shelley Beach promenade steps, down to the chilly stuff, crazy Kiwi.

Crawled into me pit at about 4.30 a.m., thoroughly pissed.

Thurs 21st

Woke up with a thick head, still aching from the surf sessions of the previous days. Recuperated in front of the box for a couple of hours, watching *The Making of Cleopatra*, and *Only Fools and Horses* vids, then launched into the 'shitchen', for a mass wash-up and clean sesh, all spotless for the mo, not for long no doubt! After a wee stretch, went surfing with Tim, Daz and Dan off the Corso. Tim has no job at the mo, so he's in twice a day, and had one of his best sessions off the Point this morning, while I suffered in my pit. Daz and Dan came back from work early again, so skinned up, suited up, and off we went for a good couple of hours, bit messy, but OK.

Got caned in the evening, with a few stubbies to wash down the day.

173

Fri 22nd August

Lazy day – went surfing with Tim, Steve and Michel, off the Corso, short but sweet, I'll miss the old place! Tim started his job washing up at the Shelley Beach restaurant, which he assures me is full of fit chicks. A book is running to see if he comes home with a date! After surf, came back for smoke and films, *Bachelor Party* on.

Not much sleep, then Bam Bam, Double A and Michel get back from their night out in Sydney (5.30 a.m.), so came out for a smoke with them. Handshakes and hugs again, then out the door for the last time, and Stevo's giving me a lift to Sydney Central so I could catch a train from there to the airport, all too easy. I don't really get too bothered about moving on, only the hassle of wondering whether the luggage suffers any mishaps, but I will miss the Bower and Manly, because it's so easy-going there, always waves, and nightlife, if not outstanding, at least acceptable.

New Zealand, and Fiji Journals, 24th Aug 2003 to 25th Sept 2003

SOUTH ISLAND, NEW ZEALAND – CHRISTCHURCH

Got the flight without grief, just running late because of the baggage escalators. Small plane, but only took 3 hours. Into Christchurch for 4 p.m., bus to city, and walk to find the digs, looking like a pack horse. Settled in at the backpackers', with a room to myself, went out for a mosey, bought some thick woolly socks and hat to combat the nippy temps in New Zealand, plus an alarm clock for the hectic schedule ahead.

Again I find a place very similar to home, very English, a bit like Oxford, or Cambridge, with its canals and gondoliers, but perhaps more so because of the crispness of the air, which I quite like. But also the trees, parks and general architecture, albeit a very small-town version, and not a huge amount of people about for a Saturday afternoon.

Sun 24th August

Up and off early to catch the **Tranzalpine train** across to the west coast. Cold fresh morning and nice warm train. Soon into the scenery of alpine mountains with crisply covered virgin snow, blue skies behind making a clear contrast. Mountain passes shrouded in mist, deep ravines with green icy-looking rivers running through them (made me thirsty just looking at them). The train has a viewing carriage (open air) for taking pictures, cold but cool! Streams of people running back and forth every time the intercom tour guide indicates an upcoming photo opportunity. Stopping at designated scenic attractions such as **Arthurs Pass**, **Lake Moana** and others. Warmer after crossing through the pass into the west and different (slightly) landscape. Intercom guide occasionally injecting humour to the commentary, e.g. **Lake Pearson** named by **Josef Pearson** after his wife because it's 'deep, mysterious, and lays around doing nothing all day'. Also, stagecoach horses that plied this route in bygone days that had an 18-month working life before being shipped to Australia for the Melbourne cup!

Intercom woman also tells us which side of the train we'll find the station platform!

Picked up outside **Greymouth** station on the west coast by the 'Kiwi Experience' coach, only ten people on board! First night stopped in **Mahinapua**, just a photo op stop and chance to get to know the new fellow travellers that night in the **Poo Pub**. Walked along the wild-looking beach strewn with remnants of the dead trees which had toppled from the coastline sand dunes, crossed over the road to the lake through the rainforest tunnel for the first of many to come mountain reflection shots.

Mon 25th

Off at 9.30 a.m. from Mahinapua and on the road through pretty much lush green dense vegetation either side of the road most of the way, each green growth being home to more plentiful green and mossy growth wrapped around it filling in the spaces like an untouched 1,000-year-old forest, damp, deep and mysterious. Quick stop at an outdoor centre to see some native culture stuff and get some feed from their not-too-healthy-looking display.

Back on the road to **Pukekurra** stop, offering paintball-ing, gold panning or bush walks. I opted for a walk along the nearby glacial river followed by a bison burger and freshly made 'hot billy tea'. Off to Franz Josef next, passing 'kettle lakes', mountain views, narrow box-girder bridges, and grey stone bottomed almost dry rivers with icy green water running from the glacial peaks. Bumped into the guy and his girlfriend I've been crossing paths with since arriving in New Zealand (third time so far), they're off to Wanaka. They'd offered to take me with them from the first day! Presently at the Black Sheep backpackers' and booked onto a half-day glacier hike tomorrow, all heli hiking suspended owing to adverse weather. Went out in the evening to cement relations with the mob I'm travelling with, got battered on beer and shots.

Tues 26th

Up early again, this time for the half-day hike up the **Franz Josef Glacier**. Kitted up with all the necessary warm stuff, waterproofs, boots and talons, which are spiked metal plates which fix to the soles of the boots. Then six of us plus guide set out in the pouring rain through the mountain valley, across the shale and gravelly ex-river bed, all grey at first, but up close the rocks are layered or striped with white quartz veins like bubblegum stretched across the stones. The rain has all the waterfalls fired up, vaulting down the steep mountainsides and fuelling the rapid streams below. After a 45-minute hike, and checking out a really cool ice cave, we reached the point low down on the glacier where we put on our talons, ready for the full-on ice trek. Dirty-looking with all the rock dust mixed up with the ice, but clearing as we ascended and becoming bluer (is that a word?). Lots of really cool crevasses and 'moulins' which are deep holes in the ice with changing shades of blue. Bit of an effort getting used to the talons and trusting them, especially on the downward tread. Took two tumbles, once snagged between two rocks and fell over in slow motion, second time the

177

talons snagged and I slid down a few metres of ice on my back, laughing all the way, no harm done. Not as cold as I'd expected, we kept warm through hiking and negotiating the ice steps and paths which needed constant working with the pickaxe by the guides as they go. Cameras soaked and film ruined so no pictures unfortunately, but an enjoyable half-day of something a little different for me. Also it was really nice drinking cupped hands full of icy-cold rainwater from the glacial streams running down as we went. Waterfalls and cascades kept my attention up as we headed down. Into the hostel bar for the evening and won the killer pool comp with a prize of a free day's snowboarding in Queenstown. Nice!

Wed 27th

Don't remember hitting the pit last night so obviously celebrated the triumph well. Very early start, 7.30 a.m. left the **Black Sheep Backpackers**, on the Kiwi bus. Stopped at **Lake Mathieson** for brekkie and scenic photo ops of Mount Cook reflecting out of the still water. Moved on past the rugged coastline in the continuing rain on our way to the **Haast Pass** and its mean mountain rapids. Stopped for bus repairs (windscreen wipers) at **Thunder Creek Falls**, more photo ops. Currently weaving our way through steep-sided mountain passes packed with moss-covered rainforest and plenty of natural carnage in amongst it all. The snow-capped summits all cloaked in mist, and occasionally low-lying mists laying like a long scarf along ridges in the forest canopy. After a three- or four-hour journey we arrived at the **Wanaka** township with Lakes Wanaka and Hawea either side of it. After checking in at the Hotel Wanaka I went for a look around, it all reminded me of where I stayed in the Hartz mountains in Germany while on a school exchange. It's still raining so I have continuously wet feet as my trainers leak like a bitch. The room we're in has a balcony with a decent view of the alpine town, and mountains behind, currently shrouded by the heavy mists. Now sat by the open fire in the hotel lounge with its impressive windowed wall and comfy lounge chairs. The view of the mountains and lake only interrupted by the upside down 'V' sections of drawn floor-to-ceiling curtains. Not at all bad for 20 bucks a night, can't be bad if the American skiing team are here too, as in, they wouldn't use shabby digs, now would they?

Thurs 28th

QUEENSTOWN

Left Wanaka at 9 a.m. and heading into the **Karawau Gorge** in all its bleak, rugged and sometimes daunting splendour. Only an hour's drive but plenty of viewage along the route with the green icy rivers running at full tilt and impressive rapids. Pulled into **Queenstown** and booked up activities, booked into the Black Sheep backpackers', then went walkabout. Took a trip up the mountain in a gondola, took some pics of the awesome views of the town below and surrounding lakes, rivers, and snow capped mountain range. Had a go on a luge up there too, 1.5k winding track in a little cart which can pick up a hair-raising speed. Out cementing relations again in the evening, no recall so must've been a little battered. Earlier picked up my free snowboarding pass and told to return to collect the free hire clothing for the day.

Fri 29th

Went to get the coach up the mountain only to realise at the last minute that I hadn't picked up the the ski clothing. Mad dash to the snow centre in town, got sorted and caught the next coach. Just an hour lost so still all good. More glorious views on the way to the **Coronet Peak**, picked up the boots and board up there and straight into the first lesson. Absolutely wicked!! What a day, so cool, I'm addicted. Aching all over now, even after a long stretch and booked and paid for two more days of snowboarding, supercool! Quiet few beers at the Pig and Whistle in town with the Aussie Richard.

Sat 30th

Up at the crack and aching all over, quick stretch and out for another day on the slopes. Quickly pushed up a couple of groups, three different instructors in a day, finding things a tad more demanding there with tricks and suchlike but all great fun and another beautiful day weather-wise. Speedy Gonzales on the downhill, that's me now, death or glory! Quiet night at the hostel watching vids, deep aches set in.

Sun 31st

Last early start for the Coronet Peak, real struggle moving first thing, stiff as a really stiff thing everywhere. Quick stretch then up and at 'em! Doing OK on the slopes until people get in the way but no real dramas. Picked up the stance properly (almost) now. Instructor says I'm ready so we head off up to the very top on the Coronet Express chairlift, and it looked a bloody long way down to this novice. Half-way down and one of the group stopped bang in front of me and I bounced off her like a spring straight on to my left butt cheek, ooh the pain!! Still struggling to walk, sit, stand, lie down, get up, dress, and pretty much anything else which requires movement, hurts. Not looking forward to tomorrow morning getting on the bus to Christchurch, it was agony just coming back from the mountain! My left butt cheek feels as if it's had a bowling ball implanted in it. Even lying here and writing this hurts. I'd kill for a hot bath. Cramps in feet and toes now setting in, just reminding me they want a mention! And breaking wind hurts too, now that's just plain nasty!!! Limped out for a few evening beers.

Mon 1st Sept

Back on the road, left Queenstown heading once again through the Karawau Gorge in all its wicked, stark magnificence, on our way back to **Christchurch**. Short stop at fruit capital **Cromwell** then onwards through the **Lindis Pass** onto another stop at Lake **Tekapo** and its view of **Mount Cook**. Booked in at **Star Times Backpackers Hotel** in **Cathedral Square**, right opposite the Gothic-looking cathedral itself, central Christchurch. What a star backpackers', cool bar with big screen, also sound washing and sleeping facilities.

Refreshed and changed, now off for a look around. Evening in the Star's Bedrock Bar watching films on the big screen and sipping coldies.

Tues 2nd

Nice lay in, stretch (brief and uncomfortable), and shower followed by relaxing coffee and read of today's paper in the common room. Body still crying out all over from the snowboarding but a little less. Bit of a stroll around the city centre taking pics along the way. Cruisey rest of day taking it easy, evening beers and early kippage.

NORTH ISLAND, AUCKLAND

Wed 3rd

Up by 8 a.m., quick coffee and pack up kit once more, check out and head across the square to get the airport bus. Scribed a few postcards while waiting for the boarding call. Looking out of the window seat to the southern alps in the distance, snow-capped and lit up by the sun through the clouds. That's the South Island done and dusted in ten days, seemed longer as I look back but at the same time it shot by. Wicked memories of a wicked place, and one more place that I'd definitely like to return to with more time. Cool views of the North Island as we fly over, looking a bit like a geography map with the shades of greens highlighting the contours of the fields, and fields divided up like patchwork quilts. On the bus into the city of **Auckland**, passing more of those fields divided by large fern hedges neatly trimmed into green walls, and eventually into the outskirts of a grubby, unattractive city suburb. Bit of a San Francisco/Brighton feel to it with its steep-hilled city roads and old-style buildings, and modern skyscrapers with their reflective glass walls. As I stepped off the bus at the corner of **Queen Street** and **Darby Street** it looked more like a part of Tokyo than New Zealand with so many oriental-looking dudes swarming through the streets, just strange at first, but cool especially the Asian influence in the food halls and shops. Booked in at the ACB then went for a stroll down to the quayside, lots of tall, regal buildings and more skyscrapers. Out for a few beers in the Globe Bar below the backpackers for the evening.

Thurs 4th

Nice long lay in, much needed rest. Left butt cheek and back of left knee black and blue from my last snowboard fall, pictures taken for the record. Walked around town but basically another lazy day. Got to the final of the Globe Bar doubles pool comp with a German girl with the most confused mixture of accents I've ever come across, speaking English while switching from Scouse, to broad Yorkshire, cockney, Irish, and god knows how many other variations. We got pipped on the final black ball for 100 bucks bar tab. May have been a good thing as my bus leaves in the morning.

Fri 5th Sept

In the zone! That impenetrable, untouchable time of bullet-proof self-confidence. Maybe it's the gorgeous green valleys and densely wooded hills with tiny awkward lambs unsteadily trotting playfully around, announcing another spring arrived, life springing eternally. Or running water everywhere, long-expired volcanic cones now thick with vegetation and stepped where past Maori tribes used them as fortifications. Steep winding roads making travel slow, so time to soak it all up. Maybe it's that whole 'land that time forgot' vibe, like some five-legged, horned, hairy beast with scaled head and feet could stroll across the road, stopping the coach, and everyone would look to the driver for confirmation of this being a perfectly common situation. Or *maybe*, my hangover's wearing off!! Heading into **Hot Water Beach** now for the **Cathedral Cove** walk down to the limestone rock beach. Half-hour hike down to the beach but not a bad view when there, a little like some of southern Thailand off the coast of Krabi, with little volcanic eruption islands covered in green growth dotted about **Mercury Bay**, so named by **Captain Cook** again; that man certainly got about. He called it Mercury Bay because it was bright in the sky then, and part of his trip involved gauging its distance from earth for purposes of navigation apparently (I know

183

some stuff!!). Snapped away for a while before we set off for the final leg to **Whitianga** ('wh' pronounced as an F). Homely backpackers', **Buffalo Peaks** in another scenic setting. Lots of stuff named Buffalo after **HMS Buffalo** which grounded in the bay in the 17 or 1800s.

Quiet night reading in sleepsville.

ROTORUA

Sat 6th

Left on the kiwi bus at 7.30 a.m. for Rotorua, uneventful journey, picturesque as ever. Stopped at Rotoruas geothermal park on arrival and spent an hour or so looking around at the bubbling mud, steam vents and geysers blasting occasionally through the rocks, all pretty cool stuff. Booked in at the **Hot Rocks backpackers**', then in the afternoon, went to the Polynesian Spa for a thermal soak, very relaxing in the outdoor rock pools at 38–40 degrees, and the water even had a kind of 'essential oil' feel to it. In the evening we all went out for a Maori challenge welcome and *hangi* (feed) at a reconstructed authentic old-style Maori village. Five coachloads turned up for the ceremony where the 'warriors' put on a display of the sort which would have been accorded to unknown visitors in their tribal days. After the 'confrontation' and acceptance of friendship, the crowd were invited to look around the tribal village. All very moody and backlit for effect. After the look around we're herded into the main hut for entertainment from the traditionally dressed tribal Maoris, as they explain each song and dance, and their meanings and relevance to tribal life. And finally a big *hangi* feast of fine foods served up buffet-style, fit to pop after. Throughout the evening we're introduced to Maori words and meanings and encouraged to repeat them. (*pukky pukky* – applause, *waka* – canoe). On the way back the bus driver was singing such classics as Glenn Miller's 'In the mood', but in Maori, most entertaining. Too full to drink after, so early night.

Sun 7th

Went for another amble around town again, checked out the park across from the backpackers' with its bubbling mudpits and semi-boiling water pools, steam issuing up all over among the flower beds. Brekkie at the Fat Dog and walked it off looking around at the lakes and monuments. Went for an afternoon spa and massage for a touch of pampering for a couple of hours, nice and relaxing. Few evening beers on the old 'cementing relations' pretext. Looking forward to **Waitomo** tomorrow and the **black water rafting**.

Mon 8th Sept

Up with the alarm, feeling decidedly foggy and don't remember hitting the pit last night so it must've been good. Now at Waitomo after a three-hour journey with the new driver who seems a laugh and keeps the busload amused with his witty commentary. Checked in at **Kiwi Paka**, real swanky hostel only recently built so everything's new, and superb views of green rolling hills and volcanic cones all around. Booked up for black water rafting this afternoon, should be fun.

'Oh what a *craic*!', abseiled 105 metres down a hole in a hill and into a cavern, with sounds of water coming in everywhere. Then we're guided through a narrow passage to a platform where one by one we're hooked up to a rope slide into the pitch black ahead, nice buzz of speed over 20 or 30 metres and pull up to get unhitched. Stop there for coffee from the guide's flasks and flapjacks, unhitch the abseil harness and queue up to jump off a ledge 15 foot into the icy cave river below with our bums in tyre inner tubes, and then off down the cave system checking out the stalactites (hanging down), stalagmites (forming upwards), and glow worms in the cathedral-like steep-sided cavern walls. Turn around and make our way back, passing our jump point where we unload the inner tubes and head on towards the increasingly loud sound of thunderous running water, and the feel of the undertow getting stronger as we went. On the way back on the tubes we were all linked with lights off, checking out the glow worm crap (it's their number 2's which glow), like stars in the sky, in serene silence. Tube-free we stumbled along the uneven surface underfoot into the more rapidly running water, we began diving in to let the flow take us downstream. So, so cool (and chilly). Come to tight holes to squeeze through, head almost underwater, and then turn uphill against a much stronger current, and the real fun began as we headed for waterfalls.

I was looking forward to some H_2O freefall, but no, we were climbing upwards through the bloody things! Absolutely wicked!! Looking for, and placing feet into the natural footholds available as mountains of water powered past you, threatening to blow you out like a flushed toilet, not once or twice, but three levels to get through before eventually pushing through the last gushing inlet and out into daylight. After that we were taken back for a hot spa bath, showers, soup and bagels. A most memorable day which included the two best-looking chicks on the bus as a bonus, and a good crowd in total. Also run by two sound Kiwis. Evening beers at the Waitomo Caves Tavern.

Tues 9th

Early scenic drive through winding hilly country roads.

'Kiwi experience': Janne the Finn, Brazilian Andre and self, boarding at Mount Ruapehu, New Zealand.

Stunning vistas through the coach windows on the road in New Zealand.

More amazing Kiwi views.

'Craters of the moon'. Hot pools of mud outside Taupo, New Zealand.

Hot Water Beach, North Island, New Zealand.

Chasing sunsets: crossing Australia from east to west.

Road kill, Western Australia.

Into the sun (right) and away from the sun (left) at Lake Hart, central Australia.

Festival of Lights, Pai, northern Thailand.

Lake Dumbleyung, south west Australia.

S21, Cambodia.

S21, Cambodia.

Sacramento Delta sunset, California.

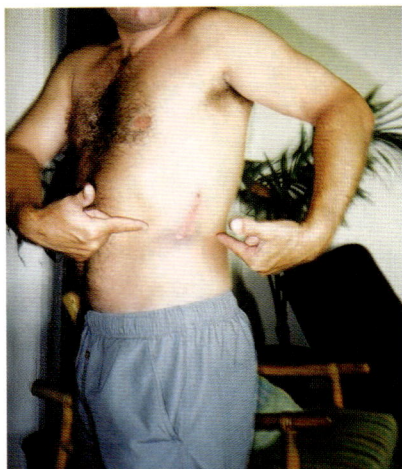

Surfboard 'bite'! Mancy, Sydney.

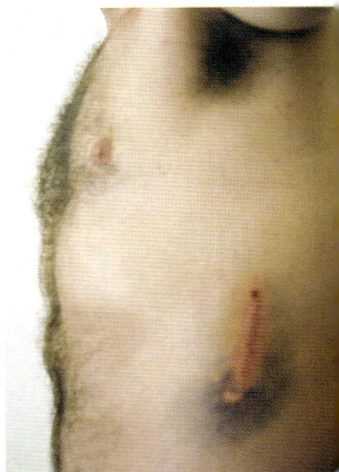

Next day.

Thai/Laos border, Mekong. Sunrise through sunglasses

'Flat flied flog'. The Pai family raft, northern Thailand.

Chiang Mai 'My Thais'.

Californian tree feller.

Siamese grass plant, south west Australia.

Mobbed up wild roos, south west Australia.

Uluru camels.

Stopped at **Marakopu Falls** for photo ops at the 35-metre waterfall set in subtropical rainforest. Then on to the **Maungapohoe natural bridge**, a phenomenon which was once part of a great cave system and now forms a giant arch as a gateway from one side of a hill to the other, quite spectacular. Gorgeous green and hilly sheep-grazing land the other side of the bridge, a few dead newborn lambs laying sadly on their sides. After our scenic detours we set off for **Taupo** and had one more stop at the **Huka Falls** just outside of our destination. Unbelievable power as the torrents pour through the narrow small canyon into the lower out spill area. Booked in at **Go Global Backpackers'**. Everyone from the bus out in the evening for fun and frolics at **Mulligans**, and the **Holy Cow** 'til the early hours (3 a.m.).

Wed 10th

Woken by Bea, the Columbian girl, as she knocked on my door at 6.15 a.m. to get me up for snowboarding. Feeling rather foggy I joined her, Janne (Finn lad), and Andre (Brazilian) for the hour-and-a-half drive to **Mount Ruapehu (Two Spirits).** Wicked mountain, much bigger than Coronet Peak at Queenstown, and longer, wider slopes with a thicker carpet of soft snow. I tutored Andre before we joined the board school. We stayed about 15 minutes and decided to go it alone with me as his instructor. At eleven we moved up a slope from Happy Valley to the Rockgardens and some awesome long runs. Great day, snowed and sleeted towards the end, but I'd already stopped with jelly legs by 3 p.m. and we wound down as we waited for our lift back. Quiet drive back as we were all knackered. After a good livening scrub-up and feed, it was out for yet another farewell drink as the bus heads south tomorrow. Lots of beer, photos and hugs. As the Kiwi crew left, I carried on drinking with some Irish lads and we moved on from Mulligans to the Holy

Cow, and progressed our session. In there I was spotted by Henry, a lad I'd snowboarded with in Queenstown, he's there with his sister Rowan and two other girls so I ended up drinking with them and we found our way to a karaoke bar of all places. Singing very badly, we kept going until they shut up shop.

Thurs 11th

Up at 11 a.m.(ish) and the Kiwi crew still around because of bus probs, so more goodbyes. Cybered off another marathon news mail to all, two hours of painfully slow typing. Big brekkie then a healthy three-quarter hour walk to the **Taupo Hot Springs** and a good few hours there soaking in their hot pools and getting massaged by the powerful jet streams and cascades, just lying back and chilling my boots. Walked back to the hostel, checked internet, and then bumped into Sarah, one of the girls with Henry from the night previous. We'd arranged to meet up but they hadn't remembered where I was staying, I hadn't even remembered we'd arranged to meet. So there I was again, with Henry the fellow Queenstown snowboard learner, his sister Rowan, girlfriend Jennie, and mate Sarah. Once again got on like a house on fire, so much so that they've talked me into skydiving the next day! – and driving up with them to Rotorua afterwards. In fairness I didn't take much persuading to remain in their company.

Fri 12th

Up nice and early to get picked up by Henry and crew in their rather flash motorhome and off we head to the skydiving centre outside Taupo. Sarah went on a different jump to us as she's having hers videoed. Poor thing had a wee sob up before going up: 'I'm so scared' she cried.

Rowan tended her, wiping away the running mascara ready for the camera, and off she went without looking back. Me, Rowan, Henry and Jennie went up next, having been kitted up and looking like extras on the *Battle of Britain* film set. Into the smallest plane I've ever been in by a country mile, and we're all held in tight against our tandem parachutists as the plane roars upwards. Henry was in first position and me second so we were right next to the sliding perspex door for a quality view of the landscape below. Twelve minutes to get to 12,000 feet and Henry's manoeuvred to the exit point. He'd been looking nervous, I thought, as we made our way up, but it turned out that he was giving 'evils' to 'Skegosaurus', the parachutist tandeming with Jennie, his girlfriend. Skeggy, this tall, bald, thin, alien-looking German, was running his fingers through Jennie's hair and using such class lines as 'I am liking the banana position, this is good ya', (alluding to the imminent jump position). So while I was erroneously interpreting Henry's look as one of sphincter contraction, he was in fact attempting, through eye contact, to convey to Skeggy to take his grubby German paws off his bird!

Once Henry was out the plane, I'm slid into position, legs out the side, knees together (not knocking, happy to say), head back, and thumbs tucked in harness straps, no turning back now, then out we go.

I can still feel that moment now. Sideways fall peacefully into the abyss, then straighten out facing down, get tap on the shoulders to signify arms out swallow-dive fashion and we're freefalling at 150 miles per hour with freezing air pushing against the face, awesome view of Lake Taupo below during the 45-second freefall, then *boosh!* as the chute opens and it feels like you've hit the bottom of a bungee drop but with the leash on your groin.

Then it's swoop and circle time as he steers the chute, navigating his way to the landing site while I just enjoy the whole experience and closing views as we drop 18 miles a minute and accurately hit the gravel bed with me punching the air like a Grand Prix driver at the winning line, feeling like going straight back up to do it again.

With all of us landed we were given a preview of our ground video which we all bought for $15. Then we hit the road to the Taupo Hot Springs a short distance from the lake and kicked back in the gorgeous hot pools for the next three hours and totally unwound. Nicely chilled, we hit the road for Rotorua, but as a cool surprise, they took me to the **Craters of the Moon** site, where bubbling mud pits and steam vents pour out from all over this eerie piece of land which looks like it could be used for the witches cauldron scene in Macbeth. They'd already been there so had a fag break while I scrambled about getting snap-happy again, trying to frame up the definitive moody shot. After that we carried on to **Rotorua** in their posh motor lounge and parked up outside the **Hot Rocks Backpackers**', where I checked in. Grabbed a box of wine and we all got started on a session, swapping travel stories, my eyes raised impressively at the mention of Sarah, who not only walked up Ayers Rock against the expressed wishes of the local Aboriginal tribespeople, but gave a metaphorical middle digit by having sex on it with the fella she was with at the time! Heaps of other funny stuff too, great crowd, especially bro and sis, Row and Henry, real lively fun characters, and not a little crazy. I'll look forward to seeing them again when I return (whenever that is!). Onto the Hot Rocks place, the **Lava Bar** after for more alcohol fuelled entertainment.

Sat 13th

Up at 8-ish feeling a bit fuzzy, no recollection of hitting the pit last night. Have to wait and see whether I was a good boy or not! Packed up and checked out of Hot Rocks. Checked the 'Welsh' crew (sorry). Apparently I did my well-honed disappearing act from the Lava Bar last night, clearly some semblance of sense not entirely subdued by the beer. Had ourselves a posh coffee and chat before another round of sad farewells, would've liked longer with them. Hugs, handshakes and emails swapped, then back on that green bus to Auckland for the last time.

FIJI TIME!

Sun 14th

Seems like I was there for ages, so much covered in just 20 days, and now here I am just outside **Nadi**, in **Veti Levu,** the largest of the **Fiji Islands**, staying at **The Tropic of Capricorn** (heard that name somewhere before??!!) backpackers'. Laying next to a pool, looking out to the islands just offshore, with the obligatory palm trees all around, volcanic black sand on the beach and pondering what to do next. Lazed and read by the pool for the day, walked a bit more on the beach. Booked up for the Fiji experience bus after a chat with some backpackers that had just done it, sounds like a great trip – so much for just lounging away my ten days here! Leaving tomorrow, me and a London lad Vish decided to give it a go. Watch this space

Ni sa Bula – hello how are you?

Fiji, oh my word! How to do it justice? First impression I'd say is like the climate of South East Asia (hot and sticky), and landscape of New Zealand (volcanic, lumpy and winding roads), with rainforest-clad mountains dropping down to smaller volcanic cones of brown and green grazing land, rivers bending round the lumps, and happy smiley waving Fijians pretty much everywhere. Mixed coastlines of volcanic black sand, gorgeous golden sands, turquoise azure waters lapping gently up to the shore, palm trees and/or mangrove-cloaked beaches affording shade when needed, and everything protected by the reef walls just offshore keeping the Pacific power at bay and making for outstanding snorkelling too.

Mon 15th

On the bus for 9.15 a.m., introduced to our guide John (Fijian), driver Kasim (Fijian Indian), and backpacking crew, then hit the road through more ex-volcanic coned hills and winding roads, all the way Fijians waving to us with happy smiles and windmill arms. Stopped at a Fijian village where we were guests of the Chief in his big hut, and shown around the village homes by the eager, super-friendly villagers, wearing our newly purchased sarongs, (a respect thing in the villages apparently).

Made our way to **Natadola Beach** for BBQ, beach football with the locals, beautiful beach walks, body surfing, and enjoying some chill time. Footy was lively and earned me a burst lip from a Dutch elbow. Plenty of claret but nothing to stop the game too long for.

On the road (dirt track!) through yet more Fijian lumpy volcanic winding roads, and everywhere the waving arms and smiling faces for us all the way to **Sigatoka**, where we pulled up for some sand-boarding down a daftly steep hill on a boogy board. Steep, knackering climb to get up there through gorse bush, black and golden sand to the top, admire the seaward view of untamed dune beach with sea debris strewn all about, and reef dump waves just offshore, then hurl ourselves down an almost vertical drop of sand dune on the boards. Great fun, went up and down half a dozen times, caked in black sand, and more blood from the lip.

Now at **Nadroga** in a very Fijian (laid-back) bar. Booked in at the **Crow's Nest Backpackers'** for the night, and now once again cementing relations. Given a tribal song and dance welcome by the locals in grass skirts and war paint, with spears, the women in brightly coloured shirts and flowers behind their ears. Beautiful harmonic singing just like the native South Africans sound; example: the singing on the film *Cry Freedom* about Steve Biko.

Tues 16th

Up early again for an 8 a.m. start to head out for today's **Matakimbal trek**. Leaving our plush settings and back out along the Coral Coast past many small villages of corrugated iron houses on stilts and a few thatched houses too (also on stilts). Always being waved at by the smiling populace as we go uphill and down dale, through the ever hilly volcanic cones either carpeted in lush green grass or hidden by rainforest with palm trees, giant fern fronds, and often encloaked by creeping ivy draped across everything.

With my board shorts on, flowerpot hat and Chiang beer 'wife beater' vest, we jump into some trucks, much like the Thailand trekking taxis, and headed for the hills! A half-hour drive followed by another three-quarter hour yomp up a dirt track in sweltering heat before immersing ourselves into the jungle of rainforest along the re-established Matakimbal (Chief's name) track up to where some upper-river villages used to be.

A good three hours of trekking through dense rainforest with the sun glinting through the surrounding growth. It was reminiscent of a Vietnam war movie, sometimes very steep and slippery, often up to the waist wading through streams, with Kasim, our driver and today's trek guide leader, steaming along barefoot, belittling our efforts, and even piggy-backing one of the young English Indian girls up and down some of the steeper and more slippery slopes. He has no noticeable muscle on him, a pot belly, and legs like matchsticks but he's clearly a strong and fit fella (smokes like a trooper too!). The two American lads (Josh and Marcus) continually shouting to each other, 'We're in Fiji', and 'this is ah-sum' (awesome), loving every minute of it.

Fantastic views all the time, be it in the streams looking up through the forest canopy, or looking down into the valleys and canyons from on high. At the end of the trek we arrived at a point along the **Navua River**, which carves its way through this range, and after a rest we jumped into some tyre tubes and floated lazily with the current of the orangey-brown river, enjoying the gorgeous views of the steep rainforest-clad mountains either side in peace and serenity, and the occasional shriek of 'Hey Marcus,' (or Josh), 'we're in Fiji'. After half an hour or so, we pulled in at the bottom of a small two-tiered waterfall, climbed up a tier and spent another half hour or so diving in, getting pounded by the falls, and just having fun.

After that it's into a longboat, barely big enough for 14 of us plus guides, then steam down the river through the occasional rock hazard, with the wake spraying out in an arced fan and pull in some way down to await our pick-up. Thunderclaps announced the arrival of a heavy but warm downpour, but nobody minded getting wet at that stage. Another excellent day and it's only day two of the 'Fiji Experience Tour'. Moved on after, on the coach up to the hectic (by Fijian standards), city of **Suva,** the capital of Viti Levu. This evening we've been instructed we're going to an Irish club for the night, and they expect us to be up for 8 a.m., we'll see.

Turned out to be a quiet affair, but we met a famous comedy Bollywood (Bombay Hollywood) star in the hotel foyer after, Johnny Lever, and he shook all our hands, so there you go, I know some celebrities me!

Ni sa moce (nee sa mo-they) – polite goodbye.
Qei sota moce – see you again.

Wed 17th Sept

Easy night so no dramas getting up in the a.m. Leaving the capital, 'Suva', on the road again, stopped at **Korovou town** quickly for grub then on through more hilly dirt track roads to a village deep in the mountain rainforest called **Wailotua village**. Another stunning location with lovely smiling happy locals greeting us excitedly. Wearing our sarongs out of respect for their custom we joined the chief and his party for the Sevu Sevu ceremony. This is a custom which all visitors (tourists or not) are expected to go through to show your friendship to your hosts, and for them to extend their welcome and forgive the visitors for any transgressions that may occur while in the village, in advance. Basically you all get tanked up on this stuff called kava, tell them a bit about yourselves, dance and sing with them, and generally smile a lot. The kava makes your teeth go numb and sometime later sends you to sleep. We sat and drank, sung and danced, drank more, sang and danced some more, drank more and more and more. Curiously they hardly touched the kava, I'm sure they were wondering when we'd say 'Enough', while we were praying they'd run out of the stuff, and soon. Eventually it came to an end, so with anaesthetised faces we were shown around their village, and while they showed us around we began to hear of their own recent adventure. As we'd come into the village on the bus, we'd noticed a white lorry stuck in the trees down the side of the mountain next to the road, and lots of villagers forming a trail like an army of ants. It turned out that a lorry full of bottles of Fiji beer had come off the road the night before and the villagers had wasted no time light-

195

ening its load which was why very few of them were interested in the kava, most of them were smashed from
consuming their windfall throughout the night.

After being shown around the village, and also joining a
couple of the local lads for a few social scoobies in their
sacred cave, we were all moved on down to the river for
some *bilibili* (bamboo) rafting action, getting punted upriver
by one of the villagers then given the easier job of steering
back with the current. Slimmer rafts than the ones I'd been
on in Thailand, and much falling off before getting the
balance sorted. Really gorgeous weather and setting with
mountainside rainforest down to the river's edge and just a
gentle current. The locals requested a song from one of us
so I trotted out the 'Just one Cornetto' ice cream ad song,
much to their amusement. They even demanded an encore –
they should get out more. I dutifully obliged though. Just
amazing place and people, love this island already.
Eventually, and sadly, left the village, with many of them
saying 'why must you go? Stay with us longer.' So, so
friendly. Next, set off for the **Navisau Adventist Boarding
School** to see how the interior island schools operate.

Really crammed dorms of more smiling faces. Everything
quite dated but doesn't seem to matter, and the kids all
appear full of life and happy as. In the boys dorm they got
strumming on a guitar and gave us an off-the-cuff concert
from around their beds, born singers all of them. After
being shown about the school, and giving them presents of
much-appreciated school supplies, everyone descends on the
school playing field to join together at volleyball, footy,
rugby or, like me, just watching (a little caned). The bus had
a flat but Kasim and John had sorted it and we were off
again for today's final destination of **Nananu-i-ra (Imagination Island Below).** More winding hilly roads through yet
more lush rainforest or grazing land until we reached
Ellington Wharf where we disembark the green bus and get

the aluminium fast boat across to the island. Quite outstanding place at the top (north) of Viti Levu. Run by Ian and Judie who own the island, this is completely off the beaten track.

Watched the glorious sunset from the **Sunset Bure** at the top of the hill, then polished the day off with an evening of eating, drinking and singing.

Ni sa moce – goodbye.

Vinaka vaka levu – thank you very much.

Thurs 18th

Up for the $5 brekkie and then mission on around the island. From the Sunset Bure (*booray* –house) at the top of the hill, I followed the path down to the beach the other side of the island and began what I thought would be a gentle three or four-hour amble around a well marked path circumnavigating the island. Think again, Sherlock! The first bay, where everybody else stayed, was an idyllic golden sandy beach with palm trees to its edge, but from there on it was mangrove central out into the sea, or an unsteady rockfest in my slippery Reef flip-flops. I ended up walking for six hours without a break through mangroves, bent double, rough track pretty much covered by natural debris, wading occasionally as I tried to get smart and find an easier route before being turned back as it got too deep. All the time wondering where the cloven hoof prints I seemed to be following were coming from (a walking shit-machine by the evidence!). Eventually made it back just before the sun set, and into the bar for a well-earned cold one. Not quite spectacular, but very different and an OK mission to have achieved unscathed. Fend-for-yourselves night for food, which I hadn't remembered about at all, so the American lads, Josh and Marcus, bailed me out by sharing their food with me, cool as. Early night as bar shut.

Fri 19th

Biscuits for brekkie (still fend-for-yourself), then mission on over to the other side of the island for some reef snorkel action. Half mile out from the shore to the reef wall and some amazingly diverse coral and other aquatic life forms in striking bright colours. Especially the bright light blue fish only an inch or two long, the soft carpet-like purple starfish, and pretty much every colour available expressed somewhere or other. Hiked back later for an afternoon siesta (1.30 to 6.30!), then fed together followed by cards (shithead), beers and bed.

Sat 20th

Up early, brekkied up, packed up, and on the aluminium speedboats to leave Imagination Island (Nananu-i-ra) and make back for **Nadi** with commentary en route from David our Fijian guide for the last stage. Tells us about Udre Udre (Oondray Oondray) a famous warrior chief that killed and ate hundreds of rival chiefs and their priests, points out the mountain with faces on all sides, before stopping for a roof-top Ruby at an Indian restaurant in the town of **Ba**. Saw a poster of Johnny Lever, the Bollywood star we met in Suva, took pictures for posterity. Out of Ba and on to hot pools just outside Nadi, mud pool where we smeared up in the hot gooey stuff and chucked around a fair bit, then into the hot rock pool to chill and clean off before the last leg and more goodbyes to yet more new found-friends.

Dropped back off at **Mama's place, The Tropic of Capricorn**, and decided to chill for the rest of my stay in Fiji. Looked after by Mama and Jerry (the owners) like a member of the family, feeding me up, getting me driven about town, and she's (Mama) mad as a hatter and full-time amusement.

Mon 22nd

Another early one last night, this'll be it from here on, just lazy days 'til I leave. Jerry and 'Mama' treat all their guests like an extended family, so it's a bit like being cosseted, which is funny (as they are).

Tues 23rd

More lazing after brekkie, then into town with Mama, and a couple of Irish girls, to shop for gifts. Ended up in a kava session with some Fijians, and being given a local cultural history lesson regarding weapons, tools, chiefs' pasts, charms, etcetera. Bought a wooden mask for F$15, and escaped. More lazing and reading in the afternoon sun. Vish, Nathan, Jez and the girls, Marie, and Lavinia (Liv), arrived off the Fiji bus, so catch-up time on travel stories again. Kava session next door at Horizon 'til early hours.

Wed 24th

Teamed up to head into Nadi for internet, shop and score weed. Back for UV's, arvo single-skinner, and chill in beach-side hammock, strung between two palm trees, watching the sun go down. Dinner at Mama's, then beer at Horizon's as a crowd, me and Vish caned, and carried on back at Mama's, after being shown the door late on.

Thurs 25th

More people arriving and departing. Louise, from Nananu-i-ra, turned up in my room, so pool action soon enough, ripping in about her ever-escaping 'white puppies'. Smoke and chill in the hammocks for a while, then game of shithead 'til dinner. Mama made us something special for our last night, so we had dhal soup, rocket salad, spag carbonara, then sponge cake, cream and ice cream, all for F$8! More farewells, and off to the airport once again.

Bye bye Fiji time, *Ni Sa Moce*.

California, USA Journal, 25th Sept 2003 to 27th Dec 2003

FLINT RIDGE, LA

Thurs 25th Sept

After a ten-and-a-half-hour flight, leaving Fiji at 10.30 p.m., on the 25th of September, I have at last achieved the long ambition of Time Travel, arriving at Los Angeles' **LAX Airport**, in California, at 2.30 p.m. on the same day as I left, thus making it the longest Thursday of my life.

My cousin, Trevessa, met me at the airport, and we were soon off into the LA traffic, in an extremely plush people carrier. Along the way, Trevessa points out some of the landmarks, such as LA Lakers stadium (basketball), and the impressive-looking entrance to the LA Dodgers stadium (baseball). Not forgetting the famous LA smog! – which hovers over the city like an unwanted guest at the party punch bowl. After a fair drive through the Freeways, passing such song-title names as, **Pasadena**, **San Bernadino** and other places made famous through TV or films, we arrived at the family home of Trevessa and James, plus the children, Christian (9), Julian (8), and Sophia (4). A really gorgeous house, much as you'd expect to see on American TV shows, with its cut and pitched dormer roofs out front, and overhung main roof for the porch entrance, with arched timber-clad surround, and balustrade. Spacious garden with pool, barbecue area, pergola/portico, extending out from the lounge, with brick-laid floor. It appears to me to be the quintessential home of the American dream I've walked into, with the three lively yet perfectly behaved children, husband away working hard, and Trevessa, the mum, keeping it all together from the home.

Sun 28th

Family back from church, and we're into the waxing of chairs, prior to lunch, and entertaining Julian and Sophia with 'Tag', and human horsey rides. More 'Monsters and Horseys' after lunch, until Trevessa whisked me off to give me a tour of LA's sights. **Hollywood** and all its seedy trappings, smog laying over the whole city in varying thicknesses. Having a good old natter as we went. Headed down the **Pacific Highway** to **Santa Monica**, and the sun disappeared under the blanket of fog, then back some way to **Venice Beach**, and out to promenade the bohemian beach front there. Long sandy beaches full of skaters, cyclists, joggers, a very diverse pedestrian scene, and curio shops and stalls all over. We took a look at a large gathering of very alternative types of people (ages, style and origins), keeping rhythm going on something like 30 or so bongos, drums and other percussion instruments new to me. The whole sound seemed not unreasonable. All arranged in a circle, with people dancing in the centre, and all performed on the sand.

A house on the beach front had been given over to a well-organised party, with all-black security, dressed like presidential aides, complete with wire from beneath their lapels, up to one ear, presumably for short wave contact. Also a batch of four Portaloos at the party entrance, and some fit young chicks in cheerleader kit as the welcoming party. I liked Venice Beach! Very bohemian and eclectic. After the enjoyable tour, we made for James's Ps for Sunday dinner. His Dad can really cook, all sorts of hand-prepared pastas and gorgeous fillings, just fantastic, still feeling fit to pop now.

Mon 29th Sept

One year away today!! The anniversary of my escape from reality, or to it, depending on your perspective. Woken by a young face (Christian), peering over me and calling my name while grinning, I think he enjoyed that. Swift toast brekkie, and then we're off in Trevessa's SUV to **Disneyland** for the day. An hour's drive of freeways in the Big Country, so much concrete and so much traffic. Arrived at Disney 10 a.m.-ish, parked on level 5 of the 'Donald Duck' car park, then caught the Disney Bus Train from car park to the attractions. We all went straight to the Indiana Jones Ride, where I got to accompany C and J, so I get to enjoy it on the pretext of looking after them. All day we kept on the move from one ride to another, with the kids' energy boundless as ever. There was a Matterhorn Ride (a bumpy downhill effort), Pirates of the Caribbean boat trip, which was fun, Indian canoe rowing, Storybook Land boat trip, Tom Sawyer Land via ferry, Autotopia, Star Wars simulation space ship, which was great, and my personal favourite, followed by the Roger Rabbit ride in Toon Town.

Tues 30th

A.M. – place to myself, except for Maria and partner, the Hispanic cleaners. Stretch and swim, then out to take a look on foot, and see what's around. Long, hot and sticky walk, with just traffic, freeways and shops to see, so terminated the expedition soon enough, the LA urban sprawl not really suited to pedestrian adventuring. Back at the Terrille residence an hour and a half later, and a few ounces lighter through sweat. Cooled in the pool after, and chilled with the book, *Endurance*, all about Earnest Shackleton and co's epic journey in the Atlantic extremes, a staggering achievement, and a great read. Evening keeping Sophia amused, with 'Hide the Eggs/Find the Eggs'. Gorgeous dinner, of swordfish steak with veg, pasta and Rosemary bread, (saying grace every meal!). Christian and Julian playing Star Wars on the computer, having found new cheats, so squeals of delight echo occasionally through the house. Finished the night reading *Endurance*.

Fri 3rd

Up early to catch James before he bolts to work, and kids to school. Trevessa off out with Sophia, so house to self again. Stretch, swim, shower, shave, then out for a mini jaunt around the Flint Ridge locale. Couldn't access the hilly terrain behind because it's all fenced off. Afternoon with Trevessa in the car, running around, pick up Christian, so he can link up with James outside his works office building in central LA, for their Scout Camp weekend away in Catalina, then off to the Party Shop in downtown Pasadena to get Barbie pom-poms for Sophia, and finally, pick up Julian from Scouts at his school. She covers a good amount of miles on any given day, so I guess it's just as well she has a plush wagon to get her about. Mexican dinner out at Cabanita restaurant, with Trevessa, Julian and Sophia. Once again she treated me, I couldn't afford this lifestyle on my travel wallet, so it's all very pleasant. How lucky am I. During the day, Trevessa also managed to organise me on a trek for Saturday, up the San Gabriel Mountains, with Sam, a 76-year-old legendary friend of theirs, starting with a 06.15 pick-up! Early night.

Sat 4th

Bright and early start, picked up by Scott Christopher (son of Warren Christopher – the former Secretary of State to Bill Clinton). Met with Polish Sam, the walkaholic real estate manager, Eric, the actor/real estate guy, and Joel, the 'cardio treatment after surgery recuperation doc'! Couldn't help wondering how I could have arrived at such a situation as to be hiking in such company. Good healthy hike up to the top, where the ruins of an old hotel remain. Trevessa had packed me off with anchovies, sardines and salmon (all tinned), with cutlery, napkins and water, bless her cottons! The other guys had cheeses, Prosciutto ham, more sardines, and bread, while Sam brought his own personal, secret blend of rocket fuel for us to drink – a thimble at a time! – the whole thing is a ritual, and I've now been initiated. Sam's amazing, 76 years old, with almost no wrinkles, no fat, and as healthy as a horse, plus being a lovely old boy, friendly, and amusing. After the hike, and goodbyes, Scott drove me up for a different view of the San Gabriels, and an idea of the snaking mountain roads. Back for coffee, and play with Julian and Sophia, before we all drove out to **Sierra Madre Villa** railway station, which runs between the Freeways into **Union Station, LA**. Like a virtual reality trip, as one minute you're looking out at all the traffic alongside, and the next you're in amongst the residential areas, and so close to the houses, you feel like you could step from the train to their back doors in one bound. Union Station has an Old World feel, with its leather upholstered seats in the entrance area, and 'non-echo', wood-clad, sectioned ceilings. We strolled through a Mexican market, and on to China Town, entertained by Mexican Indians and Chinese acrobats/jugglers/balancing act entertainers. Then got the train back from China Town Station to Sierra Madre Villa, and SUV back through the freeways home. Tried roller blading in the driveway, then a bit of hockey with Julian, before dinner and pud (bakery delights). Bath and bed for J and S, but not before they 'puppy dog' eye me into going to church with them tomorrow. Guess I'll have to shave then!

Sun 5th

Got up early, and discover last nights 'puppy dog' routine was a conspiratorial ruse to distract me while 'Mom' puts a rubber snake in my sofa bed. At least that means no church for me! Spent the day keeping Julian and Sophia amused, and finishing off the Captain James Cook biography – savage end.

Mon 6th

Packing again, after driveway volleyball with Christian and Julian. Julian said quietly, 'I'm going to miss you'. They have a way of melting you. I'll miss them all. No more young 'uns to laugh at my poor cartoon voices.

Tues 7th

Up v. early, final pack up, shower and brekkie, last morning with the family. Dropped at the bus station by Trevessa, hugs and goodbyes with all of them, before they drive off for Christian's dentist appointment (across the road!). Hear squeaky voices shouting my name, look around, and there's Julian and Sophia, jumping up and down, and waving from the opposite corner of the road, a last goodbye to bring a smile to my face.

Now on a big, swish, Greyhound coach, for eight hrs, heading out of LA's labyrinth of freeways.

Arrived **Lodi**, 4.25 p.m., and met by yet more cousins David and Sue, Driven to Dave's place near **Rio Vista**, on the **Sacramento Delta,** which is all reclaimed swampland. Cool wooden three-storey place, with river around, pub-style garden, boat moored on his own jetty.

Dinner at Dave's neighbour, Annette's, very different place, like something out of a 1970s TV show, but real homely and comfortable, also by the river's edge. Turkey dinner!

VIERAS RESORT

Wed 8th

Good kip, cereal brek and coffee, then out in Dave's boat, HMS *Bollocks*, with Sue and Dibs, for a day on the water. 45 miles, doing a 'delta loop', which took us out through the man-made water systems which used to be swampland. Passing nice riverside dwellings, under assorted bridge types in the motor launch, a nice old-style shaped cruiser, with low top awning canopy, and a 5-litre engine. Left **Ida Island,** and headed up the **Sacramento River,** winding our way to **Walnut Grove**, where we turned into the **Georgiana Slough**, all the time passing boats out fishing for the salmon which are running at this time of year, and noticing again, the many Stars and Stripes flags hoisted all over the show. The Georgiana Slough takes us into the **Mokelumne River** for a short way, before leading into the **San Joaquin River**, which in turn took us back into the Sacramento River. The delta system here apparently has over 3,600 miles of rivers and tributaries spurring off, covering a huge area. We pulled up at **Rio Vista**, a small place with a few shops and bars, but a city no less! Had a beer in the dead animal zoo (Fosters Bighorn), a bar with hundreds of of stuffed animal heads on the walls, ranging from a huge elephant head, rhino, giraffe, zebra, and deer of all differing kinds, through to fish and birds. Nearly all shot by Bill Foster, a one-time Bootlegger back in the Prohibition days. After a quick tour of the mini city, we got on the boat to return up the Sacramento River to Dave's place. Round to Annette's place again for the evening, she has foster sons with developmental disabilities,

207

Jeremiah, a big fella with the mind of a six-year-old, and a very cheery disposition, always happy. And David, who apparently is developing, but just slowly, presently they reckon he's around 16 years old mentally, (30 yrs real age). A happy house. Stayed on to watch a film at Annette's, ended up being locked out of 'The Ranch', so had to climb up to the balcony to get in.

Thurs 9th

Out in the *Bollocks* (Dave's boat) for some fishing, trawling lures from the rods splayed out each side of the boat. Nice day boating, but no luck for Dave and Dibs with the fishing. Round to Annette's again for dinner, salad starter, then lasagne and tasty Italian sausages. Evening polished off with booze, as per, TV blew, but no drama. Me and Dave stayed up late, back at the 'Ranch', debating US policy, and basically agreed to disagree! One of those 'put the world to rights' convos, except from polar positions.

Sat 11th

Up for cooked brekkie, prior to listening to the England v Turkey football match on 5 Live webcast, an edgy affair which ended 0–0, leaving England as group champs. Today is day one of the local fishing carnival week, drove into Rio Vista, and walked around the stalls, checking out American stuff, like 'wobbly' people, Harley D Hells Angels, 'Fattituders', and the usual Tat stalls, all in sweltering heat. Lots of custom cars patrolling, as well as gleaming chrome motor bikes. Back to the ranch, and prepare for the evening boat ride back to Rio Vista for the firework display, which we watched from the river, not a bad effort. Early night.

Mon 13th

Late rise, then out fishing, up and down the Sacramento River, with me at the helm, no luck with the fish though.

Tues 14th

Last day for Sue and Dibs, drove with them and Dave to the **BART** railway in **Pittsburgh**, said goodbyes, and headed back for another easy afternoon. I spent the arvo chucking rod and line out from Annette's jetty, we're house-sitting her place while she's away, and looking after her Poodle, Flipper. No luck with the fishing, TV evening.

Wed 15th

Set about Dave's redwood timber stock in his yard, resizing it, and cutting it down the middle. Good day's work on my own, then back to Annette's for dinner, TV, read and bed.

Thurs 16th

Finished up cutting down the redwood in the morning, made up some workhorses to stack it all on, and chopped up the remainder for firewood. Now kicking back at Annette's once again.

Sacramento Delta stuff

Massive labyrinth of man-made waterways
Chinese labourers built most of the early Levees
Bass (Stripers)
Salmon running
Sturgeon ('kin huge)
Chad (fish bait)
Paddle steamer history – (Delta King and Queen)

4 x 4 Chevrolet pick-ups and trailers
Screech owls
Very nationalistic with the flags everywhere

Still 16th

Dave cooked Shepherds pie for dinner. Watched NY Yankees v. Boston Redsox, NY 6–5 in the 12th.

Fri 17th

Clean and prep decking at the 'Ranch', ready for protective coat tomorrow. Internet, got an email from Jesse, so Canada open now!! Checked out San Francisco hostels and backpackers, average $20. Dave gone fishing on the *Bollocks*, came back with a 17 pound salmon! Another cruisey day pour moi.

Opinions (not mine):
an abridged version of some TV moron's programme,
The O'Reilly Factor

That America is this benevolent nation, like some Robin Hood country, making fortunes, and giving it all to the poor of the world. That Iraq should be grateful for US aid after it bombed the shit out of the place, based on outright lies, without UN approval, because it wanted to save the Iraqi people from their leader. That the Third World is jealous of 'American freedom'. That Israeli neighbouring States are the criminals.
And no shortage of believers!!***????*!!

Sat 18th, Sun 19th and Mon 20th

Daytimes, painting wood preservative on to Dave's 'Ranch' decking and balustrade, then the stairway at the back. Up late each day, then work 'til 5 p.m., shower, stretch, and back over to Annette's for dinner, house-sit, movies 'til late, and bed. Temperatures in the 90s, cooling cloud cover on Sunday. Saw two World Series baseball games between the Yankees and Florida Marlins, Sat, 5–6 by the 9th, and Sun, 6–1 by the 9th, both at the Yankee Stadium, 1–1 in games. Mon-Gridiron, Oakland Raiders lost to Kansas City Chiefs. Still reading the John Adams biography. French Revolution just kicked off, Bastille Day, July 14th, 1789.

Tues 21st

Odd-jobs morning with Dave, bit of guttering, bit of lap boarding, bit of roofing, all rough, easy, and soon done. Grocery shopping, then back to Annette's, another hot day in the 90's, Delta boats running all day as usual, chasing the salmon. Yankees v. Marlins, 6–1 to NY in the 9th, played in Florida, now 2–1 to NY in games. Watched *The Godfather 2*.

Wed 22nd

Back on the woodwork at Dave's ranch, finishing off the back stairway handrails. Another hot and sticky day in the nineties. As usual, boats running back and forth all day on the salmon hunt. Cut back Lemon tree against the wooden stairway, probably overdid it a tad. Scrub up, and back to Annette's for hot dogs and Baseball, Marlins squared it in games, taking Yankees 4–3 in the 13th, in a gripper, down in Florida. Watched *Super Troopers* after, still hilarious. Saw a Sea Lion making its way up river on return to Annette's, super-cool sight as its nose pops up and then dives down, tail flipping up and disappearing before re-emerging a hundred yards further on each time until out of sight.

Thurs 23rd

Up to the 'Ranch', working on the stair treads today, quick sand down before treating them. Delta wind blowing hard today, whipping up dust from the surrounding fields, anglers undeterred as ever. Completed sealing of stairway to upstairs door, and back decking.

Fri 24th

V. late rise, up to ranch to prep back staircase, ready for wood sealing. Prepped, but too hot to use the sealer, 80 degrees in the shade, mid nineties easy in direct sunlight, and 100 at least when sheltered from wind, which the back staircase is, suntrap oven! Having dripped more than an ounce of sweat over the job, have retired to the hammock to laze the afternoon away as I watch the Sacramento Delta world go by. Ducks and geese quacking and honking behind me, shaded and cooled by the river breeze, bliss!

Sat 25th

Up v. early, brek at Ranch, then hit the road in Dave's wagon, with trailer. Annette's poodle Flipper along on the ride to **Ben Lomond** (two and a half hrs), to Dave's other place, where we have some digging to do. Very *Waltons*-like place, in redwood mountain country, staying at Annette's daughter's place (Laura and Paul) while here. Too hot to work after midday. Nice place, right in the midst of the redwood forest, Paul runs a tree surgeon company, and he's also an American-style biker with Harley D. Went out in the evening for Octoberfest at the Tyrolean bar up the road, with Paul, Laura, Dave and Annette. Beers, shots and then bassett in the pub car park, which did for me. Blew chunks soon after, filling a pint glass with hurl, and dry hurling after that, disgraceful behaviour!

Sun 26th

Clocks went back, so extra hour's sleep on top of my early night! No hangover fortunately. Went to Spankeys for brekkie with Paul, Amanda (his daughter), John (his son) and Dennis. Paul and Amanda off out on his Harley after, no rides spare for me, so day in front of the box watching American football.

Annette spends five weeks a year in Ben Lomond, running an outreach charity project, which provides meals and clothing for deserving cases.

Hot, hot, hot! 118 degrees on the porch, warm as toast inside, Annette's sitting in the shade outside under the redwoods. Laura just returned, and opens up all the outside doors to get some air moving in this cauldron. Flipper looking wet and bedraggled after being bathed in the sink, and then speeding out the house like a rubber bullet!

Smoking bassett with Paul, Amanda and Natani, outside the garage after the sun dropped away and things cooled down. Chicken and cheese burritos for dinner, Paul and Annette digging at each other, to my amusement. Nose in my John Adams book for the rest of the night.

Mon 27th

Up early to get out to Dave's property for some digging under the perimeter walls to expose the timber, for the termite man to see. Lot of work in it, Dave shot off to **Boulder Creek** to pick up some Mexican labourers for the job. Me and the 'Three Amigos' soon got into it, Dennis and Jeremiah came along to help later, so there I was, with the 'Three Amigos', that barely speak English, and two 30-

213

year-old six-year-olds that want to talk about toys, kids' films and cartoons all day! Funny day.

Quit work by 1.30, too hot. Back to Paul and Laura's place for shower, and rest the aching back, with Flipper for company. Jacket spuds, steak, and salad for dinner with the mob. Dog tired so v. early night.

Tues 28th

Another early start for me, Dennis, and the 'Three Amigos', straight into rabbit mode as we burrowed under the glorified rabbit hutch that passes for a home and estate agents. Worked from 7 'til 3, boiled in the heat while the boss takes a joyride up to the Delta and back for the day!, not happy bunnies!!

Tired now but clean, and glad to have that day out of the way. Paul stopped at the job by chance, so I got a lift home, otherwise it would've been 'Shanks' Pony', to cap my irritation, bear in mind that my time is all a favour, maximising the piss-take!

Back at Paul and Laura's, amusement from their dog Ariel, which is better known as Pinball because, owing to its deafness and blindness, it moves around the place bouncing off the walls and furniture. On the TV the news is filled with the California forest fires sweeping through its southern area, claiming 500 properties so far. Also the news covers the low-carb beer sensation (in USA) with people apparently putting health first in their beer consumption. Forget the sugar saturation diet that remains the bedrock of American snacks, beginning with 'donuts' for breakfast, cookies anytime, and Coke with everything. Or that their idea of a balanced meal seems to be a thimble of side salad next to a kilo of meat, with potato or pasta.

Another v. early night after a heavy day with the shovel.

Wed 29th

Day off today, email check after breakfast, then out with Paul in his truck to **Henry Cowell State Park**, to check out the redwood forest, impressively huge, straight, sequoia trees, also bay trees (aromatic bay leaves), and a cool forest trail walk. Off to **Santa Cruz** after, through the winding mountain roads, stacked either side with more tall straight redwoods all the way, to see the sea, surf, pier, sea lions, cool Hollywood cypress trees, and a big dipper roller coaster ride (used on the *Dirty Harry* film set). Overcast, and a nice cool breeze at the sea, had a bite to eat on the pier, then hit the trail back to Ben Lomond, and up top for a look down into the valley, and catch a few shots with the 'point and click'.

Forest fires still roaring through southern California, from San Diego, up to San Bernadino, leading the TV news ahead of the Iraq fiasco, and idiot Bush spouting his platitudinal Bushshit over the airwaves.

Thurs 30th

Everyone gearing up for Halloween tomorrow, costumes, treats, and organising for the kids. Paul and Mike (Fat Boy/ Thor) took me off later for a Tequila OJ night around the area, and to see some of the outlying character bars. Good evening being amused by the comedy duo of Fat Boy and Rude Boy. Saw Dave's truck parked outside his place that we're working on, at late o'clock, phone him up, and a strange truth begins to unfold. In our absence, he's had a 'blue' with Laura, and had to leave the house as a result, drink-fuelled, but left some big bridges to be rebuilt. An odd story to relate, with some major apologies required from Mr Hayden.

215

Fri 31st Oct

Halloween

Log-splitting day! Snagged some work for Fat Boy and Kiwi Ross, $10 an hour to sit in front of a log-splitting machine, and knock out firewood by their joinery shop. Rain stopped play at 12.30, the first rain since my arrival in the US. Popped into Valley Churches to see Annette, and snag some feed and coffee. Then helped Dave with some bid work he's landed, just a 12x20-foot storage garage, but more paid work so that's a bonus. Back to Paul and Laura's place to scrub up and get ready to join the family crew going out 'Trick or Treating'. Me, Paul and Fat Boy, escorted the nippers around, as they hoofed off filling up their pillow cases with sweety swag from the pumpkin-decorated houses. Dennis and Jeremiah, happily bumbling along with the other kids. Loads of cool costumes, as the hordes of children everywhere in their 'Scream' masks, Goblin outfits, or E.R. uniforms, trawled door to door with their adult escorts. Food and drink at 'right on' Barbs's place, and back to Paul and Laura's later to sesh on.

Sat 1st Nov

Late start after long night of beer and bassett. Walked to work to split logs, worked 10.30 'til 3.15, when Mike (Fat Boy) came for the splitting machine, and dropped me off at P and L's. Scrubbed up and shaved. Nice fresh smell of mountain air on the walk up to the job. Found out from Laura yesterday, that she'd put my combat trousers through the wash, with my passport in them. It's now creamed!

Sun 2nd

Laura cooked eggs Benedict for brek, afterwards Paul dropped me off at the shop to stack the logs I split

216

yesterday. On to Mike's after, to help him split and stack logs at his place. Good day, couple of beers at Henflings with Thor when finished.

Back to P and L's for dinner, couple more beers, and yet more Lifetime TV chick viewing (time to read!). Invited in for a smoke with Amanda and Danny, talked about travelling, and got caned.

Mon 3rd

Off to work for 'TreeKing', working with Dave, Tom, Art and Dwayne, taking down trees, pruning, and cleaning up. Enjoyable days collar at Central Park Apartments, in Sunnyvale, real mean threshing machine wood chipper to chew up and spit out all the branches and logs. Easy day. Drove down the interstate 17 after work, beer. Dinner.

Tues 4th

Early rise for another day with TreeKing, taking a redwood down, outside the house of a Ben Lomond fireman. Dave, Art, and myself, Dave doing the climbing and cutwork, while me and Art did the groundwork, Art in charge.

Tree gear
Boot strap spikes
Hoist girdles (waist and legs)
Chain saws and straps
Lift and drop ropes
Heavy log 'drop device'
Mean bitch wood chipper
Pruning poles
Rakes, and giant plastic shovels
Leaf blowers
Beast-size trucks

217

Cool and weird-looking wild turkeys at the waste tip site. Great visuals of Dave taking the redwood down in the valley, with the background filled with green-pined redwoods.

Met up with Thor, Paul, and Dave, at the shop after dinner, where they pay out in beer for the Nascar results. Ended up on another booze cruise with Thor and Paul, got another T-shirt, this one from Joe's bar in Boulder Creek. Back late and noisy.

Fri 7th

Night in front of the box, watching Prime Time Dickhead O'Reilly talk his usual *shyte* on the *O'Reilly Factor* (O'Really Fiction), such a *twat*! Latest bullshit rant was against Public Funded Broadcast, saying they should all have to compete, and be subject to the whims of commercialism. What a fuckin' moron!!

Fri 14th

No work today as Art and Long Hair didn't fancy it (poss rain), so went with Paul to check upcoming jobs to do while he's away on his hunting trip. One at a golf course, where we pink tagged the 'to go' trees, and general cut back and clear. Then on to a really cool place in a redwood ravine, with beautiful small old wooden house, and a new one under construction, with wooden decking built around a cluster (fairy ring) of tall redwoods. Back to P and L's place for coffee, listen to Art's band on CD (Shatners Hairpiece). After that it's off to Boulder Creek with Paul for a pukka Mexican taco, and then on up the mountain to the gun range to get his rifle sights tuned in. Miserable, misty, wet conditions, so had to give up because of poor visibility.

Went to check on a downed tree afterwards, collar for

Monday. Couple of beers at Henflings after, and then back to the house for more beer, food, and bassett. Yet another messy end to the night pour moi.

Sat 15th

Woken by Sherp to go and do some more at Dave's place, pouring with rain while we pondered from Coffee 9, whether we should bother, when Dan the 'Shit King' strolls up and tells us how he can't find any labour for a couple of hours. One look at each other, and me and Sherp offer our services.

Sun 16th

Me and Dave got the last beam put in at his place, so pest control can sign it off now. After that, me and Paul drove over to Mike Finley's place to watch them work while we drank, smoked, chipped in with a little labour, and doubtless, unwanted advice. 'Dirt' and his gal Jennie turned up, and it all got messy. Pub crawl for me and Fuzzy (Paul) after, about which I remember nothing, crashed in me pit on return, while Paul (apparently) attempted to raise the dead until the early hours, happily upsetting his squatters, I slept through it all!

Mon 17th

Undisguised malcontent from the ousted parties, Paul unmoved, me staying out of it. Easy morning, work-wise, removing and clearing a felled tree and debris, before moving on to take out a 100-foot fir tree, 20 feet from a house front. Nascar Dave no-showed on the second job, so half day, and job unfinished for Art, Tom and me.

Final Nascar night (end of season), so yet another big

sesh at the Shop, and then on to Lumpy's place for me, Thor and Fuzzy, for some sushi, chat, and check out his expensive mid-life crisis road toys!

Home late and trashed again. Laura back, drinks and bassett in the Shed for all.

Wed 19th

Not an ounce of sleep, teeth grinding overtime, still charged up and feeling dirty.

Lazy day of no work, started another book, *A Prayer for Owen Meaney* by John Irving. Went walk about in the arvo, stopped and got talked at by Annette, at Valley Churches, concerning the whole soap opera *Family at War* drama, perfect material for viewing on her beloved Lifetime Channel! Survived the emotional outpouring, felt bad, weird and guilty, even though none of it in my hands.

Thur 20th

TreeKing day, removal, tidy, and clearance work at a place just outside Boulder Creek, fairly easy day. Nice place in the valley, next to a creek, and by a former railway bridge with just the column supports remaining, also the entry point once for a log flume back in the days when logging in the area was big business. Really cool 'Grove', or 'Fairy ring' of redwoods, outside the house, overlooking the creek. Nascar Dave, as usual, doing one of his disappearing acts, leaving Art to do the lion's share of the work. A good days work done nonetheless.

Fri 21st

FIREWORKS! Art finds out that Mouth Almighty Dave gets paid more than he does. On top of Art carrying him, it's the final straw for the boy. Made for a sour atmos at work. Job done and finished to the punter's satisfaction nonetheless, he even gave us a 40 buck tip each! Must've been happy.

Helped Cuz Dave throw up a wall at the Petersons after work, then back to P and L's to find Art, who tells me he's quit the firm. Over to Art, and friends Ryan, and Dom's place in **Aptos**, just outside **Santa Cruz**. Listen to their band's music on tapes, talk a little politics (anti US/UK global policies), smoked a chillum, drank some Newcastle Browns, watched *Family Guy*, and *Bowling for Columbine* DVDs, fell asleep with Art's fat cat on my lap. Their place is set in 3 acres of land, and with a row of garages opposite, in which old Ford cars are renovated for rich enthusiasts by a mechanical entrepreneur. Old rusty chassis lay around in the long grass, half-reconstructed models here and there, cool visuals.

Sat 22nd

Dropped back at P and L's midday by Art and the boys, on their way to Spankeys for brek. Off to Thor's from there, to help him and Dirt split and stack logs, then clear up his yard, job almost done, bar a few logs to split in the morning. After scrub up and feed, Thor picked me up to escape the 'hens', and do some stuff up at the joiner shop, just a couple of hours on some kitchen units, and then out to Joe's bar in Boulder Creek to play pool and drink Gold Drivers. 3–2 to Thor, and off to Finsky's rental place after, for late beer and smoke action with the 'Dudes'.

Mon 24th

Pasatiempo golf course today, for some removal and clearance work, without Art this time as he's quit. NC Dave a slightly moderated asshole today, but only slightly. I did two of the removals with Sherp, fairly easy eucalyptus trees to take out, but still require a little care and attention. Dave did the climbing work on the big oak overhanging the property, we all pulled weight. Job done, and some. A good day's collar, but sad for Art, would've been a better day with him instead of Dave.

Tues 25th

Working with Cuz Dave, Sherp and Tom at the Petersons' place, building an extension to their garage, walls up and roof on, another good day's collar, for what we have yet to agree is a worthwhile wage. Having done so much for him for nothing so far, I ought to expect he'd see me right.

Splitting more logs at P and Ls after. Hot dogs for dinner.

Wed 26th

Cold start, brrrrrr!!

Me and Sherp in action at the Petersons' place, while Dave's on shithouse repair duty at his place, prior to sale to Annette. Fairly easy day's collar, finished with me and Sherp sipping beer while watching Dave sweat over his shithouse, all good.

Thur 27th

Thanksgiving Day (Founding Fathers/Native Indians story). Up and off to work at the Petersons' on my Jack for the day, roof first fix complete, started to ply sheath it. Had lunch with Bob and Trish Peterson in their posh gaff, she's an ex-radiographer, and he's an ex-oceanographer, she's talkative, while he awaits an opportunity (rare) to get in there! Nice couple. Back to P and L's for Thanksgiving dinner, turkey, yams, stuffing, and plenty more – FULL!

Fri 28th

Back at the Petersons' with Sherp to bring on the roof. Breezy day, cruising through, just done off by the rain mid-after-noon, so tarped over the roof, and worked on the inside. Good day. Beer and bassett back at Dwayne's (Sherpa) place, his wife, Laurie, was playing Cat Stevens while she watched daytime TV. Had a bong with her, nice smooth pull.

Nice place they have here, open plan with a mezzanine gallery 'herb clinic' for Laurie's 'witchcraft' practice. Everything wood finish, and the obligatory woodburner for heating. Back to P and L's feeling somewhat light-headed, and kipped on the couch for a couple of hours, before Thor came round with some crab for me to try. Smoked a bowl with Amanda and Ali after, then off to Boulder Creek for some pool, and Gold Drivers, too wasted to play worthwhile pool, but had a good laugh, and returned late and mashed.

Sat 29th

Good old Sherp round at eight sharp for work, I was half hoping he'd 'no show', as I was feeling a little foggy still from last night. Roof done and weathered, so called it half-day.

Spoke to Canadian Jesse on the phone back at P and L's; looks like I'm heading up there December sometime!

Sat 30th Nov

Up and out with Laura, Debs (Psycho), Rochelle and Debbie (Wisconsin), off to San Fransisco for the day. Debs drove us in Laura's car, we stopped in at Rochelle's son

Shaun's place, at **15th and Market**, in the city. Him and his partner Bill have a Victorian building apartment, real nice pad. They were preparing a feast for our return from sight-seeing. A wet day and misty clouds made it difficult to see much, so I just treated it as a reconnaissance trip. We took the underground from **Church Station to Embarcadero**, and then hopped on to the 'F' train tram, along to Pier 39 and Fisherman's Wharf. Looked around the marine food stalls, grabbed a crab sandwich, and finished off Rochelle's clam chowder (real nice). Stopped in at one of the many marine theme bars for a drink, then the girls shopped for T-shirts and mementos. With no let-up in the weather, we headed back to Shaun's place, to be fed like kings, and, would you believe it, he had some prescription weed which he insisted I should try.

Tues 2nd

Sherp phoned to say Dave still doesn't want to work. Went for a walk to the job to pick up my jacket, only to find Dave there, working with Annette's foster son, David. Mr Hayden using the cheapest labour available, rather than pay me, nice way to repay a favour! Thanks cousin.

Paul returned from Wisconsin and his shooting. Amanda runs me around in her car to sort my films out. Paintball with Danny, Tom and their mate Billy, at the Chestnut Mansion estate, Billy's family's place. Great fun running around the grounds, blasting each other with paint pellets, Tom was the king shot. Watched *Pirates of the Caribbean* up in Billy's attic room, the size of an entire apartment, cinema screen-sized picture too.

Wed 3rd

Lay in 'til 10 a.m. Went hiking with Amanda and Danny,

from **Felton** to the **Lime Kilns** and the **Barrel Mills** through the **St Lorenzo Valley** redwood forest. Had a smoke at the halfway point, caned for the return, three-hour or more hike overall, plenty of pictures, great time had, really cool scenery, classic old rusty, aged, machinery. Never forgetting how lucky I am to be with such great people.

Thurs 4th

Feeling weak, picked up by Thor for work at the Guardian Angel's place (Louise) for a refurb. Dirty work, but OK. The house I've already, affectionately, dubbed 'The Shitbox'. Eve meal at Scopazzi's, for Valley Churches United's awards night, Jeremiah was made the 'Angel of the Year', for his contributions to their efforts. I was sat across the table from Jeremiah's mum, Rosy, a cool, lovely, cerebral palsy victim, she has her own radio show, and is an intelligent, amusing, amazing, and very interesting lady.

Thor led the way when it came to storming the barracks at feed time!

Fri 5th

Picked up by Thor again for more labouring for HWW. In fairness, the Shitbox should've been torched and rebuilt, it's been eaten to death by rot.

Evening beers and bassett at home, while John played quizmaster to us, talking through his voice box (nine-year-old Darth Vader), until Amanda took over.

Sat 6th

Lazy day in. Slept 'til ten. Book reading. Paul drives me to Santa Cruz to check out the waves, 2–3 foot, and heaps of surfers out there in the seaweed and sewage. Picked up a new journal, film, and photo albums. Back to P and L's, Paul cooked a gourmet crab, and stir fry, for dinner – lush! Beer, bassett, and DVD for the evening (*Nemo*).

Sun 7th Dec

Up late after a long night. Out with the family to hunt for a Christmas tree. Drove up, deep into the mountains, to a hill-billy Christmas tree farm, run by 'good ole boys', all the staff in Santa hats, and even the customers dressed in festive spirit. After being handed a saw, we trot off to select the tree, and cut it down, Paul asking Amanda to tone her language down to 'semi-trucker', and Laura telling Paul that he's the 'pot calling the kettle black', Natani geeing Amanda along, John happily oblivious, and me loving every minute of it, way better than the Osbournes. After selecting, felling and paying for the tree, we looked around the old rustic-style farm buildings, full of dated machinery, tools and historical accounts of the local forestry industry. Stopped on the way back at the **Brookdale Lodge,** an old haunt of famous celebrities in a bygone era, for Mexican coffees (tequila). Then back to the house to decorate the tree.

Out riding 'bitch' on Paul's Harley after, as he took me for a spin around the mountain roads, via a bar or two.

Mon 8th

Up and out with the TreeKing crew, as far as Coffee 9, where I disembarked, to hitch a lift with Jennie and Dirt to the workshop, and a day making up doors in the a.m., and building work, on site in the p.m., with Rob and Thor, at Louise's 'Shitbox'. Good day's collar. Quiet night.

Tues 9th December

'Shitbox', with Rob, the ageing, ex-surfer. More destruction and reconstruction. We were pulled back to the shop for some emergency door repairs, mid-morning and back to Louise's place mid-arvo, to carry on at the 'Shitbox'. Out with Paul and Thor, after a few post-work beers at the Shop with Finsky. Amanda cooked dinner, top stew soup! Smoke after.

Sun 14th

Lay-in day, and then got a pillion on Paul's Harley, over to Finsky's place, to help out on their latest rental conversion, bit of plaster boarding (sheet rocking) and roof construction, beer supplied. Quiet night in afterwards, to finish John Irving's *A Prayer for Owen Meaney*, with tears trickling down my cheeks at the end, another good book finished.

Tues 16th

Working in the spray shop with Thor again, another easy day, before being called in to the main shop, to assemble the joinery for a Thursday delivery. Lots of blustering, growling and shouts between Ross and Thor, either at each other, or anyone within earshot, funny as fuck, I call them Stadler and Waldorf, after the Muppet show hecklers.

After work beers around the work bench, with Rob, Thor, Ross, Jennie and Dirt. J and D brought home-made Tamales for all to take away with them and sample.

Wed 17th December

Another session, as me, Thor and Fuzzy, sank all the firm's

beer, and caned all of Thor's bassett, while he made a handle for P and L's woodburner door. Then hit the road to Lumpy's place for more bassett and beer. Lumpy promised me a ride in his Corvette. We'll see! Jumped out of the van, outside Fuzzy's place, to escape any further alcoholic abuse!

Thurs 18th

Weak all day. Fortunately, it was a nice cruisey day of driving to the site for delivery. Beautiful, scenic drive to **Hillsborough**, with gorgeous views (bar the smog blanket). Amazing old house, real money here! Had a quick tour around the grounds, took plenty of pics, including some of their three-legged dog. Ross bought us all lunch after delivery, and then Thor took me on an even more scenic drive on the way back, through another impressive redwood forest route of, huge, fat, straight trees, stopped for a look at a tourists' camp, with its own natural amphitheatre, and tree logs for the auditorium seats. Cool day. Taking it easy for the night.

Sun 21st

Quiet, lazy day, of laying around and reading until early afternoon. Had a few hits on a flash bong with Amanda, Natani and Stephanie, prior to making out for the Mystery Spot with them. Stephanie's an old friend of Amanda's, visiting, so we both got to see the Spot for our first time. All of us caned for the event, got a walk up ticket straight off, and had to endure a real Disneyland guide.

Real trippy stuff, with balls rolling uphill, or so our eyes believed. Lots of illusory tricks going on, but fun nonetheless, especially the wonky house. Batteries knackered in my camera, so no pics unfortunately. Souvenir shop assistant asked if I was Australian. 'Yeah that's right.' Why disappoint them?!

Jesse rang from Canada, on me way!!

Mon 22nd

Half-day at the 'Shitbox' with Rob, more demo and recon. Afternoon at the Shop, as Ross gets in another paddy over deadlines, I just laugh – soon be in the snow!!!

Laura sorted my flights out on the internet for Canada. December 28th is the day.

Tues 23rd

Thick head. Last day at the 'Shitbox', finished early. Checked out Capitola Mall with Amanda, on the hunt for an illuminated world globe, no luck. Quiet night.

Wed 24th

Started demolition at Heen Road garage, worked 'til 4 p.m., dropped off and picked up by Paul in the truck. Walk up party at the house, so plenty of beer in the 'coffin', and a pit fire outside, which we burnt my work debris on. Long night of food and drink. Paul and Laura bought me two pairs of trainers, acutely embarrassed, I gave a drunken thank you, hug and handshake.

Phoned Ma and Pa at midnight, 8 a.m. their time and had a chat, they sounded well, but I was a little non-*compus mentus*.

Thurs 25th December (Shitmas Day)

Carried on at the garage job, putting flat pack units together, and clearing the walls, ready for sheet rocking tomorrow. Just me and Amanda around for the day, picked up food and beer from Masouts, the Muslim liquor store which never shuts. Kept the pit fire going, outside P and L's porch, with more wreckage from the garage job. Danny and Natani came round, so it was a 'bassett round the campfire' occasion with the four of us. Good fire, good company, good night.

Last Christmas: Phnom Phen, Cambodia. This Christmas: Ben Lomond, California, USA.

Fri 26th

Worked with Sherpa for the day, moved the job on a bundle. After work, typed out another news mail to all. Art, Ryan, and Dom, drove over to pick me up and take me back to Aptos for a recording session at their place. Beer, bassett, and MC-ing through the night.

Sat 27th December

Art drove me back so I could do my last days work, with Thor this time. Good day. Had my last fix of the Coffee 9 honeys, how I shall miss them! No luck finding an illuminated globe, so Thor's ordering it on the internet for me. Taken out to Ciao Bella for dinner by Laura and Debbie, cool and funky place, run by an extrovert gay called Tad. The power went out when we arrived, but didn't seem to phase anyone, candlelit for first half of the meal. All sorts of weird stuff hanging from the ceilings and walls, and a headless dancing Santa on the mini stage that the staff perform on.

Back at the Casa afterwards, for goodbye beers with whoever turns up. Laura, Mike and Helen (Finley), bearing gifts and a card, Thor, bearing beer!, Amanda (touching card), Danny, Tom, Debbie and Art. Thankfully not too emotional, but sad as always. They all made me feel like a member of their family during my stay, which is incredible considering that they'd never even met me until a couple of months ago. Definitely have to come back here first opportunity, lovely place, lovely people.

Big White, Kelowna, BC,
Canada Journal,
28th Dec 2003 to 19th Feb 2004

SAN FRANCISCO, USA TO VANCOUVER, CANADA

Sun 28th December

Up pre-dawn for the off, Art drove me to **SFO airport** in Laura's car, breezed it in an hour with no traffic on the roads. Checked in for my e-ticket at the Air Canada desk in SFO.

Easy flight, with cool views of **Oregon**, and **Washington** below along the way. Grief on arrival at **Vancouver BC**, as immigration decide my passport is no longer valid owing to its 'washed' condition! After what seemed an age, I was eventually permitted to continue on my travels to **Kelowna**, once I'd signed a declaration of intent, to return to them before leaving Canada, with a new passport!

Just phoned Jesse, and now in Kelowna airport, waiting to be picked up, how lucky am I?! 2,400 Canadian bucks to blow in a month or so. Bring on the snow!!

Jesse arrived within an hour, and after the obligatory 'How ya doin' scenario and beer, we took off in his car for the **Big White Ski Resort**, my new home for the rest of my trip!!!!!

Snow-covered roads, and hostile conditions seemed no particular deterrent to the traffic, as we steamed along at a tasty old lick of speed. The Big White is a huge ski resort, an hour out of Kelowna. Jesse and Emma have an apartment there in a ski lodge, an indoor complex with pool, hot tub, bar and ski slopes to the door!!! On arrival, Jesse introduced me to the hordes of mates he has already using up the floor space, a wild bunch of snowboarding punks, with a whole new language for me to get used to, as well as tuning in to their Canadian accents, which seem heavily influenced with Irish and Scottish dialects. A wicked bunch of people, with Scott as the humour leader, closely followed by Doug, their girlfriends, Candy and Kerry, also well-equipped with wit and sharp retorts. Jesse's bro Dana, and Gav the punk band guitarist. A heavy first night soon saw me off, as much to their amusement, they discovered what a lightweight I am!

Mon 29th (Minus 11 degrees!!!)

Everybody up early and out to shred the slopes, got myself kitted out with board, boots and a two-day lift pass. Gore-Tex jacket and strides from Jesse, and gloves from Emma. Met up with the crew at the line for the Ridge Rocket Express chair lift, and that was me for the day, taking on the green slopes of Serwas, the longest slope I've been on so far. All the others long since gone on to the serious slopes for some extreme trick action, way, way, out of my league!

Predictably enough, the evening saw me off too, as I fell beside the wayside after one beer, whisky and scoob too many. Awoke on two occasions. One to do a charade which apparently no one got, then fall asleep again, only to come to life after Doug put his freshly cooked pasta down next to me, they tell me, and I grabbed the bowl, bolted down his pasta, then fell right back to sleep as they all looked on in hysterics!!

Tues 30th

Up way early again and on to the slopes. Goggles fogging on me, couple of heavy falls, more rib and butt bruises, but getting the hang of it bit by bit. A great day.

Evening's entertainment was charades, accompanied by beer, whisky, Jaegermeister, etcetera. Boys v. girls, then out for a party at another lodge, a half-hour walk through the mountain snow, to Johannes's place, to snake his beer, and abuse his hospitality. When I left, his hot tub had been taken over by Jesse, Dana and crew.

Three more boarders arrived today, Shona, Hansby and Michelle, so the floor space is filling up well. This place is like the snowboarders version of the Bower House in Manly (Sydney, Oz).

Up early, but no boarding today so I can organise my stuff, and maybe shoot into Kelowna with Gav in the arvo, to get a board and boots, and a cheap suit for the New Year's Eve party tonight. Big dump of snow overnight, so the rest of the crew hit the slopes early and mobbed up for a good day.

Gav borrowed Kerry's car to get us into Kelowna, some dickheads in a 4 x 4 jeep, driving like morons, trying to pass every car on the road, regardless of conditions, irritating Gav as they sat on our tail for a while. Eventually they passed us, and Gav mentioned, 'Drivers like that fuckin' kill people, man'. Nearly came true too, as we found out further on, when the still rolling wreckage of a green Station Wagon came into view ahead of us, with debris strewn all across the road behind it, cars pulled in, and people running around waving for phones, one guy trying to check if the blood-spattered old couple in the just halted station wagon were OK. Then, lo and behold, what should we see, but the 4 x 4 jeep, ahead 100 yards or so, in the middle of the road, absolutely totalled, and the idiots that belong with it, stood to the side of the road with a few cuts and bruises, smiling, chatting and calmly smoking cigarettes, like it had been a laugh! Gav was all for getting out and busting them up, but we were pushed for time already, and the police would

234

doubtless be on their way with the amount of people involved.

The rest of the drive went cool, and we got into Kelowna's Value Village to grab some suits for the night. Three suits for me, Gav and Lids, plus an assortment of loud shirts and ties, all for 75 bucks!

Then on to SportsMart for me to get kitted out with board, boots, and bindings, for C$423 (less than £150!!) – big day of spending. Just made it back to the Big White as the light departed, and time to get in theme for New Year's Eve action, everyone sporting suits and moustaches for the night, 14 of us in a one-bedroom apartment, but somehow it works.

Snowshoe Sam's was our venue for the night, where we paraded ourselves as music execs pushing Gav's punk band, with free CDs, all good fun and bullshit.

Thurs 1st January 2004, New Year's Day (minus 12 degrees)

Everyone weak, no boarding today. Brek at Raakel's before half the mob leave, and it's down to Jesse, Emma, Dana, Hansby, Michelle and myself. Stayed in most of the day, except for two hot tub sessions. Evening of watching films while the others went out.

Fri 2nd (minus 13 degrees)

Up at 9-ish, as Dana, Hansby and Michelle are packing to leave, and me and Jesse head off to the slopes for the day. Went down to the main ski centre, had my picture taken for, and blew 900 bucks on a season's lift pass! That's me sorted for my stay. Straight out to try the junior slopes with my new board and boots, until they felt OK, which wasn't long, then off I went back up to Serwas for some long runs. New kit feels great, and improved the runs by 50 per cent at least, pulled in by 2.30 with freezing extremities. Laze around in the apartment, stretch, hot tub and pool action for the afternoon, before a quiet night in front of the box with Jesse and Emma, watching films again.

Sat 3rd

Out on the slopes just after 10 a.m., and feeling the icy cold as the temperatures dropped to minus 25 degrees at one point, frozen burnt face on the chair lift (Ridge Rocket), and a busted finger on the second run down, as I failed to successfully negotiate two skiers that had stopped in my flight path. I toe-edged, and steamed hand-first into the crisp, icy surface, comprehensively breaking the little finger on my left hand, having built up a tad too much speed prior to the encounter. I missed them, but spilled at full tilt! Ouch. Still a fairly good few runs though, despite the icy conditions. Later, me and Jesse went to drive to Kelowna for provisions, but his car radiator blew out, we had to arrange a hire car for the trip instead, no go until 3 p.m., so I had an hour in the hot tub and pool to kill some time and loosen up.

The rental was a Ford Focus, which Jesse drove, me not being ready for driving on ice rinks yet! Got all the shopping done in Kelowna, before heading back in the dark, no mean achievement in the conditions. Little finger now purple and fat. Jesse picked up his electric guitar from the music shop while we were in town, he has three of them here now, and his playing has improved phenomenally since the Bower in Manly, he pulls off some pretty sick tunes with the Fender and amp.

Sun 4th

Temp down to minus 28 Celsius today, so only short bursts on the slopes, just an hour at a time, and keep the brakes on in the icy conditions. Started on easier Woodcutters

236

from the Plaza chair for a bit, before heading up to Serwas on the Ridge Rocket until the toes began crying out. Spent the afternoon preparing shepherd's pie, after the usual hot tub and pool sesh.

Mon 5th

Temp still minus 28 out there, so just the two short sessions for the day, with hot tub and pool after each time to get the circulation going again.

Tues 6th

Jesse cooked pancakes, Canadian style, nice and fat, with maple syrup. On the Ridge Rocket by 10 a.m., boarding down the hill straight out from the apartment. Temps warmed up to minus 18! – so a little more bearable than the last couple of days. Another two-session day, and even took on some small jumps down by Snow Pines, tumbling after the last one. Hot tub and pool after each session, then in to Raakel's Bar with Jesse and Emma for a couple of beers and games of pool. Another quiet night in front of the box and early to sleep for me.

Wed 7th

Late rise, kitchen clean-up, out by 11 a.m., nice layer of powder dumped overnight, and temp up to minus 9, so a lot more bearable. Back in by 12.30 after an enjoyable few runs down Serwas on the powder layer. Midday chill. Quiet night in.

Thurs 8th

Out by 11 a.m. with Jesse and Emma for a few runs down

Serwas for an hour, then head for the Powder Chair, and some blue run action, steep, bumpy, thick powder, and hard on the legs, tumbled a few times, more rib pain. Great views from above the clouds, as the mountain tops appeared as islands poking through the mist. The trees all cloaked in snow are called 'Snow Ghosts' and look really cool. Usual hot tub and pool session after, then a couple of beers at Raakel's in the evening after watching *Field of Dreams*.

Sat 10th Jan

On the slopes by 11 a.m., huge queues for all the chairs, as the resort has been overrun by University of British Columbia students. Checked out some different runs from the Bullet Express, and the Black Forest chair lifts, fun few hours. Picked up some vino and garlic bread to go with dinner. Hot tub and swim action for an hour, dinner, feet up, goggle box.

Sun 11th

Out again by 11 a.m., less queuing as the UBC mob off to Silver Star Mountain for the day. Visibility poor, but slopes not too busy so OK trade-off, snowing late arvo, reducing vis still further, so pulled in for relaxing hot tub and swim. Bought tickets for the bus into Kelowna on Tuesday, for a shop day. Another chill night in front of the box.

Tues 13th

Early rise to catch the bus into Kelowna for a day of shopping at the Orchard Mall with Jesse and Emma. Would have watched a movie if any cinemas had been open, but no go. Easy day strolling around the shopping complex. Picked

238

up by the return bus at 3.30 p.m., admiring the bleak dirty white scenery of the pine clad **Okanagan Valley**, with its trees on sentry duty like cathedral spires down to the roadside, white paddocks and small ponds iced over and used for temporary skate rinks. Read more of the *Memoirs of a Geisha* book, which is proving a good read. Beers and a game of pool at Snowshoe Sam's on return, picked up a vid and some wine for the evening. Hot tub and swim, before wine, cheese and oysters, while watching films: *Tango and Cash*, and *Gangs of New York*.

Wed 14th

Crap snow report, no new snow overnight, so conditions not great, may go out later for a couple of hours, just to keep the muscles working.

Went out and checked out the Bullet and Black Forest runs after the Ridge Rocket Express, visibility strange and runs awkward. Came a cropper coming down Mille's Mile from the Black Forest chair, coming down at a healthy speed for me, hit the toe edge on a brow, and flew forward, with arms at my side, smashing left shoulder first into the icy surface. *Pain*. Managed to ride down the rest of the hill with my right hand holding my left shoulder. At the bottom, after a while being sat in the snow in mild discomfort, they called in medics and whisked me off on a Skidoo, sandwiched between two girls on medic patrol. At the emergency building I was dosed up with laughing gas, to ease what was being diagnosed as either a dislocation or separation of the collar bone, ambulance on its way. No more boarding for a while. Taken to Kelowna hospital emergency ward, dosed up with morphine, X-rayed, and seen by a doc, to be told, yes it's a separation, but there's nothing to be done about it but rest, and gentle exercises for re-hab, unless of course I'd like an operation to replace the severed ligaments, which apparently they don't as a rule bother with in North America, so the doc said.

Good ole Jesse came along in a car with girlfriends of the back injury girl who shared the ambulance with me down from the mountain. Another mate of Jesse, Paul, and his Australian travel bud Zac, just happened to be coming through Kelowna on their way up to the mountain to stay, so stopped off at the hospital to pick us up at about 9 p.m. How lucky was that! Rough time with the pain and drugs, big sweat-ups and nausea. Fleece and T-shirt cut to shreds to get them off me earlier, but Jesse brought a clothing change, so all good. Back on the hill we fed and drank to drown my sorrows.

Thurs 15th

Start of R&R campaign of hot tub, pool, arm exercises, and frozen veg bag on the shoulder for half-hour spells two or three times a day. Jesse, Emma, Paul and Zac, out boarding, making use of the season pass at least. All of us out in the evening for beers and pool, a good night out, me playing one-arm pool with my arm in a sling and drowsy on painkillers. Wasted.

Fri 16th

Stretch, ice packs, hot tub, pool, read, journal. Thick head on waking up, but not too bad. Arm mobility easing up with exercise, pain manageable. Another hot tub and pool session when the others got back from the slopes. Evening scoobies, mushroom chocolate, and then out for a few drinks, Shotski at the Powder Keg bar, Snowshoe Sam's rammed with Septics, or 'Honkies', as Jesse and co call them, rowdy Yanks from Washington. Ended up back at Raakel's, with a live band playing, and heaps more rowdy

Septics, back to the apartment for more bassett, and laugh 'til the early hours, when the mushrooms finally wore off.

Sat 17th

Everyone late up after the nights efforts. Paul, Zac and Emma went out for a few late arvo runs, while Jesse saw a guy about some work around our building. Zac bailed early and brought some mince back, so I got on a shepherd's pie mission for the evening. Zac and Paul went and picked up my board and boots from the Emergency Medical Centre, which was cool of them.

Burnt the underside of the shepherd's pie, but it tasted OK. Paul, Zac, Jesse, and Emma, went to Snow Pines for a P party, I bailed and stayed in, they had a great time, and went as Prophylactics, in white bin liners with a condom taped to them. Ice packs, hot tubs, arm exercises, through the day.

Sun 18th

Another midday rise for us, morning work for poor Emma. Paul and Zac departing for Calgary, good lads and amusing company, sad to see them go, but also nice to ease off the partying and relax again. More 'stretching the shoulder' exercises, ice packs and hot tubs. Meeting Jesse's mates from Drayton Valley has been inspiring, and given me a very high opinion of Canadians. All his friends have proved to be lively, friendly, amusing and genuine people, that have been a pleasure to be in the company of. Finished reading *Memoirs of a Geisha*, OK.

Tues 20th

Early rise and down for the hot tub and pool exercises.

Shoulder coming on well, movement much improved, pain only evident on extreme extension and sudden jolts, began full-body stretches again today. Internet in the early afternoon, checked for flights home – $419 from Kelowna to Heathrow for any Tuesday in February! Back for afternoon hot tub and pool sesh, followed by stretch and ice pack. Wind down in front of the box. Arvo pics of the mountain. Evening pitchers of beer and racks of pool with Jesse and Emma at Raakel's Bar. Spoke to Bower Steve on the phone later.

Wed 21st

Another late rise, straight down for hot tub and swim therapy, managing the front crawl quite well, and general movement pretty reasonable. Stretching and ice packs continue, may try out an easy run on the board tomorrow. Now reading *The Warrior Queens*, *Boadicea's Chariot*, by Antonia Fraser, historical stuff.

Sat 24th

Back on the slopes today, just an hour, but no dramas. Arvo therapy on the bones. Eve at Raakel's on mushroom chocolate for more beer and pool.

Sun 25th

Couple of hours on the slopes today, big powder dumps for the last few days, so nice riding and soft falls in the champagne stuff. Therapy continuing after, and shoulder getting better by the day. Left knee twinging. Eve walk up to Snow Pines for smoke and chat with J and E's friends Dwayne and girlfriend, cool long walk through the still falling snow.

Wed 28th

Midday rise and out for arvo rides in the glorious sunshine, and heat wave temps of minus 1 degree. Cruisey runs and no falls, shoulder and knee holding up, no real advancement in boarding expertise unfortunately as I'm keeping the speed down to avoid tumbles and further pain from existing wounds. Beautiful views, from the top of the chairlifts, across the Monashee mountain ranges, and fresh winds blowing the champagne powder off the peaks.

Thur 29th

Slack again and slept 'til late. Had a stretch, and then out on the slopes just after one p.m, what a day for it!, snow still dumping big style. I cruised all over, and it was the best yet, with the board floating through the fresh-laid thick champagne powder, as I ploughed trails everywhere, and each time new snow instantly covering the tracks, 7 inches in the last 24 hours. Mainly around the Bullet Express chair and its various blue runs, until the 'last ride' call, as the 3.30 closing mark reared its unwelcome head. Such a good time!

Back for a stretch, hot tub, swim, more stretches, ice pack, tea and toast, before feet up and relax. Oh the hardship of it all. Chopper, the cat, amusing us all by his frenzied behaviour with plastic bags and cardboard boxes, and his sharp and playful, bitey teeth. Picked up a cheap bottle of Chilean wine for the evening, accompanied by oysters, cheeses and Ritz crackers.

Fri 30th

Up by 9 a.m. with a thick head and dodgy guts. Out on the slopes by 10 a.m., amazing thick, soft, fresh powder, as I bounced down the Bullet Run under the chairlift, stuck for a minute or two in waist-deep fluffy snow, before pushing off again. Howling winds bringing yet more snow, but my guts and head were screaming, so I came in after just an hour for a much-needed dump, stretch, hot tub, swim, ice pack and painkillers. Chilled for a couple of hours, and headed back out mid-arvo for a few more runs on the glorious powder, but desperate visibility and biting cold had me back in again after just an hour, would be just fantastic without the gales, also the ice pack chairlift seats had my backside so numb I thought it'd be frostbitten if I rode up one more time! More hydro therapy afterwards and a quiet night.

Sat 31st

Mid-morning rise, shoulder aching, so had a hot tub and swim sesh, stretch, ice pack, tea and toast, before heading out for a couple of hours around the Bullet and Black Forest runs, good fun. Back in for stretch, tea, toast and TV, with a bit of bassett through Jesse's newly made Deer antler pipes. Heaps more snow fell overnight – 35 centimetres in 24 hours! – and nearly 4 feet in five days.

Tues 3rd

Usual late rise and out for arvo 'shredding', great two and a half hrs of trying out off-piste tree runs and mini jumps, quality powder, making it feel like floating, didn't want to stop. Hot tub, swim, stretch, tea and toast, then goggle box and kip. Jesse's mate Nate, from travels in Indonesia, turned up just after midnight.

Wed 4th

More late kippage, owing to 'lack of' from night before.

Took off, late arvo, with adjusted bindings, but adjustments no good, and weather, bleak and blizzard like, so soon back in. Easy night in, and akip after *Red Dwarf*.

Thurs 5th (minus 10 degrees)

Up bright and early to catch first lift up on the Ridge Rocket. Great day all over the mountain, as I checked out the Bullet, Black Forest and Powder chairs, taking on steep stuff, trees and moguls. Had a tea, toast, hot tub, swim and stretch break, before heading back out to complete a full and quality day in the glorious sunshine.

Sat 7th

Another lazy day, set off for Kelowna in Nate's truck, to sort stuff out. My 145 Lamarr Dragon board with 'sidewalls', has started de-laminating, so we took it back and I got it changed for a 160 Rossignol Spike, capped-edge board, also spent out for a board bag for the trip home. Shopping done, had a fast food feed, and back by 7.30 to 8-ish. Followed by another quiet night for me, while the others went out.

Sun 8th

More laziness, out for a couple of hours on the new board, awkward at first, but soon got into it, quick, slick, and smooth as, fun rides. Hot tub and swim after.

Mon 9th

Late morning rise, cereal, stretch, and out after, for a couple of hours, getting used to the new board. Lots of friendly chats on the lifts, still getting mistaken for an Aussie! Clear sunny day, and very few others out on the slopes, board feels great, a really smooth ride, and easy to switch on it. Got stuck a couple of times among the trees in waste deep powder, but all fun stuff.

In for tea, stretch and TV, then hot tub and swim. Jesse and Nate cooking up burritos (some Mexican stuff).

Tues 10th Feb

Well here it is – The day I booked my flights home! Seventeen months of travelling the globe, very little of it gone to plan, but fantastic for it. It's a shame that I haven't seen more of Canada in the six weeks I've been here, but this place has been a fairly exceptional part of the ski world to get to experience. As always on my travels, there's been a large contingent of Aussies around, working all over the resort on the ski lifts, shops, bars and instructing on the slopes.

Just a couple of hours out today, with clear skies, and not too many others out riding, but wasn't really into it. My mind's elsewhere I suppose, with thoughts of home. Funny how thoughts flood my mind during the day, be it on the ski lifts, on the slopes, out walking, or just plain sitting down in the apartment, but as soon as I pick the pen up, the tide of ideas just dries right up. Irritating eh?!

Wed 11th

It's so difficult sometimes, to see the reflection, that hits so hard every reminder of life's cruel lines, when inside you feel the youth and energy of the people you're surrounded by. Youth inspires me, and I drink their energy like a grateful drunk, wishing this is the way things could always remain!!

Jesse and Nate, strumming away on the guitars, Emma

looking on at all of us laughing together after our night-time session of mushrooms. Two sessions out on the slopes today, while the others went into Kelowna to get the cat's nads chopped, and sort Nate's truck. Glorious sunshine day, and hardly any boarders or skiers on the runs. In the evening we dosed up on some mushroom chocolate, necked a few beers, and headed out for some night-riding on the half-pipe down from the Plaza Chair. Hard going for yours truly, just getting halfway up the side walls, while Jesse and Nate were grabbing air off the top edge. Eventually, with the chocolate building me up with an unwarranted self-belief, I gave it my best shot and steamed full tilt from one side, down and up to the top edge on the other side of this 8-foot half-pipe, only to realise when I got there that I didn't know what to do next. My momentary triumph turned to outright farce as the laws of nature, gravity-wise, decided my fate for me, and I descended to the ground with a heavy thud, greeted by loud howls and ouches proclaimed from the chair lifts above – I had an audience. Fortunately the combination of the heavy ski wear, and the mushroom chocolate, served to cushion the blow considerably, and once it was clear I was unhurt, laughter echoed around the place for a while. Soon after that, we called it a night, and went back to the apartment to continue our revelry, trashed and bailed, but not before drunkenly performing some of my verse for the crew's amusement.

Thurs 12th

Up early, but well hung over and feeling bleak, opted to get out on the slopes and ride, in an effort to blow it out of my system. Another clear and sunny day, with just a few others out there. Nate left early arvo, and we're back to three again. Lazy day afterwards, watching vids, stretching, hot tub, swim and feet up.

Fri 13th

Mid morning rise, yet another glorious clear and sunny day, so out riding by midday, after a leisurely wake-up. A good few hours, hooning all over the mountain while it's still relatively quiet. Easy arvo chillin' in front of the box, with Jesse strumming tunes on his guitar, he and Emma scored a load of groceries from one of the holiday house cleans, so all happy. They're out for the evening so I have the place to myself with some bassett, also picked up some beer, and another vid for the night, all good. Checked internet for flight confirmations and other mail. Chopper looking livelier this evening, having seemed a bit lethargic after his knacker session at the vets, he's now bouncing and bounding all over the apartment, clawing, chewing, licking, sniffing, scratching and chasing whatever catches his attention, for fleeting moments at a time, it's good to see the little fella full of life again.

Sat 14th Feb – Al Capone Day, 14th Feb 1929

Mid-morning rise in time to catch Capone documentary covering the Valentine's Day massacre, cool black-and-white footage news clips. Out on the slopes by 1.30, and it's snowing! Big line up at the Ridge Rocket Express, but OK over at the Black Forest, where I stayed for the arvo, riding among the trees and felled areas, in almost untouched powder, so cool, and such fun.

Watching Stephen King's *Dreamcatcher* on vid now.

Sun 15th

One more cruisey day involving all the usual.

Mon 16th

Same again, also booked airport shuttle for Thursday, and sent e-mails. Movie arvo, and then out for social with Emma's Ps who are over from Australia.

Tues 17th

Mid-morning rise, and out by lunch, great off piste in the fresh powder among the trees over at Black Forest. Cruisey rest of day, hot tub, swim, stretch, feet up, and vid.

Wed 18th

Last day, out for a brief spin on the board, out in yet more fresh-laid powder, ducking into the tree runs. Arvo prep for leaving, one last hot tub and swim sesh. Emma's Ps round for dinner in the eve, Jesse cooking another mean steak and pasta combo, and all washed down by a liberal amount of vino. Good evening of eating, drinking and chatting, Jeremy and Jo (Emma's Ps) are good company, and the night zipped by too quickly, but a very civilised last meal. Me and Jesse hit the bassett after Jeremy and Jo left, soon baked, and hit the pit.

Thurs 19th February

More goodbyes! Jesse and Emma left at 7 a.m., heading off to Silver Star mountain for the day, along with Emma's Ps, so it was hugs and bleary, tired eyes at sunrise. Kit packed and ready, last-minute look around, but sure I'll forget something. Out the door like a pack mule again, and the last leg home begins. Last chance, on the drive to the airport, to check out the sparkling, untouched snow, banked up to the roadside, and back into, and on the trees, a bit of nature's poetry.

249

Flew out of Kelowna airport, with West Jet, looking down on the Okanagan Valley and its surrounding urban sprawl, big rafts of logs laying in the waterside, as reminders of one of the areas main industries. Thin but dense layer of dark clouds, appearing compressed, both from above and below, made a curious sight to be alongside, before rising above the cloud tops, and all land views disappeared. Only a 40-minute flight to Vancouver, and then an eight-hour wait until the home-bound flight.

Much Later

I hadn't had my hair cut for about three months before I returned home, and I hadn't shaved since New Year's Day. I'd decided to wear the smart suit I'd bought from the Kelowna Value Village for the trip home. So when the family finally saw me, after 17 months away travelling, I looked a bit like the Wild Man of Borneo in his Sunday best as I arrived through the Customs gate at Heathrow, rucksacks and board bags in tow, with my favourite Quiksilver flowerpot hat on, of course.

That Friday night was the best welcome home, after the family welcome naturally, as mates from all over made it down to the Waterside pub to 'see me home'. All of a sudden you realise the magnitude of what you've just done. And much like many of the new things I'd done while away, I felt like I'd want to go right back and do it all over again! But not before I've properly caught up with all the people I've missed back here. Here's to the next time, where ever it may be!!!!!!